Never Be Bullied Again:

Prevent Haters, Trolls, and Toxic People from Poisoning Your Life

ISBN: 9781621252580

Never Be Bullied Again:

Prevent Haters, Trolls, and Toxic People from Poisoning Your Life

SAM HORN,
Author of Tongue Fu!®

Table of Contents

INTRODUCTION: WHY AM I WRITING A NEW BOOK ON BULLIES?   1

PART 1: IMPORTANT INSIGHTS ABOUT BULLIES   7

CHAPTER 1: HOW CAN I TELL IF I'M DEALING WITH A BULLY?   9
CHAPTER 2: WHY DO PEOPLE BECOME BULLIES?   16
CHAPTER 3: WHAT ARE THE SIGNS OF A CONTROLLER/MANIPULATOR?   27
CHAPTER 4: ARE YOU TOO NICE FOR YOUR OWN GOOD?   35
CHAPTER 5: ARE YOU DEALING WITH A JEKYLL/HYDE PERSONALITY?   44
CHAPTER 6: ARE IDEALISTIC EXPECTATIONS PART OF THE PROBLEM?   51

PART II: REAL-WORLD WAYS TO DEAL WITH A BULLY   61

CHAPTER 7: PROTECT YOUR SPACE, ENFORCE YOUR BOUNDARIES   63
CHAPTER 8: CLARITY IS THE KEY TO BEING CONFIDENT   72
CHAPTER 9: DON'T SUFFER IN SILENCE - DO THE YOU   78
CHAPTER 10: CALL BULLIES ON THEIR BEHAVIOR   85
CHAPTER 11: NAME A BULLY'S GAME TO NEUTRALIZE IT   92
CHAPTER 12: HOW TO HANDLE A TEASER   98
CHAPTER 13: HOW TO KEEP YOUR COOL WHEN DEALING WITH TOXIC PEOPLE   106
CHAPTER 14: STOP BLAMERS IN THEIR VERBAL TRACKS   111
CHAPTER 15: WHAT WE ACCEPT, WE TEACH   117
CHAPTER 16: DENY BULLIES ACCESS   123
CHAPTER 17: DON'T LET A BULLY ISOLATE YOU   130
CHAPTER 18: IS YOUR CHILD BEING BULLIED?   136
CHAPTER 19: WHAT CAN BE DONE ABOUT CYBER BULLYING?   147
CHAPTER 20: STAND UP FOR YOURSELF   156
CHAPTER 21: ANGER CAN BE HEALTHY   162
CHAPTER 22: PROTECT YOURSELF IN DANGEROUS SITUATIONS   169

PART III: CHOOSE A BETTER FUTURE   177

CHAPTER 23: CHOOSE YOUR BATTLES   179

CHAPTER 24: CHOOSE TO TRUST   186

CHAPTER 25: CHOOSE TO TAKE CARE OF YOUR HEALTH   191

CHAPTER 26: CHOOSE TO TURN HATE INTO HOPE   198

CHAPTER 27: CHOOSE TO TAKE THE LEAD TO ADDRESS BULLYING
IN YOUR ORGANIZATION   209

CHAPTER 28: CHOOSING TO LEAVE CAN TAKE MORE COURAGE THAN STAYING...
AND CAN BE THE BEST THINK YOU EVER DID   224

SUMMING UP: IT'S UP TO YOU NOW   234

BULLYING RESOURCES   239

ABOUT THE AUTHOR   245

Introduction

WHY AM I WRITING A NEW BOOK ON BULLIES?

"Bullying in America has become an epidemic." – rapper Macklemore

When I first wrote about this topic almost 15 years ago in *Take the Bully by the Horns*, it was because participants in my *Tongue Fu!®* programs were telling me their well-intentioned attempts to "be the change they wished to see" worked with *most* people, but not with *a specific individual* who ignored all their attempts to get along. These participants had "tried everything" to turn this situation around, to no avail.

Then, I experienced my own personal nightmare with someone who was determined to take me down. I found out for myself what a surreal experience it is to deal with someone who doesn't play by the rules.

Ironically, I was considered somewhat of an expert on how to handle difficult people. My book *Tongue Fu!®* had been published around the world. I had presented workshops on conflict resolution to the U.S. Navy, State of Hawaii, American Bankers Association and dozens of other organizations. Yet, when it came to dealing with this individual who had targeted me, all my years of expertise had no effect.

I searched for help, but found the existing approaches naïve and idealistic. The "Remove the thorn from the lion's paw and he will become your friend" mentality simply doesn't work with someone out to get you. Bullies don't want to become your friend; they want to become your tormentor.

1

The advice to "Understand that the bully probably comes from a dysfunctional family, was probably bullied him/herself, and doesn't know any better" doesn't help because sympathizing with a bully doesn't STOP him or her from targeting you.

Much to my dismay, all the recommended win-win techniques for dealing with difficult people (techniques I believed in and had been teaching for years; e.g., active listening, empathy, focus on collaboration and cooperation) ... *backfire* with bullies.

My Epiphany about Needing a Better Way to Deal with Bullies

"If you do what you've always done; you'll get what you've always gotten." – Tony Robbins

The more I delved into this topic, the more I realized we have to shift our way of dealing with bullies because standard win-win approaches don't work. In fact, they make things worse.

Why? Because bullies don't play by the rules; they make up their own rules.

Please understand, the vast majority of people care what's fair. They want to cooperate.

Then, there's the 5% who don't care what's fair. The 5% who don't want to cooperate, they want to control.

After interviewing, and asking for input from, thousands of participants in my workshops around the world, I concluded that:

95% of people:	5% of people:
• Are difficult on OCCASION	* Are difficult on PURPOSE
• Listen to LOGIC	* Dismiss LOGIC
• Try to solve what's WRONG	* Try to make YOU WRONG
• Want a WIN-WIN	* Want TO WIN
• Have a CONSCIENCE	* Don't have a CONSCIENCE
• SELF-REFLECT	* Don't SELF-REFLECT
• SELF-CORRECT	* Don't SELF-CORRECT
Win-win approaches *work* with 95%ers	**Win-win approaches *backfire* with the 5%**

What I discovered, the hard way, is that if we have the misfortune of living or working with or around a 5%er .... we need a NEW set of skills.

So, I wrote the book I needed and couldn't find. I developed actual dialogue of exactly what to say and do if someone is trying to intimidate, manipulate or control you. I recommended ways to keep perspective if you're unlucky enough to be dealing with a 5%er.

And I am happy to say many people have told me the contrarian approaches and specific, no-nonsense suggestions in *Take the Bully by the Horns* were a "godsend."

I will always remember a book event in the San Francisco area. About ten minutes before we were to start, a man and woman walked in with a teenaged girl. They came up and asked if I'd sign their book. I agreed and they proceeded to show me their well-used copy with its dog-eared pages, underlined paragraphs and starred passages.

The mom told me, "This book saved our daughter's life" and proceeded to tell me what had happened. One "normal" school day, their daughter got her lunch in the cafeteria and walked over to join her friends. As she approached their table, they *shunned* her. They turned their backs, averted their heads, and closed ranks.

At first, their daughter thought her friends were kidding. She tried to put her tray down but they sat closer together so there was no room. She said, "Hey, this isn't funny." They continued to ignore her. Painfully aware that everyone in the cafeteria seemed to be watching, she finally walked away and found a table by herself. She went home in tears.

Imagine what it's like for long-time friends to suddenly treat you like you don't exist ... and you're never told why.

The parents explained she went from being happy and healthy to being depressed and isolated. She claimed stomach aches so she wouldn't have to go to school. She stopped playing soccer because her former friends were on the team. She couldn't stop crying and wondering, "What did I do *wrong*? What did I do to deserve this?"

Desperate for help, they'd gone to their neighborhood bookstore to ask if they had any books on this topic. They bought *Take the Bully by the Horns* and read every word. They said its "take back control" advice gave their daughter the confidence to seek out new friends and get back into sports. It helped her realize she didn't want to be friends with girls who behaved like this. After several devastating months, she was finally able to put that toxic situation behind her and move forward with her life.

I'm glad *Take the Bully by the Horns* has helped people re-create and re-claim the quality of life they want, need and deserve.

The fact is though, if you were being bullied back when I wrote that book, the outcome was not always this positive. One of the many insidious aspects of dealing with bullies is they create situations where all the available options are lose-lose. The unfortunate truth was, in far too many cases, the white knight wasn't coming.

Want Good News about the Bully Epidemic?
"The only danger is not to evolve." – Jeff Bezos, founder of Amazon

Fast forward to 2015. I was watching *CBS Sunday Morning*, one of my favorite TV shows because it focuses on man's *humanity* to man.

Erin Moriarty was interviewing Tyler Clementi's parents. You may be familiar with what happened to Tyler. His dorm roommate at Rutgers secretly filmed him in his room on a date with another man. The roommate uploaded the video footage to the internet and it went viral. The breach of trust and subsequent "gay-bashing" drove Tyler to jump off the George Washington Bridge to his death.

His parents and brother elected to do something to honor Tyler in the hopes of preventing this type of cruelty to others. They founded a program called "Day One" that encourages leaders to stand up the first day their group gathers (whether that's in the workplace, at school or in a team meeting) and announce, "We agree we will not treat people differently because of their race, gender, what they look like or who they love. There will be consequences for anyone who does."

Wow. That's exactly what needs to happen to create a culture where bullying is NOT okay. There needs to be a "show of strength" - a public policy, a collective consciousness and commitment - that shifts the balance of power *against* bullying.

I went online to find out more about "Day One" and was pleasantly surprised and encouraged by what I found. I discovered dozens of new organizations pro-actively addressing this issue.

There's a "Bully Prevention Month" (October) with activities around the globe. There's even a Wikipedia entry that lists the many different resources available to schools, corporations, communities, sports leagues, government agencies and non-profits to help them develop bully-awareness-prevention environments.

I realized the cultural awareness of the toxic effects of bullying has *evolved*. The good news is, you no longer have to deal with bullies by yourself The adage "There is power in numbers" is true, and the numbers are now in favor of you.

I was inspired to write this book and include success stories of people who have reached out to me to share how they finally got past their bully experience. This book features thought-provoking insights from Lady Gaga, LeBron James, Taylor Swift, Will Smith and Amy Poehler. It addresses issues that have cropped up, such as *cyber*-bullying, which didn't even exist when I first wrote about this topic.

So, here you go. If you have the misfortunate of being bullied, I hope this "tell-it-like-it-is" book gives you:

- The confidence to speak up for yourself and stand strong
- Examples of exactly what to say and do when someone mistreats you so you no longer feel defenseless and powerless
- Tangible tools to counteract the destructive impact of bullies
- Resources for starting bully awareness-prevention programs in your organization, school and community
- Clarity that there are better days ahead and it's possible to free yourself from bullies who are trying to run and ruin your life

I hope you'll do with your copy what that teenaged girl did with hers. Highlight passages that resonate with you. Write notes to yourself in the margins about actions you plan to take. The more actively you interact with the content, the more likely you are to imprint the ideas and remember how to stand up for yourself if someone tries to bully you.

I also hope you'll share this book with people you see being bullied. If you witness bullying, intervene. Instead of being a bystander, be an upstander. Let targets know they're not alone, that people do care, and show trolls they are not going to get away with their hurtful behavior. You'll learn exactly how to do this in Chapter 21.

Together, we can create a "rising tide raising all boats" movement of mutual respect so no one ever has to be bullied again.

As author Alice Walker so wisely expressed, "Human capacity is equal to human cruelty, and it is up to each of us to tip the balance." Ready to "tip the balance" and help yourself and others who are being bullied re-claim and re-create their quality of life? Read on.

A WORD OF CAUTION

Please keep this caveat in mind. If your instincts tell you the person you're dealing with is dangerous… **it is not cowardly to remove yourself from that situation; it is *smart*.**

Honor what matters most, your health, your loved ones, your life. Put your personal safety, rather than your pride, first.

If a crazy driver cuts in front of you on the freeway, let him or her. So what if you get to your destination a few seconds later? It's not worth playing Destruction Derby at 60 mph, which could result in disastrous consequences for both of you.

If a drunk pours a beer on you or a family member (as happened in an example I'll share later in this book), do not retaliate. Instead, report the issue to an usher and ask to be re-seated. It is not in your best interests to confront someone who is under the influence.

I am not suggesting you ignore abusive behavior. I am suggesting you think first before challenging, and perhaps provoking, someone who could harm you or a loved one and put you in the hospital (or morgue).

If you are dealing with someone unstable who seems to pose a physical threat, do not corner or confront that person.

Honor (don't over-ride) your instincts. As Gavin de Becker points out in his excellent book, *The Gift of Fear,* human beings are blessed with a "sixth sense" that alerts us to danger. If your intuition is waving red flags, if your gut is warning you something is about to go seriously wrong, get yourself and your loved ones out of harm's way.

PART 1
IMPORTANT INSIGHTS ABOUT BULLIES

"You know, you don't have to be a loser kid in high school to be bullied and picked on.

Bullying comes in many different forms."

-- Lady Gaga

Chapter 1
HOW CAN I TELL IF I'M DEALING WITH A BULLY?

"Now, I've always known there were bullies in the world. You see it where people who may be stronger, or bigger, or better with verbiage than other folks... show off. To me, that's what bullying is, showing off. It's saying, I'm better than you, I can take you down. Not just physically, but emotionally." —*Whoopi Goldberg*

A participant at a *Tongue Fu!®* workshop said, "When I think of a bully, I picture a big kid slamming a small kid into a school locker. But maybe that's just an old stereotype. I've got a co-worker who's downright devious. She is petite and always perfectly put together – but everyone is afraid of her. She'll smile, all the while saying something designed to devastate you. Last week, she said, 'Linda, is that a new dress? You should wear stripes more often; they're very slimming on you.' She's about 5'2" but grown men cower around her because you never know what's going to come out of her mouth. Is she a bully?"

I was so glad she brought this up, because I have found that many people still have outdated perceptions of what a bully looks and acts like. Bullies don't necessarily have bulging biceps and black hats like the villains in melodramas. They come in all shapes, sizes, genders, ages, and professions.

Men can be bullies. Women can be bullies. Eighty-year-olds can be bullies. Eight year olds can be bullies. Managers and ministers can be bullies. Coaches, co-workers and customers can be bullies.

Some bullies are *overt*. They use verbal or physical aggression to dominate and intimidate others. Their bullying is "on the surface."

Some bullies are *covert*. They use emotional warfare and manipulation to keep you off-balance, erode your self-esteem, and control you.

Overt and covert bullies can be equally insidious.

The Centers for Disease Control and Prevention defines bullying as "unwanted aggressive behavior that involves an observed or perceived power imbalance, is often repeated multiple times, and inflicts distress in the form of physical, psychological, social or educational harm."

I agree with most parts of that definition, especially the word "unwanted," and that bullying behavior is repeated multiples times.

However, I don't agree that bullying is always "aggressive." As that *Tongue Fu!* participant pointed out, sometimes bullying is *passive-aggressive* and *subtle*. You can't put your finger on it; you just always get a pit in your stomach around this "wolf in sheep's clothing" type of bully.

Many people have told me the lightbulb came on the moment they filled out the following quiz and realized "Bullies don't have to be brutes. They're anyone who has a pattern of abusing the rights, needs and feelings of others through intimidation or manipulation."

What's the Definition of a Bully?
"A bully is anyone who has a pattern of abusing the rights, needs and feelings of others through intimidation and/or manipulation."- Sam Horn

Please note that key word *pattern*. This is the primary difference between the 95% who are simply having a bad day - and the 5% who knowingly behave badly to get their way or get you out of their way.

The "Are You Dealing with a Bully?" Quiz

The following questionnaire can help you determine whether a challenging individual in your life is an actual bully or simply an unpleasant person. The question is, does s/he mistreat you and others innocently or intentionally?

If you are dealing with several difficult individuals, take the time to fill this out separately for each one. Answer the questions, rating the frequency of these behaviors from 1 (Rarely) to 3 (Half and half) to 5 (Almost Always). Go with your instinctual response. Your first answer is usually the most honest because it comes from the gut and is uncensored.

Questions	1 - Rarely	2 - Some-times	3 - 50/50	4 - Often	5 – Almost Always
1. Do you "talk on eggshells" and watch everything you say because you're afraid you'll make this person mad?					
2. Does this person act condescending or superior? Does s/he treat you as if you are stupid or incompetent?					
3. Is this person hypercritical? Does s/he find fault with everyone else and blame them for what goes wrong?					
4. Does s/he have a Jekyll and Hyde personality? Is s/he charming in public and cruel in private?					
5. Does this person dominate conversations and talk over people?					
6. Does this person call you names ("Dummy, Ugly, Worthless") and have derogatory labels for other people?					

Questions	1 - Rarely	2 - Some-times	3 - 50/50	4 - Often	5 – Almost Always
7. Does this person insist on controlling the decisions (e.g., money, time, travel) and attack anyone who dares to question his/her judgment or authority?					
8. Has this person tried to isolate you from friends or family? Is s/he resentful when you spend time with others? Does s/he ridicule or complain about people you like?					
9. Does this person play martyr and try to make you feel guilty or responsible for his/her moods? If s/he's unhappy, it's your fault; if s/he's lonely it's because you're not paying attention?					
10. Does this person pick fights or criticize you in public because s/he knows you won't cause a scene?					

Questions	1 - Rarely	2 - Some-times	3 - 50/50	4 - Often	5 – Almost Always
11. If you threaten to leave, does this person make nice to get you back and then begin mistreating you again?					
12. If you object to this person's behavior, does s/he go on the offensive and demand to know why you're giving her or him such a hard time?					
13. Does this person indulge in crazy-making behavior, such as making/breaking commitments, reversing statements, twisting your words and then accusing you of overreacting?					
14. Does this person crowd you, hit you, scare you or use physical aggression or violence to intimidate you into giving in, going along, giving up?					
15. Are you happier when you're not around this person?					
TOTAL:					

35 or below: This individual is not a bully. S/he is a 95% - s/he will *respond in kind* to fair, ethical attempts to resolve issues. S/he may be unpleasant once in a while; however, win-win communication on your part will make it possible for the two of you to coexist cooperatively.

36-55: This person may occasionally slide into bully behavior. You need to more assertive in those situations so s/he understands their behavior will not be tolerated. Communicate from a clear position of strength and hold them accountable so they learn they're not going to "get away" with their controlling, intimidating ways.

56-75: Uh-oh. It looks like you've got a full-blown bully on your hands. This person is a 5%er, the exception to the empathetic rule. They don't play by the rules; they make up their own rules. Get a pen, sit down, and start taking notes so you can begin planning how to stop this individual from running and ruining your life.

Rest assured, we're going to address how to handle each of the behaviors mentioned in the 15 questions in this quiz.

Remember, if your answers to this quiz made you realize the challenging person you're dealing with is a 95%er: chances are they are simply stressed about something that's gone wrong and they're taking it out on you. Please pick up a copy of *Tongue Fu!®* It offers dozens of win-win techniques for dealing with people who have a conscience and who will respond to fair, ethical, win-win attempts to get along.

This book focuses exclusively on how to deal with the 5% - people who *do not respond to win-win approaches*. It focuses solely on people who don't listen to logic, who don't care what's fair, and who aren't operating with empathy. It introduces techniques on how to reverse the "risk-reward ratio" so these "toxics" are motivated to leave you the heck alone.

Are you wondering, "How is it some people become a 5%er?"

Good question. The next chapter explains what's behind bully behavior. Knowing why trolls, controllers, and manipulators do what they do can help you understand "where they're coming from" so you're not as easily knocked off balance by their dirty tricks.

Action Plan and Discussion Questions

Think of someone in your life who seems to delight in being difficult. After filling out the quiz, did you discover s/he qualifies as a bully?

If so, what pattern of behaviors does this person exhibit that makes you realize this is bully behavior?

Does this individual exhibit other hurtful behaviors that weren't mentioned on this questionnaire? What are they?

Which of these behaviors does s/he do most frequently? Describe a situation where s/he went "over the top. " What did s/he say and do? What did you say and do?

Did you suffer in silence or try to speak up for yourself? What happened?

Now, take the test for yourself. Do you exhibit any of these characteristics? Which ones? If you discovered you too sometimes behave like a bully, are you willing to read this book and look for ways to treat people more respectfully? Please elaborate.

Chapter 2
WHY DO PEOPLE BECOME BULLIES?

"For those of us climbing to the top of the food chain; there can be no mercy. The rule is: hunt or be hunted." – Frank Underwood, TV show House of Cards

Believe it or not, there really are people who think like Frank Underwood, the power-hungry lead in the HBO drama, *House of Cards*.

Thankfully, not everyone is as cold-hearted and ruthless as Frank. You've heard the phrase "knowledge is power"? Well, knowing *why* bullies act the way they do can give you power. Instead of being flustered and flummoxed by their behavior, you'll understand where they're coming from and what they're trying to achieve – which is to be on top of the food chain. Your knowledge can help you detach from their tactics so they no longer have the power to wound you.

Read these reasons and ask yourself which might be behind your bully's behavior. Note that bullies may have one, some, or all of these contributing factors. Check "yes" or "no" by the ones that might be motivating your bully to act the way s/he does.

REASON # 1: Some People Bully to Compensate for Low Self-Esteem

"The better we feel about ourselves, the fewer times we have to knock someone down in order to feel tall." —singer, Odetta

You've probably heard the classic explanation that people bully because they feel inferior. This may be hard to believe because bullies often come across as arrogant. They appear to have an inflated sense of self-esteem.

Exactly. Bullies have to INFLATE their self-esteem, be the big shot, put on a big show to compensate for the fact they feel inferior. Look beneath a bully's brusque exterior and you often find someone who compares him/herself to others ... and comes up short.

Bullies hate feeling others are more talented, popular or successful so they resort to putting others down so they can be on top. Instead of taking the mature, responsible route to improve themselves and *become* better, they take the immature, irresponsible route and try to make others feel bad so they can *feel* better.

Many of their behaviors are designed to prove to the world (and themselves) that they are superior instead of inferior.

Think about it. Confident people are secure in their self-worth. They feel no need to make people feel small so they can feel tall. They don't have to diminish others to feel dominant.

Bullies, on the other hand, can't stand it when they feel others have it "over them" so they compensate for it in a variety of unhealthy ways, including:

FAULT-FINDING. By focusing attention on other people's faults, bullies hope to keep the attention off their own. This was humorously pointed out in a classic Peanuts cartoon strip. Linus asks Lucy: "Why are you always so anxious to criticize?" Lucy responds, "I just have a knack for seeing other people's faults." Linus protests, "What about your own faults?" Lucy answers, "I have a knack for overlooking them."

Does the bully in your life pounce on your every mistake? Does s/he focus on your foibles to avoid having to examine or admit her or his own?

Yes ____ No ____

TAKING CONTROL. During a *Larry King Live* show on CNN, real estate mogul Donald Trump (and as of 2015, Presidential candidate) showed his bully stripes. A few minutes into the interview, Trump interrupted King and asked him,(disingenuously), "Do you mind if I sit back a little? Because your breath is very bad. It really is. Has this been told to you before?"

King, taken aback, obviously didn't know what to say (the purpose behind Trump's out-of-line remark). He finally mumbled, "No."

Trump pounced. "Okay, then, I won't bother."

Whew! Talk about ambushed!

What was going on? It was Larry King's show. Bullies don't want someone else to run the show; THEY want to run the show. Trump didn't want to answer to King; he wanted King to answer to him. So, he went on the attack and knocked King back, so he could be in control.

Does the bully in your life go on the attack to try to embarrass you, intimidate you, knock you back or down, so s/he can run the show, be in control?

Yes _____ No _____

NEEDING TO WIN. A man named Barry said, "My older brother couldn't stand the thought that I, his younger brother, was a better athlete. He would do anything, anything, to keep me from beating him. If we were playing hoops in our driveway, he would knock me down rather than let me score a winning basket. If we were playing chess, he would sweep the pieces off the board rather than let me checkmate him. One memorable afternoon he threw every single one of his golf clubs into a lagoon when he triple-bogied the seventeenth hole and realized I was going to win our bet." As this little brother found out, bullies resort to whatever tactics are necessary to keep from coming out on the short end.

Bullies are driven to beat you (or beat you down or beat you up) because they can't bear to be shown up. Winning gives them tangible evidence they're "the best." Does the bully in your life hate to lose?

Yes _____ No _____

DEFLATING DIGS AND DARK REMARKS. If you're celebrating something, does the bully in your life try to destroy your good mood with a dark remark? Dark remarks are designed to defeat and deflate you. You've heard the saying "Misery loves company"?

Bullies want you to be miserable because, deep down, they are. They don't want you to be happy because they're incapable of feeling that emotion. They don't want you to experience something they can't. They want you to be depressed because that means you're no longer a threat to them.; you no longer have the energy to challenge them or leave them. Does the bully in your life hate to see you happy? If you're in a good mood, does s/he say something to ruin it or make your feel bad for feeling good?

Yes ___ No ___

A woman came up to me after a seminar and said, "Now I understand what was going on with my ex-husband. He believed having fun was something we should do only when all the chores were done. I disagreed with that and regularly took our kids on excursions to the park, zoo, and pool. I always asked him to join us (sometimes the kids would beg him to come along), but he would always refuse, saying he had work to do. When we would come back into the house laughing and talking about our adventure, he would always do something to wipe the smiles off our faces. He would say something like 'Well, someone has to be responsible while you're off gallivanting around town.' In retrospect, I can see that he was deliberately trying to spoil our fun because he was jealous. He didn't like seeing us feel something he couldn't, so he would ruin it for us or try to make us feel guilty."

Marilyn Monroe said, "Success makes so many people hate you. I wish it wasn't that way. It would be wonderful to enjoy success without seeing envy in the eyes of those around you."

Bette Midler said much the same thing when she was interviewed by James Lipton on "Inside the Actor's Studio." He asked her, "What's the hardest part of success?"

She thought about it for a moment and then said somewhat sadly, "Finding someone who's genuinely happy for you."

Please note: It does not have to be this way. Confident, secure, loving people can glory in your success. They can be genuinely happy for you and want the best for you – without feeling envious and without feeling any compulsion to derail and diminish your joy.

THOSE are the people you want to seek out and be around. Not someone who is so possessive and jealous they can't stand to see you succeed.

REFUSING TO APOLOGIZE. Being a bully means never having to say you're sorry. At least that seems to be the bully philosophy.

I had the privilege of meeting Deborah Tannen, author of groundbreaking books on gender communication including *You Just Don't Understand.* Deborah shared a marvelous insight about why some men refuse to apologize. She was watching the movie *The Kid* in which Bruce Willis's character gets to go back in time and confront the bully who had tormented him throughout his childhood. This time, instead of running scared, he stands up to the bully and successfully wrestles him to the ground. What is the one thing he wants from the bully who caused him so much humiliation? What did he demand once he had the bully on the ground? "Apologize! Apologize!"

That moment crystallized Deborah's epiphany that apologizing, for some people, is an issue of dominance and subordination. For them, an apology means, "I'm wrong, you're right. You win, I lose!"

If you approach things from an adversarial point of view, as bullies do, this turns apologizing into a "one up, one down" interaction. No wonder bullies are reluctant to say they're sorry! They see everyone on a ladder. They're not about to apologize, which (in their mind) puts them lower on the ladder. Does your bully hate to apologize because s/he doesn't want to give you an advantage? Does your bully see apologizing as a form of weakness or submission ?

Yes _____ No _____

REASON # 2: Some People Bully Because They Feel No Remorse

"Psychopaths view any social exchange as a 'feeding opportunity,' a contest of wills in which there can only be one winner. Their motives are to manipulate and take, ruthlessly and without remorse. For them, language is only word deep; there is no emotional responsibility behind it. A psychopath can use words like 'I love you,' but it means nothing more that if s/he said, 'I'll have a cup of coffee." Robert D. Hare, author of Without Conscience

Remorse is defined as "distress arising from a sense of guilt for past wrongs." Bullies feel little or no remorse. They can't, or don't want to, admit they did something wrong. To do so means they would have to look at their behavior. And most bullies won't do that because it means their whole house of cards will collapse.

This means you can't expect bullies to operate with a sense of moral obligation or conscience. They won't self-examine, admit their actions are offensive and choose to hold themselves accountable. They won't make amends or voluntarily choose to treat you differently.

This lack of culpability means that bullies won't voluntarily change because they don't think about, or care about, the pain they're causing. In extreme cases, they may even enjoy the pain they're causing.

If you suspect the person you're dealing with is without remorse, I urge you to read Dr. Robert D. Hare's book, *Without a Conscience.* There are good reasons his book has received almost five hundred 5-star reviews on Amazon. He points out that psychopaths aren't always "Ted Bundy" types who commit horrific crimes. He believes there are as many psychopaths in boardrooms as in prisons. In fact, he says, "You'll find them in any organization where, by the nature of one's position, you have power and control over other people."

If you find this notion troubling, rest assured. Once we finish exploring WHY bullies behave the way they do, we'll move on to WHAT you can do about it.

You may be wondering why bullies don't feel remorse. There are a variety of reasons. Look these over to see which might be behind your bully's inability or refusal to feel empathy or responsibility.

ARROGANCE. Gore Vidal kiddingly suggested, "There is no human problem which could not be solved if people would simply do as I advise."

It's ironic that while many bullies feel inferior, some feel they are superior beings who are smarter than everyone else. This conceit means they have little tolerance for what they loftily perceive as other people's stupidity. They have a habit of disdainfully lecturing the "little people" about how things ought to be done because they self-righteously believe they know best … about *everything.* Their motto is: "I'm not rude. You're just insignificant." Does the bully in your life act as if you are beneath him or her? Does s/he treat you with disdain, as if your opinions, ideas, needs and wishes don't matter?
Yes ___ No __

HAVE "CENTER OF THE UNIVERSE SYNDROME." A teacher told me, "I have a bully in my class who's all of eight years old. If he sees something he likes, he takes it. If he's told to do something he'd rather not do, he throws a fit. I requested a parent conference, and after five minutes, I knew why Ben was so selfish. His parents, both psychologists, actually told me, 'We don't believe in saying no to Ben. We don't want to stifle his creative freedom.'"

Yikes. The teacher asked the doting couple, "What if he does something he shouldn't?" They replied calmly, "We divert his attention to something else." No wonder Ben was so ruthless. This wild child was growing up with no boundaries, no rules and no socialization. It never even occurred to him to consider anyone's feelings but his own.

Does the bully in your life only care about "Me, me, me, me, me"? Did s/he grow up in an environment where no one said "No." Does s/he want what s/he wants, when s/he wants it and woe be to anyone who gets in his or her way of getting it?

Yes ___ No ___

NO NEGATIVE CONSEQUENCES. Somewhere along the way, bullies misbehaved and no one held them accountable. They concluded, "Well, that may have been wrong, but it worked." At that point, they misbehaved again. If no one objected, they decided the advantages of bullying outweighed the disadvantages—because there were no disadvantages. What little regret they may have initially felt was removed because the rewards outweighed the risks.

You've heard the statement "Let your conscience be your guide"? Since bullies don't have a conscience, they let consequences be their guide. If there are no consequences, they have no incentive to change their evil ways.

You've heard the saying, "Rewarded behavior gets repeated"? Bully behavior often goes unchallenged, which means it's rewarded, which means it gets repeated. People often tip-toe around bullies because they don't want bullies to target them. Guess what? Tip-toeing around bullies makes it worse because bullies are learning that the worse they behave, the more people cow-tow to them. Has your bully gotten off penalty-free? Has s/he learned that bullying gets results because people become afraid and will "let" her or him get away with atrocious behavior?

Yes ___ No ___

HAVE A CERTIFIABLE PSYCHOLOGICAL DISORDER OR MEDICAL PROBLEM. Some bullies have a mental or physical disease or disorder that causes them to be unaware of, or apathetic about, their aberrant behavior. People who are bi-polar, senile, depressed, suffering from PTSD or Alzheimer's can be cruel – and they're not even aware of it. Character disorders such as antisocial personality disorder can cause sufferers to be dispassionate—devoid of the capacity to feel and act empathetically.

People in pain can also stop caring about anything but their suffering. A nurse told me, "Women who are normally kind and compassionate can become screaming banshees during a difficult labor when push comes to shove. Your world shrinks when you're in agony. It's almost impossible to think about anything except the pain you're in. I caution spouses not to take it personally if their loved one says or does something hateful when they're in pain because patients are literally and figuratively not themselves."

People can also lose the ability or incentive to judge whether their actions are offensive when they're under the influence of alcohol or drugs. Labels on many over-the- counter and prescription medications warn of dangerous mood swings and heightened irritability. Illegal and controlled substances are disinhibitors, which means the control mechanism in the brain that monitors appropriate behavior is switched off.

Is it possible your bully is suffering from a mental or physical condition that causes him or her to be unaware their behavior is inappropriate or hurtful?

Yes ____ No ____

Is s/he abusing substances?

Yes ____ No ____

REASON #3: Some People Bully Because They Feel Justified

"I found one day in school a boy of medium size ill-treating a smaller boy. I expostulated, but he replied: 'The bigs hit me, so I hit the babies; that's fair.' In these words he epitomized the history of the human race." – Bertrand Russell

Some bullies have convinced themselves they have the right to be mean. Some of their rationalizations include:

BEING BROUGHT UP IN A DYSFUNCTIONAL FAMILY.
"When I see the ten most wanted list," Eddie Cantor observed, "I always have this thought that if we'd made them feel wanted earlier, they wouldn't be wanted now."

Psychologists who have researched the origins of violence have concluded that cruelty or sadism can develop in extreme conditions of rejection and cruelty. When an individual has been maliciously bullied in his or her developmental years, that individual may retaliate and take pleasure in causing others the pain he/she has suffered.

Some bullies grew up in a home where "might was right" and feel that it's their turn now. England's George V said, "My father was frightened of his mother. I was frightened of my father, and I am damned well going to see to it that my children are frightened of me."

Is the bully in your life a by-product of this Bully Ripple Effect? Is s/he simply doing to others what was done to her or him?

Yes ___ No ___

ACTING OUT THE THEORY OF DISPLACEMENT. The theory of displacement states that for some reason, we're afraid to confront or get mad at the person who's causing our pain, so we purge our anger by picking on someone who it's safe to mistreat—someone who's lower on the pecking order. Scott, a school counselor told me he sees this played out on his campus every day. "Maybe the dad got called on the carpet by his boss. He can't tell off his boss, so he comes home and criticizes his wife's cooking. She acts out her resentment by scolding her son for not doing his chores. The son gets back by teasing his little sister about her braces, and she gets even by making fun of the new girl in school. These kids know at some level that what they're doing is wrong, but they can't take it anymore, so they release their tension by taking it out on someone else who's lower on the totem pole."

Could your bully be afraid to face the real cause of his or her discontent, so he or she is taking it out on you because you're lower on the food chain?

Yes ___ No ___

CONCLUDING THE BEST DEFENSE IS A GOOD OFFENSE. Some people didn't plan on becoming bullies but found themselves in a "survival of the meanest" environment where they felt they had to be bullies to survive. A woman contractor said, "As the only woman in a male-dominated industry, my partner was constantly being tested. Every day she faced an 'if you're not part of the steamroller, you're part of the road' situation. She finally resorted to being aggressive so she could hold her own with the macho

24

construction guys. The problem is, now she can't turn it off." Has the bully in your life adopted a "demeanor da better" approach?

Yes ____ No ____

REASON #4: Some People Bully Because They Lack Another Way

"I don't think we have to teach people how to be human. I think we have to teach them how not to be inhuman." —Eldridge Cleaver

Actually, I think we *do* need to teach people how to treat people humanely. If bullying is all someone has experienced, he or she may lack the ability to do it differently. If role models did not exhibit or teach them people skills, bullies may simply not know how to "play well with others." Unfortunately, having rough edges becomes a type of double jeopardy for bullies. Since they have so much invested in a gruff style that renders them reluctant to admit any failing, they will often continue to be a bully rather than humble themselves to seek help or admit they need assistance. Maintaining the status quo seems easier than getting out of their comfort zone.

A walking buddy of mine told me about a member of the board of their community association who fit this description perfectly. Karen said, "This woman loves to stir things up." Karen corrected herself: "Forget that, she lives to stir things up. She seems to operate on the belief that negative attention is better than no attention. This woman finds things to fuss about. If we don't have a contentious issue to handle, she'll create one just to prolong the meetings and be in the middle of things. "I've come to the conclusion that she's lonely and her life is rather empty. Her involvement on this committee is probably the only thing she has to look forward to. The problem is, she doesn't know how to relate to people. I think she says outrageous things just to engage people so she doesn't get ignored. The irony is, she feels everyone is against her. Well, everyone is against her because her nitpicky style is so off-putting. The sad part is, she ends up being even more isolated because people go out of their way to avoid her. She would never in a million years think of herself as a bully, and she would never for a minute realize she's the source of her own problem."

Sound familiar? Does the bully in your life alienate people because of his/her lack of social skills? Do they feel like the victim even though they're the ones behaving badly? Does their perception that they're being persecuted become a self- fulfilling prophecy because they're antagonizing people with their gracelessness? Yes ____ No __

Action Plan and Discussion Questions

Did you get any "Aha's" that help you understand why people become bullies? What are they?

What are two factors you feel might be behind your bully's behavior? Explain why you think this person is motivated to mistreat others.

Did you recognize any of these factors as part of your personality? Which of these characteristics do you relate to and why?

Do you feel differently about the bully in your life now that you know what's causing or contributing to his/her behavior? Explain.

Chapter 3
WHAT ARE THE SIGNS OF A CONTROLLER/MANIPULATOR?

"Someone who is nice to you and mean to the waiter is not a nice person."
– humorist Dave Barry

"If I only had paid attention to my instincts," Kathy sighed. "I had never been pursued so ardently. I met Ron at a church retreat. He asked me out the next night, the next night, and the next. By our sixth date, he had asked me to marry him. I hadn't even been thinking about getting married, but I got swept up in this whirlwind romance and his insistence that we were 'meant' to be together. He assured me he would plan everything, and he did plan everything. He planned the wedding, our honeymoon, our home . . . and the next five years of my life. The night before we were supposed to walk down the aisle, I had a heart-to-heart with my sister and maid of honor.

In the middle of our celebratory evening, my sister looked at me and asked, 'What's wrong?' I started crying and confessed, 'I want to get in a car, start driving, and never look back.'

Stunned, she asked, 'Why?' I admitted I didn't want to marry my husband-to-be. He had given me the bum's rush (if only I'd realized then how true those words would be) and I had said yes because he'd had more than enough conviction for both of us. My gut was telling me not to go through with the wedding, but I thought it was too late to back out."

"Over the next few years, as long as I went along with what Ron wanted, things were okay. When I started getting a mind of my own, life started going downhill fast. If I didn't want to do what he wanted, when he wanted, the way he wanted, he got upset. If I questioned his opinion about something, there was hell to pay. I went to a therapist to get some advice, and after listening to me for a while, she asked, 'Why did you marry such a controlling person?'

"I laughed in instant recognition of the truth. 'It never even occurred to me that he was controlling,' I told her, shaking my head. 'I just thought he really loved me.' The therapist told me that Ron had displayed the classic signs of a controller early on, I just hadn't known it. The urgent pursuit, the pressure to commit, the handling of all the details—all were indications of someone who has to be in charge.

"In retrospect, there were other danger signs; I just didn't recognize them. In that first year, he started to cut me off from the people I cared about. He never wanted to go to my folks' house for Sunday dinner and he was always trashing my friends. When I met him, he was really unhappy with his job and very bitter about his ex-wife. I just thought he had a bad boss and a witch for an ex-wife. It was only after being around him a while that I realized every manager he worked with was incompetent and every woman in his life had somehow 'screwed him over.' I wish I had listened to my intuition. When he was telling me all these terrible things about his former wife, this little voice inside me said, 'Someday he's going to be saying those kinds of things about you.' That little voice was right."

This man had indeed displayed several of the ominous characteristics of a controller/manipulator. One of the primary signs was that he rushed her into marriage. He was afraid she'd "find him out" if he waited too long, so he rushed her to the altar before she had time to discover what he was really like.

If you're getting involved with someone, you might want to compare his/her behavior to the following checklist to see how he or she stacks up. In addition to the behaviors we've already discussed (ignoring or violating other people's rights, incessant demands and "demeans"), these behaviors are a red flag that something's amiss with this individual. If you observe more than a few of these characteristics, you might want to head the other direction – or at the very least, bide your time and get to know this person better before making any long-term commitment.

The Telltale Traits of a Controller: A Checklist

"Persistence, only proves persistence; it does not prove love. The fact that a romantic pursuer is relentless doesn't mean you are special-it means he is troubled." — Gavin de Becker, author of The Gift of Fear

As Kathy discovered, and as Gavin de Becker points out, persistence, only proves persistence it doesn't prove love and it doesn't mean you're special. It could be a warning signal of a controlling personality who wants what s/he wants and will not stop until they get it. Have a person in mind while you read through these characteristics.

1. DISSONANCE. Psychologists agree that one of the primary indicators of a troubled person is incongruent behavior. As Dave Barry pointed out, someone who is nice to you and nasty to "the help" is not who he or she seems. Someone who lets slip racist remarks and then tries to laugh them off is revealing his or her true character (or lack of it). Someone who says he or she loves children but seems remote or rigid when around them is displaying dissonance—defined as "inconsistency between the beliefs one holds and his or her actions." What this means is that you cannot take this person at his or her word. Everything they say will be suspect because you won't know when they're telling the truth and when they're not.

2. POSSESSIVENESS. Someone who comes on strong and wants (or has!) to be with you constantly is showing a dangerous need to have you all to him or herself. Possessiveness is defined as "a desire to own or dominate." Bullies often don't have many (or any) friends of their own, which means they grow to resent your other relationships. Does this person pout or try to make you feel guilty for abandoning him or her when you spend time with others? Does this person want to know all about your previous partners, and somehow resent the fact that you've been with someone other than him or her? Bullies are so insecure they see everyone you care for as competition and as a threat to their dominance. This reluctance to share you with others will only get worse and become more perverse.

As rapper/singer Drake says, "Jealousy is just love and hate at the same time." Yikes. Controllers can simultaneously love you and hate your confidence, success, popularity, talent - all at the same time - because they see those strengths as threatening their power over you.

3. SECRECY. People who don't want to discuss where they work and live and don't want you to meet their friends or family may have something to hide. People who refuse to reveal anything about their past are often concealing emotional baggage. What you don't know *can* hurt you. Someone who doles out self-revelations in small quantities may seem mysterious and alluring in the beginning. In the long run, being with a person who withholds most of himself or herself gets lonesome.

4. BITTERNESS. Does this person have a lot of animosity toward his/her parents, former spouse or previous managers? Please understand you will be reliving and working out the unresolved traumas of this individual's childhood and prior relationships. You've heard the Zen saying "Wherever you go, there you are?" This person hasn't yet figured out that his/her source of enmity is internal, not external. If this individual is lugging around deep-seated resentments, it is only a matter of time before he or she starts accusing you of the same "crimes" former significant others supposedly perpetrated upon him or her.

5. CRUELTY TO DOMESTIC ANIMALS. It's one thing to dislike dogs or be allergic to cats. It's quite another to intentionally injure an innocent animal. People who see no harm in deliberately wounding a living creature lack humanity. If you see someone purposely inflict pain on an animal, don't accept any explanations. Head for the nearest exit. The next animal they hurt may be you. (Please note: hunters can be exempt from this. In certain areas, hunting is a tradition and doesn't necessarily connote an unmerciful spirit. Draw your own conclusions about the potential of cruelty based on this individual's treatment of all animals.)

6. TWISTS WORDS. Does this person take what you say and turn it into something you didn't mean? Do you sometimes feel on the defensive and don't even know why? Does this person obfuscate— make confusing statements and then accuse you of misunderstanding?

Bullies often make and break promises and then claim they never made them in the first place. This is a crazy-making ploy designed to turn you inside out so you don't know what's up.

7. HOLDS YOU RESPONSIBLE FOR THEIR UNHAPPINESS. Does this person blame you for his or her bad moods? If he's sad, it's because you didn't ask about his day? If she's depressed, it's because you don't take her anywhere anymore? If he's angry, it's because you said something that provoked him? There will be no pleasing this kind of person. Such people essentially haven't grown up, and never will as long as they hold everyone else but themselves accountable for how they feel.

8. PERFECTIONIST. Does this person nitpick or have such high standards no one ever measures up? Does this person have to do things himself because anyone else would just "mess it up"? If you're still in the honeymoon or courting phase, you may be temporarily exempt from this person's unceasing criticism. In time, though, his/her insistence on things being done a certain way (his/her way) will transfer to you, and then you'll never be able to do anything right. Jimmy Hoffa once said, "I may have my faults, but being wrong isn't one of them." Tyrants won't admit to any faults, least of all being wrong.

9. PINPOINTS YOUR WEAKNESS AND USES IT AGAINST YOU. Controllers and manipulators have a talent for ferreting out your emotional Achilles' heel and using it as ammunition. If you don't want to be considered selfish, they'll call you selfish. If you're unsure of your parenting skills, they'll attack your parenting skills. This is a classical Machiavellian method of exploiting your weakness so you're impotent (lacking power or strength) and they're omnipotent (having unlimited influence or authority). Their goal is to make you doubt yourself so you're vulnerable to their attempts to own you.

10. PLAYS THE MARTYR. Does he or she try to lay on the guilt by saying things like "Go ahead! Go skiing with your friends. I don't mind. I mean, who wants to spend time with an old fogie like me anyway? I'm sure I'll find something to do." Does this person play the long-suffering individual who's unappreciated? Is it a common theme that he or she is the only one who holds things together and everyone else is frivolous and hedonistic, thinking only of him or herself?

11. HATES TO HAVE HIS OR HER AUTHORITY QUESTIONED.

Does this person take umbrage if you dare dispute his or her facts, opinions, or observations? Does he or she come across as a know-it-all who has to have all the answers? Bullies can't stand to be challenged because they're afraid their "powerhouse of cards" could come falling down. Their "my way or the highway" communication style is based on their need to be in control and beyond reproach.

If you disagree with this person, does he or she escalate their intensity in an effort to force you to concede? If so, this means that every conversation is going to turn into a verbal battleground. It means this person will start disparaging your intelligence, expertise, and experience so you no longer have the confidence or strength to challenge him or her.

12. LIES, LIES, LIES.

Mark Twain once commented that "Truth is more of a stranger than fiction." Does that description fit the person you're dealing with? Does he or she self-aggrandize and exaggerate his or her achievements? In order to win respect, bullies often claim to have visited places they've never been, know people they've never met, and excel at things they've never tried.

In the mid-1970s, I had the privilege of working with two-time Grand Slam Champion Rod Laver at his Hilton Head Island tennis facility at Palmetto Dunes. A couple of times a year we sponsored national tennis camps. Every once in a while, someone would blow in the pro shop at the beginning of a new camp, and we would sense that we were about to deal with a type of individual the Aussies playfully refer to as "all flap and no throttle." Texans call this "All hat and no cattle." That translates into a "blowhard who talks a bigger game than they deliver."

Does the person you're dealing with display blowhard tendencies? Does he or she wax eloquent (or not so eloquent) about past accomplishments? Did this individual somehow manage in the first few minutes of meeting you to let you know how much money he made, what degrees she had, or what awards he's won? Was she so intent on impressing you with her curriculum vitae that she failed to ask about yours? Watch out. Red alert. Bellicose bully on the loose.

A man named Steve talked to me following a seminar. He said, "I think anyone getting into a relationship ought to read through this checklist first. It sent chills up and down my spine because you described my ex-girlfriend to a T. She displayed every single one of those characteristics. She chased me until she caught me; then once she caught me, I couldn't do anything right. She used to listen in on my phone calls and interrogate me about my old girlfriends. She was paranoid about me even looking at another woman. She smothered me. What's worse is that somehow she made me feel that everything was my fault. Even when I tried to end the relationship, it was because 'I was giving up on us' and 'I was afraid of commitment.' She tried to make me feel guilty for 'throwing her out,' and for her having given up her apartment, even though she was the one who had pushed so hard to move in with me. She never for a moment considered that she played any role in what went wrong. It was all on me."

Are You Dealing with a Part-time or a Full-time Controller?

A controller does his or her best to make you feel worse. Are you involved with someone who displays a mixture of these traits? Are you thinking, "Well, my partner does some of these things some of the times, but so do I! After all, no one is perfect."

You're right. The key issue is how frequently your partner engages in these behaviors and whether he or she is willing to change. Do you have any clout or leverage with him or her? Is he or she open to input or would s/he dispute anything you say?

Chapter 23, "Choose Your Battles," has a series of questions you can ask to determine whether this relationship is worth saving or whether you may need to end the relationship to save yourself. First, it's important to evaluate whether one reason this individual has been taking advantage of your good nature is because you're too good-natured.

Action Plan and Discussion Questions

Think back to a bully you dealt with in your life. Did he or she display any of these controlling behaviors in the beginning? Which ones?

At the time, did you believe those behaviors were a temporary, legitimate result of negative situations? Explain.

Is there a person in your life right now who has more than five of these traits? Does knowing these are patterns of behaviors that will only get worse motivate you to change your relationship with this person? Why or why not?

Could you be contributing to this unsatisfactory relationship? What is your role in what's happening?

Chapter 4
ARE YOU TOO NICE FOR YOUR OWN GOOD?

"Life is a fight, but not everyone's a fighter. Otherwise, bullies would be an endangered species. --author Andrew Vachss, founder of PROTECT

A single lady raised her hand in a program and asked rather plaintively, "I don't understand it. I'm a nice person. Why is it the last three guys I've gone out with all turned out to be jerks?"

The answer may surprise her and you. Bullies actively seek out people pleasers because they can count on them to go along to get along.

You may not like to fight and you don't see life as a fight. But bullies do. That's why they deliberately target nice people who "won't put up a fight" because they know they'll be able to win "without a fight."

Be honest. Are you a people-pleaser? A peace-maker? A Pollyanna type person who likes to be positive and look on the bright side?

That can be a strength, but it can also be a weakness when dealing with bullies.

Why? Webster's defines a bully as someone who is habitually cruel to others weaker than himself. Bullies don't pick on powerful people, they pick on people who won't push back. For a bully, that translates into a nice person. Bullies love nice people because nice people can be counted on to continue being kind nice even when someone's being mean to them.

One of the most important lessons-learned I've learned in the last ten years is that our strength, taken to an extreme, becomes our Achilles Heel.

Kindness and compassion are wonderful qualities, but not when someone is being cruel to us.

As William Blake said, "He has observed the Golden Rule, 'till he's become the Golden Fool." When dealing with someone whose goal is to control, ethical approaches often invite exploitation because they're interpreted as weakness. If you're playing by the rules and bullies are breaking the rules, they will win every time.

It can be disillusioning to discover one of our best qualities is being used against us. It can be disheartening to understand we've been "played," and that someone has knowingly taken advantage of our kindness.

The good news is, you can still be nice to people who deserve it and be strong when people don't deserve your kindness. *You can be NICE and STRONG.*

Is Everybody Happy?

The pleasers' motto is "Is everybody happy?"

Pleasers often come from unhappy homes in which they received limited support or love. They thought being obedient and/or agreeable was the way to get their parents' attention, so they did their best to be the good little boy or girl. Even as adults, they continue to try to ingratiate themselves to others to get the acceptance they never received as kids.

Pleasers are approval junkies. If someone doesn't like them, they quickly self-examine to see if they did "something wrong." They then adapt to get back in the other person's good graces. If someone is upset, they are the ones who try to make it right, to keep the peace at any cost. Unfortunately, the cost is often them giving in and going along, at the sacrifice of their own wants, needs and rights.

Pleasers are quick to see other people's points of view instead of their own, and frequently give up their opinions with comments like "It doesn't matter" or "I don't mind" when it does matter and they do mind. They are the quintessential "No, you go first" personality types. As a result, many pleasers feel put upon by their family members, co-workers, and acquaintances. They don't want to risk alienating anyone, so they say yes instead of no even when they don't want to be in charge of the third grade bake sale and they don't want to let their neighbor borrow their lawn mower—again.

As you can imagine, this takes a toll. Pleasers are so desperate for harmony, they pay almost any price to keep everyone happy. While outwardly, pleasers often appear to have it all together, internally they feel taken advantage of. Not that they'll complain about it. They wouldn't dare risk alienating public affection. Only to themselves will they admit their heartbreak because everyone seems to take their generosity for granted.

Are you wondering, "What's this got to do with bullies?" Bullies partner with pleasers for several reasons. First, bullies are often disliked and they want to feed off the popularity of their well-liked partner. They're hoping that associating with a charming mate will cause people to hold them in higher regard.

Second, bullies are often obsessed with status. They want to prove they're big shots, which is why they often have fancy houses, expensive toys, and trophy spouses. It's a "look at me" attempt to loom large in people's eyes and inspire envy.

Third, bullies are privately envious of pleasant personalities. Harville Hendrix's groundbreaking research into relationships says that we seek mates who complete us. We look for qualities in our partner that we admire and that we lack. Since many bullies lack social graces, they're consciously or unconsciously hoping that their mate's social skills will rub off on them and they'll acquire the characteristics they lack but secretly long for.

Finally, tyrannical bullies know that pleasers will kowtow to their domineering ways. The compulsive need to live in harmony that pleasers feel means they often end up acquiescing in an effort to avoid unsettling conflict. Bullies know all they have to do to get a pleaser to give in and give up is to get ugly. They know pleasers will capitulate rather than risk the dreaded unpleasantness.

Is Your Willingness to Take Responsibility Working Against You?

So do you have a "pleasing" personality? If so, this otherwise attractive quality may have attracted the wrong kind of individuals— people who are more interested in exploiting your pleasantness than appreciating it.

I've discovered that kindness and compassion often go hand in hand with empathy and accountability. Kind people are quick to look at THEIR behavior to see if they did something wrong. Compassionate people are quick to see how they may have contributed to something that went wrong.

Taking ownership of a situation and self-examining to determine what role we played in a relationship gone wrong is an excellent characteristic. And this "three fingers pointing back at me" philosophy can be taken too far.

In fact, bullies pervert your willingness to "own" a situation and use it against you. Now, everyone's finger is pointing at you – holding you solely responsible for why the relationship isn't working.

"Boy, does this strike home," a man named Daniel said. "I was the only child of a distant and cold mother. Nothing I did was ever good enough. My childhood was a vain attempt to get her to notice me and love me. So what did I do when it was time to get married? I found someone just like 'dear ole Mom,' of course.

"I tied myself in knots trying to make my wife happy. No matter how hard I tried, she always found something wrong with it or me. Sound familiar?" he asked, smiling at his own expense. "If I took her out for dinner for our anniversary, she wanted to know why I hadn't gotten her flowers. If I got a raise at work, she wanted to know why I hadn't gotten one sooner. If I bought her a dress, she wanted it in a different color. There was just no pleasing this woman." He laughed out loud at what he had just said.

The truth, as Daniel found out, is that it's impossible to please some people. In particular, it is impossible to please tyrants because they don't want to be content, they want to be in control. They want you to continue to feel you're "never enough."

Efforts to cajole a bully never work because a bully wants to perpetuate the cycle of his or her partner's never obtaining approval and therefore trying harder to win it.

Why? **The emotionally distant person in a relationship rules that relationship.**

That's such an important insight, I'm going to repeat it. *The emotionally distant person in a relationship rules that relationship.*

By withholding what their partner wants, bullies keep control. Bullies adopt aloofness as a way to keep pleasers on an emotional leash.

Bullies are disapproving on purpose because they know appeasers can't stand rejection and will renew their efforts to "keep the please."

Who Am I Trying to Please and Why?

"The reward for conformity is that everyone likes you but yourself." --author Rita Mae Brown

The question is, how can we change what is, for some of us, a lifetime habit of relating to others? Next time you're about to say yes to a request or give in to a command—whether it's agreeing to cover for a co-worker while she takes a long lunch or going to see a violent movie you rather not watch, take a moment to reflect on the following questionnaire.

Am I doing this because . . .

1. I owe this person a favor and it's a fair exchange?
2. It's a tangible expression of my love or respect for this person?
3. They deserve what they're requesting?
4. It's a way to honor them or say thank-you?
5. It's a present for a special occasion?
6. It's my "job" and I'm required to?
7. I know in my heart it's the right thing to do?
8. I truly want to? I'm doing it willingly and without coercion?
9. I want to contribute to this person (or to mankind) in a positive way?
10. It will serve me and give me something I want (money, status, satisfaction, pleasure, more time)?

Or, do your motives fall into the following categories:

11. I'm trying to buy this person's approval?
12. I don't want this person to get mad at me?
13. I have a sense of obligation and feel I should say yes?
14. I don't know how to say no?
15. I don't want to hurt this person's feelings?
16. I'm afraid people will think less of me if I don't go along?
17. This person is pressuring me with "Everybody else does it"?
18. I'm afraid this person will cause a scene if I don't give in?

19. I habitually agree to do what people want?

20. I don't have the strength, clarity, or courage to say no?

Answering "yes" to the first ten questions means you have valid reasons for granting this person's request. You are agreeing for all the right reasons.

Answering yes to the second set of questions means you would be abdicating your own rights, needs, and desires. It is not in your best interest to give in to what this person wants.

Four Steps to Saying "No" When Being Pressured to Say "Yes"

The path to confidence requires learning how to respectfully refuse people's unreasonable requests. If being agreeable has become a habit, you can begin reversing it by resolving to take these four steps to saying "No" when being pressured to say "Yes.

From now on, when people ask you to do something you don't initially want to do, vow to:

1. TAKE TIME TO MAKE YOUR DECISION. A friend has a coffee mug that says, "Patience comes to those who wait." Well, wiser decisions also come to those who wait. Say, "I want some time to think this over. I'll get back to you later today (or tomorrow)."

If the other person tries to pressure you, simply say, *"Fine, if you want an answer right now, the answer's no."*

Then get away from this person so you can think this through in private. Bullies often loom over you as a way of getting their way. They are well aware that your momentary "unsureness" is no match for their intimidating presence or charming seductiveness. Delaying your answer and removing yourself from their sphere of intense influence prevents bullies from mentally crowding you. You are literally and figuratively giving yourself some space so you can get perspective on this issue and determine whether saying yes is in your best interests.

2. REVIEW THE HISTORY Of THIS PERSON'S DEMANDS. Has this person consistently been over the top with coercive requests? Have you been a "guilt sponge" and absorbed more than your fair share of the responsibility for making this relationship work? Have you consistently given up what you want while this person has been getting almost all of what he or she wants?

3. DETERMINE IF SAYING NO IS WHAT'S REQUIRED TO KEEP A BALANCE OF POWER. Understand it's your responsibility (not the other person's) to make sure your needs are met, your rights are respected, and your desires are granted. If saying yes will perpetuate a "one up, one down" relationship— with you on the bottom, again!—it's time to refuse this request so the relationship will be more equitable.

4. KEEP IT BRIEF. The more succinct you are, the more convincing you'll be. Do not offer long-winded explanations. The more reasons you give for your decision, the more ammunition you give aggressive individuals to shoot down your answer. The more you hedge, the harder they'll press. Simply say, "No thank you." Or "No, I'm not going to do that." If they "demand" an explanation, simply look at them and say, "Because I don't want to. End of story."

Don't Get Drawn Into Debating Your Position

"Most fears of rejection rest on the desire for approval from other people. Don't base your self-esteem on their opinions." – Harvey McKay

Anticipate that manipulators will try to make you feel bad for not giving them what they want.

If, for example, a co-worker says, "But you've always covered for me before," simply repeat what you said and do not get drawn into defending your decision. As Mark Twain observed, "it is easier to stay out than get out" of an argument. If you try to justify your refusal by saying, "Well, I have too much to do today," a habitual exploiter will quickly say, "I'll only be gone a little bit." If we weakly protest, "Violent movies make me uncomfortable," a controlling person will sense your ambivalence and pile on extra pressure: "Come on. It got good reviews. Do it for me."

Explanations lead to debates. It's better to refuse over-the-top requests without justifying yourself. Keep the responsibility ball in their court by saying, "You're welcome to find someone else" or "I'm not going to see violent movies anymore. Period." You can also say, "My mind's made up" or "This is non-negotiable." They may stomp off, but remember, they are hoping that throwing a tantrum will motivate you to capitulate.

Maintain your clarity that you are no longer going to try to please everyone at your own expense. As Harvey McKay points out, don't base your self-esteem on whether other people approve of you. You don't have to be mean, just mean what you say.

From now on, reverse the "disease to please" by:

- Understanding the unhealthy pathology behind needing everyone's approval
- Recognizing it is fair (and your right and responsibility) to balance your needs/ wants with those of others instead of constantly giving in to others' needs and wants
- Asking the "Who Am I Trying to Please and Why?" questions to see if you're agreeing to this person's request for wise reasons
- Firmly refusing over-the-line requests without apologizing or defending your rationale
- Becoming clear you want the self-respect that comes from saying "No" vs. losing self-respect because you gave in to go along
- Remembering that in the final analysis, what matters is whether *you* approve of what you do and how you behave

The moral of this chapter is that happiness is best achieved by serving yourself in balance with serving others. Being nice should not require the ongoing sacrifice of your rights and needs. Being clear about this is central to having the assurance to not give in to intimidating tactics.

Action Plan and Discussion Questions

Are you a people pleaser? If so, what do you think contributed to you becoming one? Do you mostly seek approval from men or women, family members or authority figures? Explain.

What's a relationship with a significant other in which you traditionally go along to "keep the please?" Who is that person? What are some ways you try to win approval or keep harmony?

Have you recently agreed to a favor even though you didn't want to? Talk yourself through the "Who Am I Trying to Please and Why?" questionnaire. Why did you say yes? How are you going to say no and honor your rights and needs - without weakening under his or her pressure, defending yourself or being drawn into a debate?

Chapter 5
ARE YOU DEALING WITH A JEKYLL/HYDE PERSONALITY?

"Sticks and stones can break my bones, but words can break my heart." – author Robert Fulghum

Financial columnist Michele Singletary wrote an insightful article in *The Washington Post* about how we often don't follow our own advice. Michele has repeatedly warned readers to never give private information over the phone. On this particular day, she had gone to the gym for a workout. She walked out of the health club only to find her car window shattered and her purse gone. Devastated, she still had the presence of mind to report the theft to her bank and credit card companies.

A short while later, she received a call from her bank manager on her cell phone (which she'd kept with her). He explained they had caught the burglar trying to use her ATM card. Relieved, Michele burst into tears. She was especially appreciative of the manager's solicitous manner. He asked for a few details so he could confirm her account information, explaining he wanted to make sure the thief didn't have an accomplice who would try to use her card at another branch. Thankful for his thoroughness, she gave him the information and promised to meet him at her bank as soon as she could get there.

As she started driving, it struck her. She had given a stranger her PIN number. Oh no! She arrived at her bank and, as you might have suspected, her worst fears were confirmed. No one knew what she was talking about. The person she had talked to was the thief, not the bank manager, And yes, in the short time it had taken her to realize she'd been had, he had withdrawn the maximum amount of funds from her account.

Michele couldn't believe she had fallen prey to such an old trick. She was especially angry with herself because she realized the reason she never suspected the truth was that the caller had such a courteous, urbane voice. She realized that somewhere in her mind, she must have thought someone with such a sophisticated, caring manner could never be a crook.

Welcome to the world of Dr. Jekyll and Mr. Hyde. As the movie of that title so impressively shows, good and evil can exist in the same person. This can be a hard thing to wrap our mind around because we tend to think of people as good or evil, not both. Remember the old nursery rhyme "When she was good, she was very, very good; and when she was bad, she was horrid"? Well, that's how Jekyll and Hyde personalities work. They are one person in public and another in private.

Bullies Are Masters of Deception

"There are only two things I don't like about him. His face." -- author, Dorothy Parker

In her book *Not to People Like Us*, author Susan Weitzman addresses a surprising bias that she discovered through her counseling practice. Namely, that society doesn't believe domestic abuse happens to middle and upper class women. Her research has revealed just the opposite— that up to 60 percent of the women in her practice have suffered from what she calls "upscale violence." She says many of these women are successful in their own right, have a college degree, and live in a household with a combined income of $100,000 or more.

The article makes the point that not only does society discount this as a possibility; the victims themselves don't believe it's happening because they've never been exposed to abuse before. They are bewildered that someone who supposedly loves them can at the same time be so cruel. Weitzman explains that many of these women are accomplished high achievers who have never had anyone be mean to them. They conclude they must be doing something wrong and redouble their efforts to "fix the problem." Further complicating the issue is the fact that these women are confused. On one hand, their spouses are charismatic, high-profile leaders, active in their community or church. On the other hand, these same "role model citizens" are capable of shocking brutality.

One of the terrifying aspects of these on-off personalities is you never know which one you'll wake up to, which one you'll come home to, or which one will walk in the door. This means you live on a constant roller coaster of apprehension. Anyone who lives or works with this type of individual never knows what's coming next. Things can be going swimmingly, and the next thing you know you're in hot water.

A psychologist friend once reported an interesting finding she'd heard at a conference she'd just attended. The lecturer had said that children are remarkably resilient and can learn to cope with almost any parenting style (short of out-and-out abuse) ... as long as it's *consistent*. What's actually more difficult to deal with is a parent who's affectionate one day and heartless the next.

Children never feel secure with this type of "hot-cold" behavior because they don't know if what they were allowed to do yesterday will be punished today.

Anxiety can be defined in two words: *not knowing*. Not knowing if what they say/do next is going to change their parent into a raving lunatic keeps these children in a never-ending state of emotional limbo.

Sound familiar? Those who live or work with a Jekyll and Hyde often end up nervous wrecks. Since they can't predict what will set this person off, they don't know how to prevent it from happening. They monitor everything they say lest they trigger a tirade. They often end up "dulling themselves down" to minimize the chance they'll do something the bully will find offensive and use as an excuse to turn on them.

As you can imagine, this guessing-game lifestyle takes a toll. To make matters worse, people on the outside often tell J & H victims how "lucky" they are. Acquaintances only see the public behavior of Mr./Ms. Hyde, which is purposely kept "perfect," so everyone wrongly concludes they're a "perfect" couple. Partners of J & H bullies rarely go public because their accounts of abuse are met with skepticism. A horrifying reality is that if victims finally dare to speak up about their torment, people tend to discredit their "outlandish" charges against this "pillar of the community."

Whistle-blowers are often the ones pilloried instead of the one doing the damage. The sad fact is that people who are not privy to what goes on behind closed doors tend to look askance at the accuser rather than the abuser. At some level, people simply can't or don't want to believe that an acquaintance they admire could be capable of atrocious behavior.

What's worse is that police can take action only if there's tangible evidence of a crime. This makes trying to hold a Jekyll/Hyde accountable even more of a no-win proposition, because verbal abuse does not leave physical marks. It leaves emotional scars (sometimes for decades after the fact); but since psychological wounds cannot be visually substantiated, somehow they don't count. The deliberate destroying of a human being's spirit can't be proven so it goes unpunished. Furthermore, the bully has often warned the victim not to report him or else. The victim is frightened into silence because s/he knows from experience the abuser has the obsessive determination to make good on his or her threats.

So what to do? Decide that your mental and physical health is a higher priority than the "false" security of a marriage, house, and income—especially if that marriage, house, and income come attached with an abuser. Realize that your sanity and safety are more important than maintaining the status quo. It's especially important to realize that if you have children, staying in this relationship means you're teaching them this is what marriage is like and this is how men and women treat each other. You're teaching them a parent's role is to martyr him or herself and to silently suffer and stay in a relationship—no matter how horrible.

Is that what you want your life to be? Is this what you want as your future? Is this what you want your children to mimic— because they will. If you've been telling yourself that maybe this Jekyll-Hyde person will change, they won't. Research shows again and again that abuse doesn't "go away" of its own accord; it escalates. As a psychologist explained, "It is better to be from a broken home than in one."

Years ago, a woman told me her story. "I was one of the millions of married people who thought divorce was not an option and that it was important to 'keep the family together at all costs.'"

She added, "I know how trite that sounds, but the statistics and studies at that time backed me up. They all reported that children suffer terribly as a result of divorce, and I thought, 'I can't do that to my kids.'

My dad had always played devil's advocate around the dinner table and taught us to defend our decisions with logic, so I placed an inordinate amount of importance on what the 'experts' said. Research showed there was no such thing as an amicable divorce for children and that kids suffered devastating consequences because the parents couldn't get their act together and behave like grown-ups. So, I was determined to do everything I could to provide a healthy home for my kids and give them a good upbringing."

She continued. "My husband was a very public person, active in his industry and the recipient of many awards for his 'community service.' But, at home, he was increasingly abusive to me. I told myself I was an adult and could deal with it … as long as the kids weren't being harmed. Then I discovered that my husband, the same man who had all these pictures of himself with politicians and celebrities on our walls, was not really in construction, as I had believed all our married life. He was connected to the mob.

Then, my kids started having problems, and I realized it wasn't just me who was being abused. "I told him I had found him out, and that I was leaving and taking the kids with me. Big mistake. He warned me that if I even thought about leaving, he would have me declared insane and put away—and I knew he could do it."

This terrified woman left in the middle of the night with her five (!) children, drove cross-country, and lived, frugally and incognito, on the West Coast until her kids were grown. She said, "My children constantly thank me for having the courage to do what I did. My three sons are all married and they are wonderful to their wives. My two daughters don't let anyone mistreat them. I guess that's my legacy. My advice to anyone who is in an abusive relationship is 'You may not know how you're going to pull it off and it may be very hard, but you will never regret leaving. You will only regret not leaving . . . sooner.' "

Are you living with someone who is charming in public and cruel in private? Does this person have a Dr. Jekyll and Mr. Hyde personality – you never know who's going to walk in the door, who they're going to be on any given day?

This is crazy-making behavior because you can never relax. You never know who this person is going to be TODAY. You are constantly on edge, because you never know what's coming next.

F. Scott Fitzgerald said one sign of intelligence is the ability to hold two conflicting thoughts in the mind at the same time.

This is one of the most confounding aspects of dealing with a bully. They are not ALWAYS evil. They can be "normal", but then turn on you in an instant.

The hard thing to understand is that bullies can be BOTH. They can abuse you one moment and apologize the next. Which to believe? This dichotomy of behavior causes a roller-coaster of emotions.

What is insidious about this is that, in your mind, you may believe that someone who is kind can't also be cruel. You think such diametrically-opposed behaviors couldn't exist in the same person; they must be mutually exclusive, one OR the other. So, if this person is kind one moment and cruel the next, you see their cruelty as an aberration. It was a "mistake," a "one-time" thing to be forgiven and forgotten.

No, Jekyll and Hyde personalities will always be both. And cruelty is a deal-breaker. If they've been knowingly cruel to you once, twice, three times ... they'll do it again. It's a fatal flaw. And it's not going away and it's not getting better.

As Robert Fulghum noted at the beginning of this chapter, hurtful words are not harmless things that can be taken back, again and again, They can break the heart and spirt of everyone around them.

If you are dealing with someone who has a pattern of Jekyll/Hyde behavior, and who has ignored your attempts to improve the situation, it is time to seek outside counsel.

If this is a personal relationship, please see a qualified specialist – whether a psychologist, therapist or domestic abuse counselor – to explain the situation and explore next steps.

If this is a professional relationships, please document the behavior with the W's and report the unacceptable behavior to the proper authorities. What was said and done? By whom? When? Where? Who witnessed it?

Action Plan and Discussion Questions

Do you work or live with a Dr. Jekyll and Mr./Ms. Hyde personality? Who is that person? What's an example of their public-private behavior?

Does this person keep you on edge because of their on-off behavior? Do you believe this person will change or that circumstances will improve? Why or why not?

If this is a "public" person, are you afraid people won't believe your version of events if you reveal what goes on behind closed doors or when no one else is around? Elaborate.

Does this person mistreat you and then recant ("I'll never do it again") and ramp up their efforts to "win" you back because they don't want to "lose" you or they don't want you to leave? Do you believe them because you choose to see the best in people? Then, they do it again? Explain.

Do you see now that the pattern of Dr. Jekyll-Hyde behavior will re-occur and get worse, not better, and that it's in your best interests to report the behavior and/or to get away from this person? Explain.

Chapter 6
Are Idealistic Expectations Part of the Problem?

"Expectations are resentments under construction." – *Anne Lamott*

Many of us have idealistic expectations of how people ought to act.

These "wishful thinking" beliefs undermine our effectiveness and destroy our ability to deal effectively with bullies. Why? Our naïveté' means we're constantly caught off guard when people behave in ways we think they shouldn't.

Simply put, we can't respond to bullies the way we have in the past, or we'll reap the same unsatisfactory results.

We need to examine our expectations and see if they're helping us or hurting us. This chapter identifies several idealistic expectations that make matters worse. It then recommends replacement "realistic expectations" that can contribute to, rather than compromise, our bully-busting efforts.

As you read through these, ask if your default beliefs about how people are supposed to act could be undermining your ability to neutralize the controllers, intimidators and manipulators in your life.

In case you're wondering, "Okay, what if I discover I have been idealistic and optimistic about the bully in my life treating me better; how is that going to help me?" … rest assured, the upcoming chapters will teach you exactly what to do if someone is abusing your good nature. For now, simply ask yourself if any of these idealistic expectations might have unwittingly encouraged the bully in your life.

Idealistic Expectation # 1: Silence Is Golden
Realistic Epiphany: Silence Emboldens Bullies

"People told me that if I ignored you, if I pretended that you didn't bother me, you'd eventually give up and move on to the next victim. So why didn't that ever happen?" – Laurie Faria Stolarz in Dear Bully: Seventy Authors Tell Their Stories

Many of us have been taught to "turn the other cheek" and "hold our tongue." In fact, Calvin Coolidge said, "I never regretted a single thing I didn't say." Unfortunately, when we turn the other cheek with a bully, they'll slap that one, too. Bullies perceive silence as permission. Remember, bullies are not going to reflect on their actions and realize the error of their ways. They won't admonish themselves with "This person doesn't deserve this. I'm going to apologize." No, bullies think, "Great! I mistreated this person and s/he didn't protest. I'll interpret that as a green light."

From now on, realize that silence sanctions. As you'll discover in Chapter Seven "Protect Your Space, Enforce Your Boundaries," bullies will continue to invade our emotional turf unless we establish and enforce verbal boundaries. You may be thinking, "But my mind goes blank and I get tongue-tied when someone's mean to me. That's why I don't speak up. " Don't worry. I'll teach you exactly what to say when you don't know what to say.

Idealistic Expectation #2: Active Listening Promotes Understanding
Realistic Epiphany: Active Listening Perpetuates Abuse

"Listening is being able to be changed by the other person." – actor Alan Alda

"Normal" people understand that the willingness to put yourself in the other person' shoes and hear their thoughts, needs and desires, is the key to mutually-rewarding relationships. Healthy relationships rely on being willing to listen and care about the other person's point of view, not just our own.

This works though only if the other person is equally interested in listening to you. It works only if the other person is open to seeing things from your point of view, to being "changed" and influenced by you.

This is why giving bullies empathetic attention often backfires. Listening to controllers, intimidators and manipulators gives them an undeserved "bully pulpit." Active listening to someone who's on a rant grants them unwarranted carte blanche opportunities to dump their vitriol on us and dominate our mind and time.

Dr. Jacob Azerrad, author of *Anyone Can Have a Happy Child*, believes Americans attend more to bad behavior than to good behavior. He believes this is due to "kiddie gurus who repeatedly urge parents to soothe, comfort, and talk to a child who screams, throws things, or otherwise acts in obnoxious, infantile ways." He points out that the more faithfully parents follow this foolish advice, the worse their children behave. Azerrad suggests that "Instead of playing therapist, parents need to teach their children how to calmly handle things that don't go their way."

Agreed. It's time to stop playing therapist to adult bullies who throw tantrums when they don't get their way. We need to stop giving them a willing, sympathetic audience and start teaching them they can't get away with obnoxious, infantile behavior. Chapter Eight, "Clarity is the Key to Being Confident" teaches you how to cut bullies off mid-sentence so they can no longer bend your ear or will. You will learn that interrupting a bully is not rude, it's the right thing to do.

Idealistic Expectation # 3: Crying Purges Emotions
Realistic Epiphany: Crying Produces More Emotion

"At first you might wonder what you did to deserve such treatment. Nothing, probably, so that doesn't matter. What matters is that, eventually, the abuse becomes the status quo. It's no longer about the whats and whys ("what did I do?" "why are they doing this?") but the whens and hows ("when are they going to do it?" "how are they going to get me?"). Persecution becomes inevitable, inescapable. And once you get into the victim mindset, you're **ed. The bullies don't even need to hurt you now; your poor, warped, pathetic brain is doing half the work for them." –Nenia Campbell, from Freaky Freshman: A Memoir of Bullying and Social Anxiety

One of the biggest lessons I've learned about dealing with bullies is that, past a point, crying makes us weak. For months I was in a state of shock as the bully I was dealing with disobeyed court orders, and the authorities did nothing to hold this person accountable. The constant barrage of character assassination designed to break my spirit almost did just that. I wore out the phone talking to a couple of close friends looking for advice, solace, and (I now realize) sympathy.

In essence, I was feeling sorry for myself. Although my despair was justified, my sister, bless her heart, finally told me that my "Poor me" and "Ain't it awful" attitudes were perpetuating the problem. She was right. Self-pity preserves the bully-victim loop.

Tears have been called the safety valve of the heart and summer showers to the soul. Crying can be a healthy, tangible way to purge grief. Pouring out the tidal wave of frustration to a trusted friend or therapist can help us survive and find a solution.

However, as Voltaire said, "The longer we dwell on our misfortunes, the greater is their power to harm us." In other words, weeping keeps us wounded. There comes a time when it is to our advantage to stop crying and start trying. Once we have mourned and allowed ourselves to feel the sadness that accompanies being bullied, it's time to regain our strength and self-respect. One way to do that is to stop complaining about the situation and start planning what we're going to do about it.

Idealistic Expectation #4: Bullies Are Responsible for Fixing the Problem
Realistic Epiphany: The Person Being Bullied is Responsible for Fixing the Problem

"I was a gawky, skinny girl with big teeth and that made me an easy target. I had two bullies who tortured me all through junior high school. Only later could I see that I was showing them my fear and that's what they were pouncing on. When I finally stood up to my bully, that's when things changed for me. I'm sure those experiences explain why I've been so anxiety-ridden in my adult life." --actress Eva Mendes

We need to accept that even if what's happening isn't our fault, it is our responsibility. This may seem grossly unfair. It is also the way it is, and the sooner we learn this lesson, the better off we'll be.

Why is this so important? Because *"There are no victims without volunteers."* You may protest, "I don't agree with this. Innocent children don't volunteer to be abused." You are absolutely right in pointing out that innocent children are not responsible for being mistreated.

There are also adult exemptions. A man in a seminar objected, "I'm a victim of a drunk driver, and the idea that I somehow created this offends me. I was sitting at a traffic light waiting for the light to turn green when this guy who was ten sheets to the wind plowed into the back of my car. I was in a hospital for three weeks, and I've spent the last ten months in physical therapy. My car was totaled; the driver didn't have insurance; and I've spent hours on the phone trying to take care of bills that I shouldn't have to pay for in the first place. You can't tell me that I somehow asked for all the misery this guy has put me through."

This is an important distinction. I am not suggesting that we necessarily attract bullies into our life, and I am not saying we're to blame for what's happened.

I am saying we have to take responsibility for fixing what's happened, *because the bully won't.* We may not have provoked these unfortunate circumstances, but we can't wait for bullies to come to their senses and make things better . . . *because they won't.*

Sally Kempton said, "It's hard to fight an enemy who has an outpost in your head." Waiting for wrongdoers to do right by us means our peace of mind is in their hands. This incident and individual may be out of sight, but they are not out of mind. For our own mental health, we need to move on, and the way to move on, even if we're still in the midst of an ugly situation, is to see it as our trial by fire.

At some point in our lives, all of us have probably had some cross to bear. We have suffered, or will suffer, a disaster or an injustice. At that point, as fellow speaker W. Mitchell says, "We have a choice. We either focus on what we can no longer do or on what we can do."

Mitchell ought to know. Riding his motorcycle through the streets of San Francisco, he was blindsided by a laundry truck. The resulting crash and fire left him with no fingers and a disfigured face. Being the original eternal optimist, Mitchell recovered from those injuries and continued on with his life— becoming the mayor of Crested Butte, Colorado, and running for congress.

Then, while taking off from a small airport, the private plane Mitchell was piloting lost power and crashed. After helping his passengers to safety, Mitchell found he couldn't get out of the plane. He was paralyzed from the waist down.

For many people, two life-shattering incidents in the span of a few years would have been the proverbial last straw; they would have descended into despair. Not Mitchell. At last count, he has traveled to more than fifty countries and spoken to more than half a million people in his mission to share his inspiring message "It's not what happens to you, it's what you do about it."

As Mitchell knows from experience, when life (or a bully) knocks us down, we can stay down, feeling sorry for ourselves, lamenting all the while how unfair this is, or we can get up, brush ourselves off, extract insight, and move on. As Ernest Hemingway said, "The world breaks everyone, and afterward many are strong at the broken places."

**Idealistic Expectation #5: If I Try Hard Enough, Long Enough, Smart Enough, The Bully Will Ultimately Come Around, See the Light, Apologize, and Make Amends
Realistic Epiphany: Believing This Keeps You in The Bully's Power**

"Bullying builds character like nuclear waste creates superheroes. It's a rare occurrence and often does much more damage than endowment." --author Zack W. Van

Did you see the 2015 Academy-award winning movie *Whiplash?* Actor J.K. Simmons won an Oscar for his lead role as Fletcher, an abusive band leader who creates an atmosphere of fear in his classes. He mercilessly taunts a talented drummer, Andrew, causing him to become depressed, abandon his relationships and ultimately get expelled.

Later in the movie, Fletcher and Andrew bump into each other. Fletcher explains the only reason he pushed Andrew was so he "could achieve greatness." (Right!) Fletcher invites Andrew to play at a music festival, but then sabotages him by playing a different song for which Andrew has no score. This IMDB plot synopsis summaries what happens next:

"Andrew leaves the stage humiliated, but returns and begins playing 'Caravan.' The rest of the band follows his lead and joins him. Andrew ends the performance with an impressive drum solo. Fletcher is at first angry, but then gives a nod of approval to Andrew as he finishes."

Unfortunately, as my friend Jeanne Sullivan said in her TEDx talk, *How to Deal With Bullies, Bozos and Buffoons* ... *"That only happens in movies."*

This "Hang in there and ultimately an abuser will give you respect" is a downright dangerous bunch of hogwash. It's why many people stay in roller coaster, abusive relationships because they think if they're just "good enough", the bully will finally recognize their value and give them the respect they want, need and deserve. They keep trying to impress the bully in the hopes the bully will "come around" and apologize and make amends. That is *not* going to happen.

First, why spend years trying to get the approval of someone who treats you terribly?

Second, to somehow imply, that a two second "nod of approval" is worth months (years!) of misery is totally messed up.

Third, it is not in a bully's DNA to self-reflect and self-correct. Their whole M.O, is to stay on top. They are not about to acknowledge your success; that threatens their superiority. If for some reason they do, watch out because it's only a matter of time before they take you down a notch so you don't get "too big for your britches."

Bullying Is a Test of Your Self-Respect

"People always say I didn't give up my seat on the bus because I was tired, but that isn't true. No, the only tired I was, was tired of giving in." -- Rosa Parks

One of the most important things I've learned in the fifteen years that I've been writing about, speaking about and researching this topic of bullying is ... that bullying is a test of your self-respect. It essentially comes down to, "How are you going to let people treat you?"

Being bullied is a defining event in your life. It is a test to see what you will stand for – and what you won't stand for. It is a test of what you think relationships should look like, and how passive or pro-active you're going to be about creating a quality life.

Soon after J.K. Simmons won an Oscar for his role as the abusive music teacher in *Whiplash*, I read a wonderful review of the movie *Seymour*, which is about a revered piano teacher.

In a stroke of luck, the movie was premiering at a nearby theater the next day, and Seymour Bernstein himself was going to be there for a Q & A following the film. I immediately went online and bought a ticket.

I watched this exquisitely beautiful movie with tears running down my face. Why? Because THIS is how a REAL teacher behaves. The movie showed Seymour sitting side-by-side with his students, praising what they did well. Diplomatically showing them how to play a passage better. His teaching honored the gift of creative expression. Not one abusive word. Not one act of intimidation, manipulation or bullying.

It's easy to see why Seymour's students love him and love music. Seymour doesn't *abuse* people to become their best, he *encourages* them and shows them how to become their best.

What a stark contrast. Don't ever believe a verbal abuser who is telling you they're doing it "for your own good," who's claiming it's because they "want the best for you." Those are the Fletchers of the world. Their bullying is about control, not about caring.

Instead, seek out the Seymours. Seek out people who support you, not sabotage you. Seek out relationships where mutual respect is the norm.

Is It Time to Update Expectations and Take Back Control?
"The only thing necessary for the triumph of evil is for good men to do nothing." –
Edmund Burke

Are you tired of giving in to and going along with a bully who has been undermining your self-respect and quality of life?

Have you realized that, at some level, your unrealistic expectations were keeping you in a toxic situation because you thought that, someday, somehow, things would get better?

Do you understand that how you respond to a bully is a defining event? That what you put up with or not - shapes who you are and how you perceive yourself?

As Edmund Burke pointed out, doing nothing is not an option. If you do nothing, the situation will stay the same or get worse. Continuing to operate with the same naïve expectations will perpetuate the problem. The bully in your life will continue to control you, intimidate you, manipulate you, take advantage of you.

The next chapter teaches how to start holding bullies accountable so you start receiving the respect you want, need and deserve.

Action Plan and Discussion Questions

Did you relate to any of these idealistic expectations? Which ones?

How have these beliefs compromised your effectiveness in neutralizing a negative individual's impact? Has your kindness or silence made the situation better or worse? Explain.

Have you "cried buckets," as one lady confessed? How has it helped? How has it hurt? Is it time to dry your tears? Why or why not? Could it help to see the bully as a defining event, as your trial by fire? How so?

Do you agree with the idea that "There are no victims without volunteers"? Why or why not?

Do you see yourself as a victim? Is that a story you tell? If so, what benefits do you derive from considering yourself a victim?

Do you agree it's your responsibility to fix what's happening, even if it's not your "fault?" Are you ready to take steps to solve this - even if the bully is the one causing the problem? Why or why not?

PART II
REAL-WORLD WAYS TO DEAL WITH A BULLY

"The willingness to accept responsibility for one's own life is the source from which self-respect springs." – author Joan Didion

Chapter 7
PROTECT YOUR SPACE, ENFORCE YOUR BOUNDARIES

"I believe each individual is naturally entitled to do as he pleases with himself and the fruit of his labor, so far as it in no way interferes with any other man's rights."
-- Abraham Lincoln

Bullies do just the opposite of what Lincoln suggested. They feel entitled to do exactly as they please even when it interferes with other's rights. In fact, they deliberately invade our boundaries in an effort to establish dominance. That's why we need to assert ourselves and back bullies out of our physical and psychological space. They will continue to push us around if we don't.

You may be thinking, "Easier said than done. Someone violating my space is such an abstract concept. What space? Is there a way to make this gray issue more black and white?"

Matter of fact, yes.

Every animal (including humans) has a safety circle. This is both a physical and psychological space around us that is "ours." This varies from culture to culture, and situation to situation, but picture a hula hoop around you. That's your 'space." No one should intrude in that space unless you invite them, trust them and want them to be there.

If another animal (including humans) encroaches upon that imaginary yet real boundary, s/he is too close for comfort. S/he now poses a threat and we feel at risk.

Wild animals (lions, deer, zebras) and domestic animals (dogs, cats, horses) have clarity about not letting others violate their boundaries. For a variety of reasons, we human beings frequently allow others to breach our physical and psychological boundaries, and therein lies the problem.

Many times, when someone is behaving in ways that are not right, fair, or kind, it's because we have not explained or enforced our boundaries. This chapter explains how to identify, communicate and enforce our boundaries.

A surprising example of boundary enforcement happened one morning while I was walking my Jack Russell terrier (known for their feistiness). JR spied a cute little furball ahead and dashed up to check her out. This little doggie dynamo, less than half of JR's size, launched herself at him and yapped fiercely.

JR jumped back in surprise. The little Pekingese stood there glowering at him. JR decided to give it another go. He approached, a little more cautiously this time, to try to sniff noses (or whatever). She was having none of it. She lunged at him again and barked even louder. JR got the point and bid her adieu.

Notice that little Pekingese didn't rationalize JR's behavior with "Well, he probably had a dysfunctional puppyhood and doesn't know any better." She didn't passively submit while reflecting, "Well, he's young and just hasn't learned his doggie manners yet." She didn't pardon his unwelcome approach with "I need to put myself in his paws and see things from his point of view." She didn't mull over his actions and acquiesce resignedly with "Well, he's probably feeling needy because he's new to the neighborhood and doesn't have any friends."

No, that little furball let JR know in no uncertain terms that his behavior was not welcome. She was quite clear that he had crossed the line, and barking was her way of communicating "Back off!" which JR promptly did.

If only we humans were as clear about barking (I mean marking) our boundaries. Many people in my seminars share tales of woe about bullies who have behaved atrociously. When I ask, "Have you said anything to them about this?" a surprising number admit they haven't.

Unlike the fuzzball, we sometimes rationalize a bully's unwelcome intrusions with "He must have had a frustrating day," "She didn't mean it," or "He's under a lot of pressure." We silently submit to unwanted impositions out of some mixed-up sense of social obligation or manners. We internalize our dismay, thinking, "I can't believe he or she did that!" These are indirect and ineffective paths to protecting our rights. You've heard the phrase "His bark was worse than his bite"? If we bark, we usually won't have to bite because bullies will back off and stop bothering us.

What to Do When Someone Invades Your Hula Hoop of Space

Our physical space is an arm's length away, literally. Stretch your arms out in front of you, to the side, and then as far as you can behind you. That's about three feet, and that's your safety circle. People shouldn't come into that "hula hoop" of space unless you invite them in or unless they're someone you trust who has permission to be in close proximity. And yes, the size of personal space varies with different cultures and changes when we're jammed together in a public place. That's why people who are on a packed bus or subway car often avert their eyes. It's a way of honoring others' space and maintaining your own.

From now on, if someone inappropriately crowds you, don't internalize your discomfort, express it with body language or articulate it with words. You can raise your eyebrows as if in surprise they'd violate your space and look at them as if saying, "Yes?" Your body language is sending the unspoken message of "What do you want and what are you doing in my space?" If the person doesn't back away, look rather pointedly at his or her feet and then up and say, "Little close, aren't you?" If the person still doesn't get the hint, put your hand up and say, "Hey, back off" to reestablish a proper distance.

What if you're in your office, and someone approaches you from behind and hovers over you. Turn toward him or her and give them a "What the heck?!" look. Or say, "There must be a reason you're crowding me. What is it?"

People who violate your boundaries may be doing so innocently. However, if you don't establish from the beginning that you control your space, not them, they will conclude they can intrude anytime they want. When you don't determine who can get "near and dear," you abdicate your power. Ethical people won't take advantage of this, but unethical people will. Allowing people to trespass when you don't want them to sends a sign that you can be pushed around and acts as an unfortunate precedent that people can have their way with you.

If someone continues to physically pressure you, use your words in addition to your body language. Hold your hand up with your palm out. This is a universal gesture meaning "Stop!" An outstretched hand wards off unwanted advances because it means "Don't come any further." Say out loud, "Back off" or "Give me some room." This lets people know that you will not passively acquiesce to any attempt to crowd you.

There was a fad a few years ago where kids would put their palm out and tell someone who was bothering them, "Talk to the hand, not to the face." That was a tangible way of letting whoever was trying to get under their skin know, "Whatever you're trying to do – isn't getting through."

Doing this in polite conversation isn't appropriate, however if someone is clueless and getting too close for comfort, it can be an effective way of keeping them out of your space and face.

If you're at work, and someone approaches you from behind or in the hall and puts an unwelcome hand on your arm or shoulder, shake it off. I'm not channeling Taylor Swift, I mean physically *shake them off.* Shake your shoulder to dislodge their hand and say out loud, "Hands off!"

And yes, do that even if this person is your boss. They're the one out of line. You need to let them know you're not going to let them cross the line or they will not think twice about doing it again, and again.

Do Not Forgive Those Who Trespass

You may be wondering if bullying is an international problem and if these techniques work in other countries? The answer is "Yes" and "Yes."

I was asked to speak at the Asian Leadership Conference in Seoul. Other speakers included Prime Minister Modi of India, President Park Geun-hye of S. Korea, Former Prime Minister Kan Naoto of Japan, former President of Germany Horst Kohler, Secretary General of The United National Ban Ki-Moon, and Jack Ma, founder of China's Alibaba Group.

While there, I got a copy of the May 16-17, 2015 *Korea Herald* and found this in an advice column called *Annie's Mailbox.*

"My next door neighbor has made my husband and me feel like prisoners in our own home. The day we moved into our house, she stood in our front yard and asked where each piece of furniture was going to be place in the home. When we have family over for a backyard barbecue, she walks right over to the grill and interrupts our meal. Anytime one of us it outside, she immediately comes by to gossip about other neighbors.

I want to put up a fence, but my husband is concerned what people will say. We now have to open our door and look around before going anywhere. We are considering moving. How do I deal with this situation?" - Trapped by Nosy Nellie

The columnist replies, "By all means, put up a fence. You are entitled to your privacy, and if your neighbor doesn't like it, too bad. Stop worrying what she will think. Be polite, but do what you need to do to enjoy your home."

Hmmm. What would you suggest these people do?

I don't think they should have to foot the bill to put up a fence they don't want. I think they should enforce their boundaries because this woman is trespassing. Their yard is their property and they have the right to allow only who they want on it.

Ideally, in the beginning, when she planted herself on their lawn and started asking where they were putting their furniture and why, they could have realized they didn't have to respond to her questions just because she asked them. They could have put the ball back in her court with, "Why do you ask?" If she said something like, "Just curious." They could have said, "Oh," and gone about their business.

When she trespassed into their yard, they should have spoken up and said, "Nellie, this is a private party." If she didn't take the hint and leave, then it was time to stop being subtle and start being direct. "Nellie, this is our back yard and we did not invite you. Please leave." When she approached them on their driveway or sidewalk to gossip, they should interrupt and say, "Nellie, don't want to hear it."

Are you thinking, "You're going to hurt her feelings" or "Oh, that's so rude!" Please note, you are not being "rude" when someone ignores hints, social cues and polite requests to respect your space. If they insist on physically or psychologically trespassing, do not worry about hurting their feelings. They are not worried about hurting yours. They will continue to violate your space unless you are crystal clear in backing them off.

Over the years, I've come to understand that articulating and enforcing boundaries is the "first line of defense" when dealing with bullies. They will throw out "test" insults to see how we react. They will physically crowd us to see if we back down. They will use a sob story to play on our emotions to see if we're easily manipulated. Like this neighbor Nellie, they will continue to encroach on your space as long as you let them.

When you call them on their behavior, they may not like it but they'll stop trying to get away with it.

Guarding Your Emotional Space?

"If anything, we should feel sorry for people who want us to feel bad about ourselves, because they are the ones struggling for approval. In school, bullies tortured other kids because they thought it would make people like them more." — singer *Ariana Grande*

It's easy to tell when someone is physically crowding us. It's harder to tell when someone's mentally crowding us. You may be wondering if there's a way to make this "cross the line" concept more concrete.

Yes, there is. Picture an old-fashioned seesaw like the one you used to play on in the schoolyard. Imagine yourself on one end and the person you're dealing with on the other end. Understand that the success of any relationship (whether it's between you and a friend, you and your spouse, you and your boss, you and whomever) depends on whether this Rights/Needs Seesaw is kept in balance.

You've heard the expression that "every relationship has its ups and downs"? That's true, and as long as the ups and downs are fairly even (catch the significance of those words), this remains a mutually rewarding relationship.

As long as both people are sensitive to each other's wishes, as long as both are willing to make the adjustments that are part of living or working together, as long as compromises are somewhat equitable, and as long as both have equal say about how the ride operates, this will be a healthy partnership.

Bullies Don't Want an Equal Ride

"I was very tiny. I spent most of my time stuffed into lockers. Thank god for cellphones, or I'd still be in there." -- Chris Colfer, actor in TV series Glee

The thing is, bullies don't want a partnership with a balance of power; they want a dictatorship where they have all the power. They want to, as Ariana Grande pointed out, make you make you feel so bad, you'e down and can't get up. Their idea of give-and-take is for them to take, take, take while you give, give, give.

Picture your relationship with a domineering individual in your life. Do you have equal say-so about how your ride (relationship) operates, or are you stuck on the bottom all the time? Do you hardly ever get your way and the other person almost always gets his/her way? Do you feel like you're along for the ride, whether you like it or not?

Can you picture how wrong it is for one person in a relationship to always be in the driver's seat, to always be on top, the other always on the bottom?

Can you see it's appropriate for you to get your fair share of needs/rights met? From now on, if a bully tries to (metaphorically speaking) stuff you in a locker, understand you need to stand up for what's fair despite his/her efforts to keep you down.

A manager named Norm said, "I have an employee who drives me nuts. Tracy is so manipulative. She is always complaining about something. She comes in late, leaves early, and is always taking time off to run errands she insists can't wait until after work. In the beginning, I agreed to her requests because she always had a good excuse, "My other is coming in from out of town and I need to pick her up at the airport," "My best friend is in the hospital," but after a while it got to be too much. The other employees resented that she was getting special treatment.

"Tracy walked into my office last week and told me she was taking Friday off to attend a networking event. Normally, I support employees who want to participate in industry programs. However, I thought this was just another of her ploys to get out of the office.

"I mentally pictured the history of her demands over the last few months. It was obvious that she had taken more than her fair share of favors. I told her she couldn't go, that she was behind on her projects and needed to get caught up. She tried to get me to change my mind by saying it was too late to cancel because she had already paid. I didn't buy into it and told her she was needed to be in the office all day Friday.

"She was not used to not getting her way. She upped the ante by accusing me of not supporting her professional development. Instead of responding to that ludicrous accusation, I stayed on track and said, 'Tracy, you are the one who has repeatedly taken time off and not made up for it. You need to fulfill your work obligations or start looking for another job.' She stormed out of my office, but I didn't budge and didn't apologize because I was clear she was the one out of line, not me."

From now on, if someone is trying to manipulate you into giving them what they want, picture the Rights/Needs Seesaw. If they have a pattern of getting their way, it's time to enforce the rules and hold them accountable for what's fair to you and others.

Action Plan and Discussion Questions

Who is someone in your life who is trying to emotionally manipulate you? What is this person doing to get his/her way?

Picture the history of the Rights/Needs Seesaw with this person. Are the ups and downs fairly equal? Is this person on top and you're on the bottom, most of the time? Do they consistently get their needs met, and you hardly ever gets yours met? Explain.

Can you see it's up to you to keep this relationship in balance, and that means saying "No" next time this person wants you to do something you don't want to do?

Do you have someone in your life who is physically crowding you and/or intruding on your physical space? What has she or he been doing or saying?

Did you enforce boundaries in the beginning? Did you give subtle hints or polite requests that were ignored? Did you not speak up at all? Explain.

Do you now understand it is your right and responsibility to keep bullies from abusing your psychological and physical boundaries? What are you going to say to back this person off so they are no longer encroaching on your physic territory?

Chapter 8
CLARITY IS THE KEY TO BEING CONFIDENT

"If you're horrible to me, I'm going to write a song about it, and you won't like it. That's how I operate." -- Taylor Swift

Clarity is the key to having the confidence to confront bullies.

Why? Confusion immobilizes. When we're not sure what we believe, we're not sure what to say or do, and when we don't know what to say or do, we usually don't say or do anything. Bullies capitalize on this uncertainty to press their advantage.

At one point in my battle with a bully, the tactics being used against me were unconscionable. I was exhausted but needed to keep running my business and making money to pay bills and support myself and my sons. I was flying to a speaking engagement in a small town on a prop plane. I was right next to the engine so it was incredibly noisy.

Who knows why, but all of a sudden my brain was on fire and the "Clarity Rules" you're about to read poured out of my mind so fast my fingers could hardly keep up.

I wrote them down on the only piece of paper I could find. (Yes, I found it in the seat pocket of the plane, and you can imagine what it was. That will teach me for not carrying a notebook with me.)

I will be forever grateful for that divine guidance or whatever it was that "downloaded" these Clarity Rules in a matter of minutes. They came to me "pure" and they are as heartfelt and relevant as when I first wrote them down almost 15 years ago.

Clarity produces conviction. Conviction keeps us strong. Think about it: If you're clear that your health is your top priority, it's easier to go out for that walk, run or workout – even when you don't feel like it. When you are clear about the RIGHTS in the Clarity Rules, you don't allow people to mistreat you or the people around you. .

Imprint the following "Clarity Rules" in your mind. Believe them in your gut. Post them where you can see them throughout the day. Carry a copy in your wallet so you can pull them out when the occasion warrants. Review them frequently for a shot of courage. The clearer you are about what's important to you, the less vulnerable you'll be to a bully's effort to knock you down and keep you down.

If you live in the United States, you studied the Declaration of Independence and the Emancipation Proclamation that address the human bill of rights. Yet some of us forgot that we each have inalienable human rights. For whatever reason, we gave up control of our lives to someone who sought power over us.

Emancipation is defined as "to free from restraint, control, bondage, or the power of another." Our goal is to develop and adopt our own personal Bill of Rights so we can emancipate ourselves from individuals who have been bullying us. Understand that bullies will not just go away and voluntarily leave us alone. Why should they? They've got a good thing going. We must take responsibility for ending a dominant/doormat situation or it will continue.

The Clarity Rules

"When your values are clear to you, making decisions becomes easier." -- Roy Disney

I have clarity that I choose to believe the best of people, and I give them the benefit of the doubt until they prove me wrong.

I have clarity that I will be kind and compassionate until someone tries to take advantage of my good nature.

I have clarity that I will seek win-win resolutions until it is obvious the other person refuses to play by the rules.

I have clarity that it is my responsibility to speak up if someone crosses the line of common decency and tries to intimidate me.

I have clarity that suffering in silence perpetuates the problem.

I have clarity that I will walk tall so bullies won't perceive I'm weak.

I have clarity that I am a worthwhile person who has the right to stand up for my needs if someone tries to trample them.

I have clarity that I will ask myself, "What's my culpability?" so that I do not unwittingly contribute to or perpetuate a bully's mistreatment.

I have clarity that I will set and state limits in advance so people know my boundaries and ethical threshold.

I have clarity that I will no longer "keep the please" at any price.

I have clarity that I want to serve as a role model for my loved ones that we do not passively endure someone verbally abusing us.

I have clarity that my definition of a healthy relationship is one in which both parties have the freedom to think and act for themselves.

I have clarity I will not volunteer to be a victim. I will remove myself from a relationship in which someone is trying to own/control me.

I have clarity that words can hurt and haunt. I will not demean others and I will not allow others to demean me or a loved one.

I have clarity that life is a blessing, not a burden. I will not allow bullies to intentionally undermine my quality of life or that of my loved ones.

I have clarity that I am responsible for my physical and mental health, and I take appropriate action to improve unsafe situations.

I have clarity I do not give myself up and I do not give up on myself.

Get Clear That What You Accept, You Teach

"What impresses me about America is how well parents obey their children."
—*Duke of Windsor*

Remember earlier in the book we clarified that bullies come in all shapes, sizes, and ages? These "Clarity Rules" apply to our relationships with children as well. As the Duke of Windsor observed, some adults answer to their children instead of the other way around.

"Talk about confused," Abigail said. "My 22 year-old daughter had me turned inside out and upside down. I was supposed to be the parent in the relationship, but she had me twisted around her little finger.

"I had always dreamed of those close mother-daughter relationships where you went shopping together, were the hang-out house, etc. It was never like that with us. Tiffany's teen years were a nightmare. My friends told me her behavior was typical adolescence and she would grow out of it. She never did.

"Tiffany came home after college because she couldn't find work. A couple of months stretched into six months, six months stretched into a year, and she still hadn't found the 'right' job. During this time, she was online, texting her friends or lying around watching soaps. Every time I tried to talk to her, she'd turn things around and say I was unsympathetic.

"I finally went to a therapist to get help. The therapist just let me pour out my frustration the first session. Over the next few weeks, she helped me see that I was being bullied by my own daughter and that I had enabled this situation by not setting up and enforcing ground rules. She helped me understand that the way out of this mess was to keep asking myself, 'Who's the parent?' and by giving Tiffany what she needed rather than what she wanted. She also suggested I pull a mea culpa."

Abigail continued. "Mea culpa is Latin for 'my fault.' The therapist told me turning this situation around was going to be tough because the precedent was set that Tiffany could do whatever she pleased. The only way to change this losing game was for me to take responsibility for letting things get out of hand. After all, Tiffany was only doing what I had let her get away with. In a way, I had taught her that her behavior was acceptable because I hadn't held her accountable The therapist helped me write up 'House Rules' and told me how to enforce them.

"I told Tiffany we were going to have the first of what was going to become a weekly family meeting. The therapist had emphasized how important it was to make this a formal ritual rather than a casual get-together, so we sat down at the dining room table. I took responsibility for letting her take advantage of the situation, told her I realized the error of my ways, and *that things were going to be different from now on.*

"I explained that if she wanted to continue living in our home, she needed to obey the rules and contribute to the house upkeep. If she chose not to do that, she had a week to move out."

"Tiffany just sat there, stunned. I told her I should have done this a long time ago, but hadn't been clear about my role as a parent. I now realized I wasn't helping her by helping her, and I was going to hold us both accountable for being responsible adults."

"I also told Tiffany, 'A condition of you continuing to live here is that we go to counseling together once a week. If you have issues with this, we can work them out with the therapist.'

I wrapped up by saying, 'I have absolute clarity about this. There will be no excuses or exceptions. Begging, crying and name-calling will NOT motivate me to change my mind. I told her I was looking forward to us living together in harmony, and hoped this would be one of the best things that ever happened to us. It was."

A woman who heard this story asked skeptically, "Do you really think that she would have thrown her own daughter out of the house?"

I told her, "She needed to be prepared to do just that or otherwise she was teaching her daughter to take advantage of her."

Empty threats serve no one. That's why it's so important to be clear about your proposed action. The mother was doing the right thing by claiming mea culpa and by outlining the new policies and consequences. If the daughter chose to break the rules, it would be her fault she's out of the house, not her mother's. Tough love is simply a way of teaching people that they will be held accountable for their behavior, whether they like it or not. Instead of the world revolving around them, they learn that if there are consequences if they choose not to play by the rules.

Are you in an untenable situation right now? Have you given yourself a bad back by bending over backward to accommodate someone who is breaking the rules? Has your confusion about your role or rights perpetuated this problem?

Remember to pull a mea culpa so the people affected don't feel they're being unfairly blamed for behavior they were never held accountable for in the first place. That's the catch-22 of not enforcing policies. Rule breakers may know what they're doing is wrong, but if no one complains, they conclude it must not be that bad. Their logic is "If it was really important, you'd stop me, so I guess this must be okay."

Action Plan and Discussion Questions

Did anyone ever teach you that you had rights? If so, who was that person and how did he or she tell you this?

Do you agree with the rights in the "Clarity Rules"? Are there any you would like to edit or add? Which ones?

Are you in a situation that's overdue for some rules? What are they and how are you going to establish them?

Visualize meeting with this person. What exactly are you going to say to claim mea culpa and agree to a fresh start? How are you going to let him or her know that things are going to be different from now on?

Chapter 9
DON'T SUFFER IN SILENCE – DO THE YOU

"The need for change bulldozed a road down the center of my mind."
—*Maya Angelou*

If someone has been bulldozing a destructive path down the center of your life, it's time to hold that person accountable.

And the way to do that is, instead of being hurt and internalizing what that person said or did and keeping it to yourself, is to ... SPEAK UP.

In particular, it is to speak up using "You" words instead of "I" words. Let me explain why. My research shows that many people responded to bullies in one of three ways.

AVOID: Many people think that if they tiptoe around bullies and don't say anything to "make them mad" ... bullies will leave them alone. Wrong. What they're not taking into account is that bullies pursue their targets. Once a bully has fixated on you, trying to stay quiet and steer clear is ineffective because the bully will find you. He or she will seek you out even if you're doing everything you can to be invisible.

ACCOMMODATE: People who are conflict-averse often end up making unhealthy compromises to prevent confrontations. The problem is, bullies know this and purposely play it to their advantage.

Accommodating bullies perpetuates their intimidation because they know people will back down in the face of their aggression. People who go along to get along better learn how to get along without their self-respect, because they won't have much.

ASSERT: Well-meaning psychologists and conflict resolution experts often recommend you assert yourself by using "I" words because it is a way of "owning" your beliefs and behaviors. That is absolutely the right thing to do when both people are playing fair. However "I" statements backfire with bullies. Telling a bully "I don't think this is fair" or "I don't deserve this" is exactly what s/he wants to hear. The whole point is for you to be bothered by their behavior. "I" statements don't dissuade bullies, they delight them.

Are you wondering, "If these three approaches don't work, what does?" The answer may surprise you. I am going to suggest something that probably flies in the face of everything you've been taught.

DO THE YOU: Start using "YOU" statements with bullies. "You, back off." "Shame on you." "You are out-of-line." "Doing the You" is more effective than avoiding, accommodating or asserting – because it keeps the attention on the bully's inappropriate behavior.

Do the You

If there are no heroes to save you, then you be the hero. -- Denpa Kyoshi, fictional hero of the manga series Ultimate Otaku Teacher

Actress Melissa McCarthy showcased how to "Do the You."

While appearing on the TV show *Ellen*, Ellen Degeneres asked McCarthy to share her response to a film critic who had accused her of looking "hideous" in the movie *Tammy*. He claimed she was "only effective when she was attractive," and she shouldn't allow herself to look so terrible in public.

McCarthy ran into this critic at the Toronto Film Festival. Instead of avoiding him, she walked right up and asked , "Would you have said that to a man?"

He waffled, so she asked a follow-up question, "Do you have children?"

He said, "Yes, I have a daughter."

McCarthy asked, "How would *you* feel if your daughter came home and said she'd been told, "You can't have a job because you're unattractive." Would *you* say, "That's right."

"No," he said, "I would never want that to happen."

She said, "Please think about this. Every time you write about women and tear them down, little girls read that and it chips away at their self-esteem."

Kudos to Melissa McCarthy. Notice she didn't use "I" words. "I was hurt by what you said." That would have made her seem "emotional" and might have led to a thoroughly unsatisfying debate that went something like this, "Well, that's too bad you didn't like what I said. I'm a movie critic. I was just doing my job."

No, she asked him questions that caused him to have to answer for himself. By using "You" questions, she caused him to have to express and experience what it would have been like to be on the receiving end of his caustic comments.

President John F. Kennedy said. "A man does what he must—in spite of obstacles, dangers, and pressures—and that is the basis of all human morality."

WE need to do what we must – and that is to NOT stay silent when people are not acting with morality. Remember, silence sanctions and gives haters and trolls a bully pulpit.

A young woman showed the importance of "Doing the You" when someone tried to ruin a special moment for her. She was graduating from Georgetown University and her father showed up, uninvited. Her dad had been abusive to her mom and was persona non grata following their divorce.

Her father approached her moments after she had received her diploma. True to form, instead of congratulating her, he started in with his typical criticism, "You just wasted four years of your life. Why'd you get a degree in political science, anyway? You're never going to be able to find a job. You just threw away thousands of dollars."

He would have continued his verbal assault, but she put her hand up, looked him in the eye and said, "*Dad, stop. Do I look like my mother?*"

His mouth dropped open. She continued, "I'm proud of myself for graduating from this university, and I'm glad I got this degree. If you are here to help me celebrate, you're welcome to stay. If you're not, leave."

Bravo. Notice, she didn't go on the attack, she did what was necessary to stop his attack. She didn't lose control and start calling her father names. Neither did she back down under his mean-spirited remarks, break into tears and cry, "I don't deserve this. Why are you doing this?" She didn't turn the other cheek only to end up depressed, angry and resentful years later, lamenting that she never had successful relationships with men because her dad had been such a jerk.

She "Did the You." In no uncertain terms, she interrupted her dad and told him his behavior was unacceptable. She spoke up instead of suffering in silence and held him accountable for his hurtful words. She also posed a constructive option that gave him a face-saving out.

Look at that phrase, "in no uncertain terms." That is a prerequisite for speaking up to bullies. You can't waffle or be wishy-washy. You'll learn in upcoming chapters how to be crystal clear when holding bullies accountable so they know you mean what you say.

Like this savvy young woman, we don't want to be a wimp and we don't want to go on the warpath. We want to have the strength and skills to speak up on our own behalf, instead of passively allowing others to manipulate and intimidate us.

Sometimes, people bear bully behavior because they're passively hoping that time will heal all wounds. If they're insulted, they brush it off and think, "I don't mind." If someone mistreats them, they think, "It doesn't matter." It does matter, and you *should* mind.

Bullies count on us being afraid of them. Their modus operandi is to manipulate you into a moral cul-de-sac where you're forced to be the "bad guy." Since you don't want to be the bad guy, you end up tolerating situations you would never endure otherwise.

This was what was happening to a woman who consulted with me. She was a single mom of six adult children. Her one daughter had married an extremely possessive man who had emotionally blackmailed her into breaking off contact with her family. When they did show up at holiday gatherings he would ruin the occasion by barking orders at his wife, interrupting people right and left, and offending everyone at the table with bigoted, racist opinions. This woman was heartsick about what was happening to her daughter, but felt helpless. Her daughter had been so co-opted, she wouldn't listen to warnings.

The family had put up with this man's antisocial behavior because they wanted to maintain contact with their daughter and sister, even if it was just a couple of times a year. The mother confided, "We've come up with a plan. This Thanksgiving, if he starts in on one of his tirades, we're all going to get up and leave the table. That ought to teach him."

I looked at her, dismayed.

She asked, "You don't think that's a good idea?"

I said, "This analogy might give you an insight into what's happening. A young couple bought their first home and filled it with brand new furniture. The next weekend they went to the animal shelter and got a cat. The cat had been in its new home for only a few minutes when it started sharpening its claws on the sofa. The wife rushed over, picked up the cat, and put it outside. Later that day the cat started kneading the sofa again with its claws. The husband rushed over, picked it up, and put it outside. So from then on, whenever the cat wanted to go outside, guess what he did?"

Hmmm. This couple wasn't training the cat, the cat was training them.

"Abandoning your holiday meal won't teach your son-in-law the lesson you want. He's training you to continue to accommodate his abominable behavior. Think of the satisfaction and power you give him by getting up and leaving your own table in your own home.

"I know you feel he's got you over a barrel because you don't want to lose your daughter. The point is, he's holding everyone hostage. It's time for him to pay the consequences for his behavior instead of everyone else. When dealing with bullies, we need to honor the majority. Instead of many people sacrificing their rights to honor one individual's misbehavior, the one individual needs to change his or her behavior to honor the group's rights."

The woman asked, "What should we do?" I suggested, "Act as the matriarch and take charge. Tell your daughter your plans first so she's prepared, and then take him aside alone before everyone sits down. Tell him, 'Things are going to be different from now on. We value family, and our holiday meals are going to be a celebration of that. That means you will treat my daughter and everyone else in our home with respect. That means you will not share hateful, bigoted opinions at the table. That means you'll listen to what other people have to say without interrupting. This is our home and these are our rules. If you want to join us, you need to abide by them. If you choose not to honor these rules, you will be asked to leave and our daughter will stay. This is not open to discussion or second chances, so don't test us on this.' "

I told her, "Then walk away. Don't engage him in conversation. You are laying down the law; this is not open to debate. It doesn't matter if he likes it, what matters is that the family's values are being honored. Don't let him put you on the defensive. You are not being heartless, you are simply holding him accountable for decent behavior.

"If he acts up, stand, point to the door, and say, 'Roger, get your things and go.' If he turns to his wife and blusters, 'You're coming with me,' increase the intensity of your voice, look him in the eye, and say distinctly, 'Don't you dare put her in the middle of this. Margaret is staying here and finishing her dinner. You knew the rules. Now, leave.'"

I shared this story with a colleague and she said, "What if that son-in-law browbeat his wife into leaving with him anyway, and he cut off all communication with the family?"

I said, "You're right, there is a risk of that, and it would be unfortunate. It's important to understand, though, that the son-in-law is using the family's fear as a way of coercing them to put up with his offensive behavior. This is what bullies do; they make everyone else pay while they get their way. They create double-bind situations where your only options are lose-lose.

"If that happened, I hope the family reminds themselves that they didn't ask for or want this unfortunate situation. The bully has perpetrated it upon them and it's up to them to put a halt to his emotional tyranny. The alternative of continuing to tiptoe around his tantrums serves no one.

"In the final analysis, I still think it's better to call him on his behavior because if the family doesn't stand up to him, the daughter never will. Refusing to indulge his manipulative behavior may produce a period of painful estrangement, but hopefully, in the long run, their decision to no longer submit to his bullying would give their intimidated [look at the root of that word!] daughter the strength to do the same."

You may be thinking, "I don't know if I have what it takes to take on a bully." I assure you, you do have what it takes. If you don't put a stop to this, who will? Get clear that you will no longer allow anyone to intimidate you.

Action Plan and Discussion Questions

Do you have someone in your life who is trying to own you? What does he or she do to lord it over you?

Do you feel you've been forced into an double-bind situation where your only options appear to be lose-lose? Describe that situation.

Has this person intimidated you to the point you're afraid to speak up? Do you realize the bully has "trained you" to give in and go along? Are you clear it's your responsibility to speak up and put an end to the bullying? Are you ready to become your own hero? Explain

Chapter 10
CALL BULLIES ON THEIR BEHAVIOR

"People treat us the way we teach them to treat us."
— Jack Canfield, co-creator of Chicken Soup for the Soul books

Remember the lyrics of the classic Beatles song, *Let It Be?*
"When I find myself in times of trouble,
Mother Mary comes to me,
Speaking words of wisdom, let it be, let it be."

Tolerance can be an admirable trait. But when dealing with intimidators and manipulators, *intolerance* is the more admirable trait.

This was demonstrated to me while attending a convention presenters' dinner. On my right was a screenwriter-agent from Los Angeles, and on my left was a self-described Southern belle who had helped organize the conference. We were discussing the not-too-impressive lot of movies that had been released over the last few months. The woman on my left decried the decline of values and then added, almost as an afterthought, "A lot of this is the fault of all those homosexuals in Hollywood."

The screenwriter and I both blinked, not sure we had heard what we had just heard. I was offended by her remark, but was going to "let it be."

The agent wasn't going to let her off so easy. He looked at her in shock and asked, "What did you say?" She quickly backpedaled. He made one more comment, "That was really inappropriate" and then moved the topic on to something else.

I remember thinking, "Good for him." He was absolutely right not to "let it be."

Hopefully, expressing his intolerance of her sweeping generalization will make her think twice about her homophobic remark. She may even decide that not only will she not say anything like this anymore, she won't think it anymore either.

That's the power of positive intolerance. We don't want to give silent assent by ignoring inappropriate remarks. It only supports, encourages and perpetuates them.

My son Andrew and I were doing the weekly laundry when he was in junior high. He came in with an armload of basketball T-shirts and casually remarked, "Oh, yeah, Mom, I need some more 'wife beaters.'"

I looked at him, stunned, and asked disbelievingly, "What did you just say?"

He explained, "Wife-beaters. You know, the shirts with the cut-off sleeves you wear under your basketball jersey."

I told him, "Andrew, that's an offensive term."

He protested, "Mom, that's what everyone calls them."

I responded, "Andrew, other people may call them that. The question is, are you proud of calling them that? Is that the kind of term you feel good using? Please think of some other name for them."

He nodded and easily agreed, "Okay, Mom."

If I had said nothing, Andrew would have thought nothing of continuing to use that offensive phrase.

Please commit this to memory: When people say or do something that offends you, if you don't let them know it, they will continue saying and doing things that offend you. After all, you didn't protest, so it must be all right, right?

From now on, resolve to keep these "positively intolerant" responses at the ready so you are ready to call them on their offensive remarks:

- "Keep those kinds of thoughts to yourself."
- "That's offensive. Please think of a different way to say that."
- "You might want to reconsider that. It doesn't reflect well on you."
- "What?! You can't mean that."

- "Do you want to repeat that?" (said incredulously with raised eyebrows)
- "I'm sure I didn't hear that right. Do you want to rephrase that?"
- "Don't say stuff like that when you're with me."
- "Use different language. That is unacceptable."
- "What makes you think I want to listen to that?"

The above phrases can convince garbage mouths (as my mom used to call them) to change their tasteless tune.

There is another, even more tangible way to persuade people to clean up their off-color act. I used this technique at an airport and can vouch for its effectiveness.

My delayed flight landed after midnight. The complimentary hotel shuttle bus had stopped running, so I needed to catch a cab, even though my hotel was only five minutes away. I got in the backseat and gave the driver my destination. As soon as he heard the name of the hotel, he went ballistic and started swearing a blue streak.

I knew why he was upset. He had probably waited in line for a long time and was hoping to get a fifty-dollar fare, not a five- dollar fare. I understood his frustration, but screaming obscenities was not an option. Someone spewing profanity at you is a clear case of verbal abuse.

Instead of yelling back at him, I simply pulled paper and pen from my purse, leaned over the front seat, looked rather pointedly at his driver's license, and asked, "How do you spell your name please?"

He stopped, mid (invective-filled) sentence, and drove the rest of the way in silence. As soon as we arrived at my hotel, he jumped out and came over to open my door. He took my hand in his and pleaded, "Please don't report me. I can't afford to lose my license." He was as contrite as could be, and I marveled at the simple effectiveness of asking someone how to spell their name.

From now on, if people vent their vitriol at you, don't verbally lie down and take it. If you suspect this is a rare overreaction, you may choose to first use a sympathetic "Has it been one of those days?" Your caring question may be just the thing to let them know you're on their side and they'll stop directing their rage at you. If they don't respond to your attempts to work things out, you might want to make a last-ditch win-win effort with, "This has been upsetting for both of us, and I'm sure we can resolve it if we focus on solutions, not fault."

If they continue to rant or if you are simply not willing to tolerate their outburst, take out paper and pen and ask pointedly, "How do you spell your name?" or "What was that you said?" Rather than becoming belligerent yourself, these simple questions let them know their verbal abuse is not going to be allowed. Making a memo is a way to inform insolent individuals you are making a written record of their inappropriate remarks, which is often sufficient incentive for them to zip their lip.

Remember, people who act objectionably are testing you to see what they can get away with. That's why it's so important to establish and enforce boundaries in the beginning of any relationship.

Teachers know the importance of starting the school year tough. As my Aunt Carol, a kindergarten teacher in California for more than twenty years, said, "You can always loosen up as time goes by. But if you don't let 'em know who's boss that first day, you'll be playing catch-up the rest of the school year."

Consider what Aunt Carol said: "We've got to let them know who's boss." Boss is defined as "one who exercises authority or control." That is why bullies come on so strong. They're trying to establish themselves as top dog. If we allow would-be bullies to boss us around, we'll end up as the underdog.

The first day of class, Aunt Carol always laid down the laws. One of the most important rules was that when she clapped her hands three times, everyone was to get silent immediately. She would practice with the class until everyone, and I mean everyone, got it right. "Right" meant no talking: not one giggle, whisper, or tailing-off conversation. Those five-year-olds respected Aunt Carol because they knew they were loved and would be held accountable for courteous behavior. Aunt Carol didn't believe in wishy-washy rules that were enforced one day and not the next, applied to one child and not the other. Her standards (boundaries for behavior) were clearly stated and consistently enforced. As a result, there was order in the classroom and those kindergartners behaved like angels (well, most of the time).

Do you have standards of behavior for the people in your life? Are they too low or inconsistently enforced? If so, it's not too late to declare a do-over. Remember do-overs from when you were growing up? Do-overs are the child's equivalent of a golfer's mulligan. Perhaps you were playing jump rope, and three jumps in, you slipped and stepped on the rope. "Do over?" you asked hopefully.

Declare a Do-Over

A woman named Carla said her husband had gotten into the habit of coming home in a black mood. He'd slam the door on the way in, throw his briefcase on the table, and stomp around the house until his funk wore off. Anyone unlucky enough to get in his way got an earful.

"I put up with it for a long time because he worked in a golden-handcuff job that he hated but couldn't afford to leave because it paid so well. On top of that, he spent at least an hour commuting each way, so I thought he deserved some slack.

After years of this, it occurred to me that I had bad days at work, too, and I didn't take it out on everyone else. Sometimes the kids were upset about something that happened at school and they didn't think it gave them the right to make everyone else miserable. I decided we'd had enough. That evening George made his normal grumpy entrance. I picked up his briefcase, took him by the arm, and marched him back outside. I closed the screen door in his face and announced, 'We're tired of you being such a grouch. We have bad days, too, and we don't take it out on you. From now on, when you walk into our home, treat us with the courtesy we deserve and leave your rotten moods outside.'"

She said with a smile, "He got the point. The word 'Do-over' is our 'code' now. If anyone in our family – and that includes me - starts taking our bad mood out on others, someone just says, 'Do-over' and it's over."

What Do We Do with Customers Who Are Out of Line?

A public seminar audience got into a heated debate about what we should do if we're dealing with a customer who won't respond to reason. A financial consultant contributed her opinion: "At my first job, the rule was 'The customer is always right.' That may work in theory. However, it doesn't always work in practice. We deal with some very demanding clients who seem to think they can treat us any way they want. My mother and father taught me I have the right to be treated with respect, and that doesn't include having someone order me around like a servant.

"One of our VIP clients launched into a tirade over the phone one day because she wasn't happy with how her investments were performing. I listened patiently for a while, sympathized about the market downturn, and then tried to focus on what action we could take. She continued using me as her personal wailing wall. I finally interrupted and said, 'Mrs. (who shall remain nameless), I want to help you, and please speak to me with respect.' She continued calling me every name in the book. I said it one more time. She kept venting, so I ended the conversation with 'Mrs.   , I want this conversation to be productive, and it's not. I am going to hang up, and you are welcome to call back when you are ready to speak to us with respect.'

"I knew there was a chance she would call our branch manager to complain about my impertinence, so I quickly documented the call so my supervisor would know what she had said and why I responded the way I did. She did call to complain, and thankfully our manager backed me up."

A savings and loan officer said, "I agree with this. Our policy is that the customer is right most of the time, but not always. We give our employees the right to make judgment calls about over-the-line behavior. We have an unwritten policy that our workers do not have to tolerate extreme behavior. We're even willing to lose a client if they insist on abusing a staff member. I got a call from one of our tellers who was being browbeaten by a customer. This teller, Lynne, has worked for us for years and is unfailingly polite. I knew the client must have really been a tough customer if Lynne hadn't been able to win him over. I asked that the man be put on the phone and started with my usual 'How can I help you?' combined with 'I'm sure we can work this out.'

"Most people calm down with that line because they feel they're talking to a senior employee who has the power to resolve their situation. It also helps that I assert the belief that we'll be able to come to a satisfactory conclusion.

"It didn't work with this customer. He continued ranting and raving. I kept trying to steer the conversation to a solution, but he was having none of it. After ten minutes of futility, I interrupted and said, 'Sir, it seems like we're not going to be able to satisfy you today. If you'd like to give the phone back to the teller, I will ask her to draw up a cashier's check for the amount in your account, and you are welcome to find a financial institution that fits your needs.'

"He sputtered a few times and then admitted, 'I don't want to close my account.' 'Fine, then,' I told him. 'Let's focus on how we can settle this issue and move forward.' That worked with him, but there are some people who refuse to respond to reason. I tell employees it's okay to 'fire' a client who repeatedly refuses to cooperate. I trust their judgment. I would rather they spent their time servicing our thousands of satisfied customers than spend all day trying to turn around a permanently disgruntled 'I'm going to be difficult until the day I die' individual."

WARNING! BEWARE OF THE VIOLENT BULLY

Freya Stark said, "Tolerance cannot afford to have anything to do with the fallacy that evil may convert itself to good." Understand that intolerance can convince many controllers and manipulators to cease and desist.

Intolerance can carry risks though. If you're dealing with a truly evil person, a Frank Underwood type who is willing to do anything to get to and stay on top of the food chain, it is better to steer clear of that person.

If your instincts are waving red flags, review the checklist in Chapter 23, *Choose Your' Battles* to decide whether being intolerant could put you at risk.

Action Plan and Discussion Questions

Do you know someone who has a history of spewing prejudiced, bigoted, sexist, hateful remarks? What have you done about it in the past?

How are you going to practice "positive intolerance" from now on? What are you going to say when someone makes an offensive remark?

Can you think of a time when someone said something out of line and you documented what they said? Did it convince them to cease and desist? Explain.

Were you taught that the customer is always right? Do you agree with that? What are some exceptions? Do you have a client who is behaving inexcusably? Are you prepared to hold them accountable even if that means "firing" them? Explain.

Chapter 11
NAME A BULLY'S GAME TO NEUTTRALIZE IT

"Let's address the elephant in the room. YO ELEPHANT!" – Pulitzer Prize winning humorist Gene Weingarten

Syndicated advice columnist Carolyn Hax is an ever-flowing fount of wisdom. I always look forward to her no-nonsense tips in *The Washington Post* because she can be counted on to call them how she sees them.

Many of her columns deal with some variation of the theme, "What do I say when someone is clueless and asks something that's none of their business?"

Carole believes in coming right back with, "That's none of your business," accompanied by a smile (or not) depending on the level of egregiousness (and if that's not a word, it is now.)

That's called "naming the game" and it works. Instead of tip-toeing around the issue of their inappropriate behavior, which is the elephant in the room, address it head-on.

As mentioned before, bullies often float trial-balloon taunts to test you. If they get a reaction, it WORKS and they'll do it again.

Often they don't even believe what they're saying; they're just saying it to get a rise out of you. They like to stir things up and create drama because it's a power trip for them.

Whatever you do, *don't deny or defend an outrageous accusation* because you'll end up arguing their point. Denying an outrageous accusation with "I never said that!" or "That's not true!" rewards bullies, because you are reacting to their attack, which is what they want.

If someone says, "You women are so emotional," and you say, "We are NOT EMOTIONAL," you've just proven their point. If a bully taunts, "Now don't get mad," and you say, "I am NOT MAD," now you are.

As said in previous chapters, "I replies" backfire with bullies. Anytime you "reply with an I" to an accusation, you just rewarded the manipulator because you bought into a back-and-forth, no-win argument.

If you're dealing with someone who likes to throw out disparaging remarks, lob the verbal hot potato right back in his/her lap. If someone says huffily, "Well, this is a technical issue and I'm not going to waste my time explaining it to you because you're not smart enough to understand it," interrupt and say, "What did you just say to me?" and then stop talking.

Making people repeat their snotty remark lets them know they're not going to get away with it. This simple question puts them on the spot instead of you. The query "What did you just say to me?" forces verbal hit-and-run artists to explain themselves.

Dame Helen Mirren demonstrated how to do this right in the middle of a media interview. The reporter referred to her as a "seductress" and asked, "Is it hard to be taken seriously as an actress because of your (gesturing toward her breasts) ... 'equipment?'"

She wasn't about to let him get away with his sexist remark. Instead of answering his question, she put the ball back in his court and asked one of her own with, "Explain yourself."

He blanched a bit because he knew he'd been called out. He said lamely, "You know ... your physical attributes."

"You mean my fingers?" she asked, waggling them, refusing to play along and accept this unflattering characterization.

Point made. Want a wonderful example of NOT answering an inappropriate question just because it was asked. It's far more effective to respond with a question, "What makes you say that?" or "Why do you think that?"

Remember, the onus (responsibility) isn't on you to respond to the content of an offensive remark. That justifies unfair, unkind or untrue accusations. You are arguing their point (no matter how outrageous) which is their goal. Their goal is to knock you off balance and have you on the mental ropes.

Keep your cool and call them on their tactlessness, "Why would you say something like that?!" "Shame on you." "Really?!" "You either take that back or you get reported. Which do you prefer?"

While I was out shopping for groceries, a man named Rob who had attended a *Tongue Fu!* workshop walked up, beaming, and reported a success story. He explained, "I work with a guy who seems to go out of his way to be condescending. I've been on the job longer, but he's got the higher degree and rubs his academic credentials in my face at every opportunity. The Monday after your workshop, Jack walked up to my desk, looked over my shoulder at a project I was working on, and said loud enough so everyone in our office could hear, 'Having trouble with that spreadsheet? You should try college. They teach that freshman year.'

"That did it," Rob said. "He had humiliated me in public for the last time. I stood up, got right in his face and said, 'What did you just say to me?'

You should have seen him. His mouth dropped open and he just stared at me in shock. I don't think anyone had ever challenged him before. I didn't say anything else; I didn't have to. I just kept looking at him, waiting for an answer. He finally mumbled something under his breath and beat a hasty retreat."

Bravo. Another reason the phrase "What did you just say to me?" works so well is because it uses the word "you" instead of the word "I."

I'm going to emphasize again the importance of making this shift. Responding with "I replies" is habitual for many of us. By all means, continue to use "I replies" when dealing with individuals who care about cooperation. If someone is "situationally upset" and you happen to be their lightning rod, go ahead and say, "I don't like being yelled at. Please speak to me with respect so we can focus on finding a solution to this." That helps them become aware it's not fair for them to take their anger out on someone who's trying to help them fix what went wrong.

If you use "I replies" with people who only care about control, they'll laugh in your face. Telling bullies "I don't like how you're behaving" doesn't motivate them to quit, it motivates them to continue. They *want* you to dislike what they're doing.

Furthermore, bullies try to make you responsible for how they treat you — the "You made me do it' rationale that is their stock in trade.

Using an "I reply" boomerangs back on you because it plays into their strategy to keep you on the defensive and makes you seem reactionary.

"Doing the You" keeps the attention where it belongs—on the bully's inappropriate remark. Imagine someone calls you fat. Saying, "I don't like it when you make fun of my weight" makes your reaction the problem. The bully will probably come right back with, "Then you should stop feeding your face."

It's better to say, "Rob, put a sock in it" or "Who asked for your opinion?"

Please note, reversing this habit and using "You" statements may feel awkward, even wrong, at first. That's why I've provided a variety of "I Replies" and "Do the You" responses below. Practice them out loud so you become comfortable with them and have the confidence to use them with bullies when it's time to trot them out in real life.

As you say them out loud, listen to how "I Replies" can come across as whiny or weak. The "Do the You" responses work better with bullies because they rebuff attempts to intimidate you, put you on the defensive.

"I REPLIES"	"DO THE YOU" RESPONSES
"I want you to stop."	"You need to back off."
"I've had it."	"Enough! You have gone too far."
"I don't appreciate having to wait.	"You need to apologize for being late.
"I don't think that's very nice."	"Stop that. Clean up your act."

A disc jockey at an Arizona radio station shared a "Do the You" success story. Following our in-studio interview, this deejay, who had been in a wheelchair for most of his adult life, told me about the rather frightening time he had had when firing an employee. "This guy was really upset. He stormed into my office and lit into me. He was leaning over, shaking his fist in my face. Instead of backing down in the face of his threats, I looked him in the eye and said, 'We'll have this conversation as soon as you sit down in that chair.'

"I was kind of surprised, but he sat down. If I had said something like 'I don't like being yelled at,' he would have probably shouted back, 'Tough! I don't like being fired' and kept letting me have it."

This deejay was right. An "I Reply" would have made him come across as a wimp. "Doing the You"—that is to say, "You need to speak to me with respect"—commanded the employee's compliance because it was a command instead of a cowardly plea. The deejay's strong rather than sympathetic response was exactly what the situation called for.

One woman had a problem with this idea. She said, "Isn't 'Doing the You" and naming the game just a form of attacking back? I've always been told that an aggressive response just leads to more aggression."

Good question. Surprisingly, I've found that most people aren't angry when you call them on their over-the-line behavior, they're appreciative. Situationally difficult individuals who are stepping on your emotional toes can be so caught up in venting, they're not really considering what it's like to be on the receiving end. They either don't have the discipline or self—awareness to police their own behavior, they expect you to police it for them. They figure if you don't like how they're acting, it's up to you to do something about it.

Addressing Issues (vs. Avoiding Them) Saves Everyone Time
"Decide what your minimum level of acceptable treatment is, and then do not accept less that that, even from someone you love, love, love."
– advice columnist Carolyn Hax

A woman named Nina told me, "My cousin was downsized when her corporation was acquired in a merger. She called almost every night to report her latest job-search nightmare. At first my heart went out to her because I imagined how awful it must be to go from employed to unemployed through no fault of your own. As the weeks went by, though, I got fed up with her nightly calls. She seemed to feel I didn't have anything better to do than to listen to her gripe. She kept telling me I was the only one she could talk to about this, but I finally got so frustrated, I let her calls go straight through to voice mail and didn't respond. I know that wasn't nice, but I was tired of listening to her. How should I have handled it?"

I suggested she could have pictured the Rights/Needs Seesaw to see that it wasn't rude to let her cousin know her nightly calls were over the top, it was the right thing to do. Instead of avoiding her cousin—which doesn't solve the problem and often aggravates it—she could have put a stop to the free therapy by saying, "I'm really sorry about what happened. I'll be glad to help you brainstorm how to find a new job. I'm not willing to listen to you rehash every night how unfair this is. You're right, however that doesn't help either of us."

Nina got back in touch with me to report she did contact her cousin, and much to her surprise her cousin admitted it hadn't been fair to hog Nina's evenings and apologized. Nina said, "What an eye-opener. I could have saved both of us a lot of time by speaking up instead of agonizing over this issue for weeks."

Remember Nina's lesson. Many people are glad when we clarify our boundaries because it means they don't have to second-guess how we feel. Honest communication is such a relief because we don't have to wonder if the other person is telling the truth or saying something "just to be nice." Instead of having to read between the lines and worry about hidden agendas, we can take each other at our word. It's a marvelous thing in a relationship to trust that other people will let us know if we're doing something that's bothering them.

We can't expect people to intuit how we feel. Communication can't be left to chance or coincidence. "Doing the You" is a clear way to let people know we consider their behavior objectionable. If they're ethical, they'll appreciate the heads-up. If they're unethical, they'll understand that we won't buy into their taunts, tirades, and power plays.

Action Plan and Discussion Questions

Have you been taught to use "I replies" when communicating with others? Do you see how they backfire with bullies who already blame everyone else for their behavior? Give an example where an "I Reply" just made the situation more frustrating.

Who is someone in your life who accuses you of things that are unfair, unkind or untrue? Do you deny or defend? As Dr. Phil would say, "How's that working for you?"

How are you going to "Do the You" and put the responsibility ball back in this person's court so they have to explain themselves or experience/express what it's like to be the recipient of their taunts/insults?

Chapter 12
HOW TO HANDLE A TEASER

"I don't deserve this, but then I have arthritis, and I don't deserve that either." –
Comedian Jack Benny

An often-used bully tactic is to say something mean and then follow
up with "Just kidding." Bullies claim their dig was unintentional, but it
was planned all along. If we protest their thinly disguised insult with
"Hey, I don't deserve that," they retort with mock innocence, "Stop
being so sensitive" or "Why are you making such a big deal about this?
It was only a joke."

Teasing is defined as (1) "to tear in pieces," (2) "to disturb or annoy
by persistent irritating," (3) "to attempt to provoke to anger,
resentment, or confusion," (4) "to goad," and (5) "to pester." Whew!
As you can see there's no "just" or "only" when it comes to teasing.

While it's true that some people's teasing is innocent banter that's
part of normal social interplay, bullies use teasing as a passive-
aggressive weapon. It's their way of saying something offensive without
taking responsibility for the damage they're causing. It's a malicious,
indirect way of rousing our wrath and weakening our self-esteem. It's a
sneaky way to get our goat while making us a scapegoat for their
unresolved anger or envy. What can we do about it? We can take the
sting out of poisonous barbs with these "Cease the Tease" steps.

7 Steps to "Cease the Tease"

"Most comedy is based on getting a laugh at someone's expense. And I find that's just a form of bullying. I want to be an example that you can be funny and be kind. You can make people laugh without hurting feelings." – Ellen DeGeneres

1. REMOVE THE INCENTIVE.

Teasers do not pick on people who are immune to their taunts. They target vulnerable individuals who reward them with satisfying overreactions. Stammering, blushing, crying, or becoming offended are all signs of victory to a bully. Desensitize yourself and understand that anything you're embarrassed about is ammunition to a bully. If you're overweight or have acne, you're going to hear about it. A young man I know in Hawaii who's a talented pro surfer is also pigeon-toed. He says, "It used to bother me when kids gave me a hard time about it, but then I realized I better learn to shrug it off. Now if someone brings it up, I tell 'em they're just jealous because being pigeon-toed lets me grip my board with my toes and gives me better balance surfing."

As Ellen points out, bullies are trying to get a laugh – *at your expense.* It's "money" to them if you are bothered by it. If you shrug off or laugh off attempts to get under your skin, they'll give up because teasing isn't fun when it doesn't work.

2. FIGURE OUT WHAT THE TEASER IS TRYING TO ACCOMPLISH.

Check facial expression to see if the teaser is being playful or punitive. If teasers have a spiteful gleam in their eye, they may be deliberately trying to one-up you. If they have more of a twinkle in their eye, this could simply be an example of their adolescent sense of humor. A teaser is usually trying to rile you by tossing out a taunt that elicits an emotional rebuttal. However, teasing can also be a socially clumsy way of engaging you in conversation and getting your attention. It's an immature way to get a reaction, any reaction, rather than be ignored. This could be an awkward way to try to connect with you.

3. GIVE THEM A DOSE OF THEIR OWN MEDICINE.

Beating teasers at their own game makes this a losing proposition for them. If you have fun with them, it's no longer fun for them to make fun of you. Turn the table on the teaser with "Look who's talking." or "This is a little bit like the pot calling the kettle black, isn't?"

The truth is, teasers like dishing it out, they don't like getting it back. When you meet teasers tit for tat, rap for rap, they're not controlling the situation, you are.

Taylor Swift's statement, "If you're mean to me, I'm going to write a song about it, and you're not going to like it" prevents anyone from messing with her. They know in advance they'll pay a penalty if they do.

4. WORK THE CROWD.

Is the teaser playing to an audience? If there are people around, the teaser is hoping to heighten his or her status by taking you down. The key in this situation is to talk to the group, not to the teaser. "Joe's at it again, picking on people he wishes were his size." In this way you're linking yourselves with them. Now it's not him against you, it's you and the group against him. Outnumbered, he'll probably slink away and think twice before taking you on again.

5. HEAVE A SIGH AND ROLL YOUR EYES IN MOCK EXASPERATION.

Teasers want to aggravate you. Adopting an "I'm so bored with this" posture frustrates teasers because this is the opposite of what they're trying to achieve. Look heavenward and say resignedly, "Here we go again. This didn't work last time. What makes you think it will work this time?" Meet their attempts to irk you with apathy. A weary "You're wasting your time" will cut 'em off at the passive-aggressive remark.

6. EXPOSE THEIR MOTIVES.

As soon as you take exception to his remarks—"I do not color my hair!" or "I was not coming on to you!"—the teaser has succeeded. Instead of going on the defensive, go on the offensive. "Why do you do this? Does it make you feel good to try to make people feel bad? Do you get some kind of cheap thrill out of it?" Uncovering a teaser's agenda and putting her "on trial" will quickly convince her that this is not worth her while.

7. AGREE AND EXAGGERATE.

Another way to take the fun out of teasing is to agree with a taunt and then add your own twist. If someone ribs you about your lack of computer know-how, say, "Yeah, if someone asks me what kind of laptop I have, I say, 'Gray'." This type of verbal martial art – Tongue Fu! - means you go with the flow instead of fighting it.

One of the best "agree and exaggerate" practitioners I've ever met is former Pittsburgh Steeler quarterback and Super Bowl MVP Terry Bradshaw. Terry is one of the most likable individuals you'd ever want to meet. When people give him a hard time about being "ugly" (he's not), he says, "I'm glad I'm not good-looking. If I looked like Brad Pitt, it'd take me an hour to shave!" If someone gives him grief about his several marriages, his good ole boy response is, "My mama told me, 'You're marrying outside the family—you're gonna have problems.' " If someone ribs him about his supposedly less-than-brilliant IQ, he goes along with it by saying, "Face it, how smart can I be? I made my living by putting my hand on another guy's rear end." Terry makes it difficult for other people to be difficult because he refuses to take himself too seriously.

WHEN A MAN TEASES

Deborah Tannen, the author of the book *You Just Don't Understand*, told me about an experience that added insight into the differences between male-female communication styles. She said, "I was sitting in a plaza on a sunny day watching children play. A little girl was daintily eating her ice cream cone and a boy walked up and pushed her. She immediately started wailing and the girl's mother scolded the 'bad boy' for being so rough. A few minutes later, the 'trouble-maker' spied a boy about his own age on the other side of the plaza. He ran up to and gave the boy a shove. The boy shoved back. The pair ended up in a tussle and minutes later were happily playing together, having a great time."

Deborah said it was a perfect example of how the impact of behavior can depend more on how the receiver interprets it than on how the sender intends it. The little girl was threatened by the roughhousing; the little boy welcomed it. The little girl's day was ruined; the little boy's day was made.

That's why it's important to ask if our reaction could be a gender issue. What people say is not always what others hear. Next time someone says something you regard as offensive, look past the behavior to the intention. Maybe teasing is this person's socially awkward "stick the redhead's pigtail in the inkwell" way of getting your attention. He's trying to connect and doesn't know what to say. Maybe this person's put-downs are a playful cultural or family tradition. Unless this person has a history of being a bully, you might want to give him the benefit of the doubt. If, however, you know from previous experience that this person is trying to mess with you, use the next idea to ward him off.

Are You Up to the Teaser's Test?

"Your humor never fails to abuse me." – line from the movie The Lion King

Remember, bullies push, push, push to see what we're made of. Think of it this way. For verbal abusers, teasing is a test. Does it fluster us, frustrate us? Knock us off balance, knock us down? If so, it's working.

The goal is to let bullies know that we're up to their test. If we're able to successfully parry their verbal jabs, they'll usually leave us alone because it's "no fun" to pick on someone who gives it right back.

An attorney friend is a perfect practitioner of this concept. Pam said, "I got sick and tired of hearing all the lawyer jokes. I know some people have had unsatisfying experiences at the hands of the legal system. However, it gets old hearing for the umpteenth time, 'How do you know when a lawyer is lying? When her lips are moving' and 'What do you call a hundred lawyers at the bottom of the sea? A good start.' An associate finally told me that being made fun of comes with the attorney territory, and I better develop a thick skin or my sensitivity about this was going to drive me nuts.

"She was right. Now I collect lawyer jokes and post the best ones on a bulletin board in my office. If I'm at a cocktail party and someone starts in with 'Hey, have you heard the one about … instead of inwardly groaning, I add my two cents worth. One of my favorites is 'Why don't sharks attack lawyers? Professional courtesy.'"

Another example of someone who wisely decided to lighten up instead of tighten up is Joseph Heller. He said, "When I read something saying I've not written anything as good as *Catch-22*, I'm tempted to reply, 'Who has?'"

Good for Heller. Heller's *Catch-22* was a masterpiece that included a phrase that has become a watchword of our time. Only a handful of authors have achieved enduring impact on popular culture. Whether he liked it or not, his follow-up books would all be compared (probably unfavorably) to this once-in-a-lifetime novel. It was smart of him to anticipate this public reaction and handle it with humor.

A man named Art who was "follically challenged" said he agreed with my friend's decision to not take herself so seriously. He explained, "I started losing my hair when I was only thirty-five years old. I went the rug route and should have taken out stock in Rogaine. After about five years of sinking thousands of dollars into hair plugs and everything else on the market, I realized I was fighting a losing battle and decided I might as well learn to live with and laugh at my baldness. If someone tries to make a joke at my expense, I come right back at 'em with a joke of my own, like 'I'm not losing my hair, I'm gaining face.' Sometimes I say, 'I'm not bald, I'm a man of scalp' or 'I'm not bald, I'm a hair donor.' Once people realize I'm not self-conscious about it, it takes the fun out of it for them and they usually drop it."

Art had a good point. When bullies discover they can't get our goat, they go elsewhere. Their goal is to make you feel embarrassed. If you're not bothered by their verbal darts, they'll stop slinging them because they're pointless.

Here's another example. A woman in a seminar told us she'd gone to high school with a gossip queen who was one of those "If I never see her again, it'll be too soon" types. Monica said, "Every girl in our school was afraid of her because she was such a mean girl. She'd give you these backhanded compliments like 'Did you get a haircut? Your face looks thinner.' I knew I was going to run into her at our reunion and I was determined not to let her ruin my evening. Sure enough, as soon as she saw me, she started walking across the dance floor with that spiteful gleam in her eye. Before she could say a word, I put my hand up and said, 'Beth, don't even start' and turned and walked away." Kudos.

Are You Letting Bullies Push Your Hot Buttons?

Did you ever watch the TV sitcom "Mad about You" with Paul Reiser and Helen Hunt? There was a classic episode where "Helen's" mother was coming to visit. Her mom was a notorious perfectionist, a "travel agent for guilt trips." Helen spent the day cleaning the apartment and fixing an impressive meal. When her mother showed up, nothing was good enough. This was wrong, that was wrong. After an extremely frustrating evening, her mom left and "Paul" and "Helen" went to bed. She's laying there, looking at the bedroom ceiling, reliving everything that happened and getting more and more upset. She finally looked at her husband and says, "I don't understand it. I'm thirty-years old. Why is it my mother can still push all my hot buttons."

He looks at her and comes back with the perfect response. "That's easy, she installed them."

Bingo. What are you hot buttons? If you're sensitive about something, you're going to hear about it. If you're overweight, skinny, bald, have an accent or a disability; you're going to hear about it. Those issues don't have to be "sore spots" unless you let them. Come up with comebacks and people will never again have the power to push your hot buttons, because you dis-installed them.

Being funny with someone who's crossed the courtesy line may not be our first choice, but it's worth a try if everything else we've tried has failed. "The sound of laughter has always seemed to me," observed Peter Ustinov, "the most civilized music in the universe." Sometimes humor is a civilized yet effective way to get through to someone who's not listening.

This was demonstrated by a veterinarian's assistant who told me about her boss's clever handling of a client who wouldn't take no for an answer. This client was a well-known cheapskate who was always questioning her bill. She had called the vet's office because her dog Fifi had hurt her paw and the owner was trying to figure out whether it was serious enough to bring her in. Actually, she was trying to get free advice so she could treat the injury herself instead of having to pay a visit to the clinic.

After ten frustrating minutes of back-and-forth, the vet finally said, "Mabel, put down the phone, go get Fifi, and bring her to the phone." "What?" squawked Mabel. "Just do it," the doctor ordered. So Mabel put down the phone, found Fifi, and brought her back to the phone.

The vet said, "Now hold Fifi up so I can look at her paw and see how bad it is." Mabel protested, "You can't see Fifi's paw over the phone!" The doctor pounced. "That's right, I can't see Fifi's paw over the phone. Now bring her in so I can make a proper diagnosis and we can get this treated." Bravo!

Oscar nominated actress Gabourey Sidibe, the star of the film *Precious* also demonstrated the power of "having the last laugh." She said that, over the years, she has constantly been teased or "trolled" about her weight. She decided she was not going to let it get to her anymore. A perfect example of this? *Entertainment Weekly*, in its June

19, 2015 issue, printed her Twitter response to the mean comments made by online haters about her appearance on the red carpet for the Golden Globes.

Her response, all in under 140 characters? "I mos def cried about it on the private jet on the way to my dream job last night." Snap.

Action Plan and Discussion Questions

Are you sensitive about something? What do you say if someone brings this up? Are you tongue-tied or do you have a reply at the ready?

Can you create some comebacks so teasers no longer have the power to push your hot buttons? Who are you going to ask for help to develop these responses so, from now on, you'll be up to the teaser's test?

Have you witnessed a situation where someone used humor to defuse a situation? What happened?

Is there someone in particular in your life who likes to tease you? What does s/he say? Do these remarks get under your skin?

What is his or her intent? What does he or she hope to accomplish?

From now on, what is one specific way you're going to interrupt them and "give as good as you get" so they're no longer able to get your goat?

Chapter 13
HOW TO KEEP YOUR COOL
WHEN DEALING WITH TOXIC PEOPLE

"I don't want to be patronizing – that means talking down." – comedian Wendy Morgan

How can you keep your cool when dealing with toxic people? How can you stay centered when someone is targeting you?

A friend named Jeff was diagnosed with ADHD. He told me, "I have the attention span of a gnat." Actually, he's not alone. Harvard researcher Nancy F. Cohen found that goldfish, yes, *goldfish,* have longer attention spans than we humans do. Nine seconds to our eight I actually wrote a book about that topic called "Got Your Attention?" that teaches how to capture and keep busy people's attention in our culture of INFObesity and impatience.

However, *getting* people's attention was not Jeff's challenge. *Keeping* his attention on any one thing for any amount of time was compromising his relationships with others because he always seemed "antsy." For years, he searched for something that would help him counteract his hyperactivity and nervous energy. After trying Ritalin, hypnosis, biofeedback, and just about everything else, he finally discovered something that helped control his fidgeting ... a rosary.

He carries it in his pocket wherever he goes. If he's in conversation and his thoughts are all over the map, he brings out his "worry beads." He's found that giving his hands something to do quiets his mind. "Sitting through a long meeting used to be the impossible dream.

Working this rosary gives me an outlet for my impatience so I can stay focused on what people are saying instead of being a nervous wreck."

You may be wondering, "That's nice, but what does this have to do with bullying?" If giving his hands something to do quieted Jeff's mind, giving your hands something to do may quiet yours.

A goal of bullies is to dominate your thoughts. Dealing with them can be a "mind battle." You may find it hard to focus because you keep reliving something the bully said or did.

It can be helpful to keep something tangible in a pocket, purse or wallet that has positive symbolic meaning and that gives your hands (and mind) something to do. Every time you look at it and touch it, it reminds you of who and how you want to be, who and what is important to you. It could be a picture of a loved one, a quote that inspires you every time you read it, a lucky key chain a friend gave you.

Take Your Touchstone
"To be yourself in a world that is trying to turn you into someone else, is the hardest battle you'll ever fight and keep fighting." – e.e. cummings

While browsing for a gift in a boutique, I spied a lovely tiger eye stone in the shape of a heart. I knew instantly I wanted to give it to a young friend who was being bullied at school. He was a gentle soul, and gentle souls don't do too well in an environment where rowdiness rules. Sometimes I could see his confusion when he watched the popular kids with their loud, brash ways. Their constant jockeying for position simply wasn't him. He wanted to be included but didn't want to become someone he was not. There didn't seem to be any middle ground.

That's where the heart rock came in. I told him I hoped it would be a visual, tangible reminder that he could be nice *and* strong. I hoped it would be proof that he could be solid as a rock and a beautiful soul.

This weekend, check out a museum shop, nature store, or a craft boutique. Find a beautiful stone that fits in the palm of your hand. Carry it with you in your purse or pocket so you have a tangible talisman to keep you strong in stressful situations. When dealing with challenging individuals, wrap your hand around it to remind yourself you can be hard without being heartless. If someone's trying to push you around, use it as a reminder to be solid as a rock. It can help you keep your cool by giving your hands something to do so your mind doesn't get riled up.

One of the by-products of being in a battle with a bully is it's easy to start living in your head. Like a tongue probing a sore tooth, you can't stop thinking about the latest insult or outrageous stunt. The problem with this is, the more you replay the tapes of what they've said and done, the more shell-shocked you become. Their destructive influence begins to infiltrate your every waking moment. This, of course, is exactly what bullies want. Their goal is to be all you can think about.

Your goal is to stay grounded in reality so bullies can't ruin your quality of life. One way to do this is to surround yourself with tangible reminders of the still-wonderful world that exists outside the bully. It could be a touch-stone or it could be a touch-*shell*. Here's what I mean.

When I lived in Hawaii, a couple in our community had a nightmarish experience with a private contractor they'd hired to remodel their home. After several lengthy delays, the builder basically demolished one section of their house and then absconded with the money they had foolishly prepaid him for supplies. Not only were they out the $20,000 they had planned for the project, they had several unusable rooms with structural damage where interior walls had been torn down.

My friends couldn't get past this debacle because every time they looked at their house, they were confronted with the mess they were in.

My friend told me this during a walk/talk on one of Maui's user-friendly beaches. After hearing her tale of frustration, I suggested we start looking for "thumb-shells."

"What are those?" she asked.

I explained I used to get homesick when speaking on the mainland. One day, at Keawekapu Beach with my sons, I found a small white seashell that fit perfectly on the end of my thumb. I asked her, "You've heard of a thumbnail sketch? Well, this was a thumbnail shell. From then on, I kept one in my pocket. If I was missing my sons or dealing with fallout from the bully, I would slip it on my thumb and instantly be back on the beach with the boys, happy and healthy. I suggested Janice do the same. If she started getting upset about the damage done by the contractor, she could bring out her touch-shell and switch her attention to what's right with her world instead of what's wrong.

Keep a Tangible Talisman or a Meaningful Quote Nearby

"Peace of mind for five minutes, that's what I crave." — Allanis Morrisette

Talisman is defined as "an object held to act as a charm to avert evil and bring good fortune." What "lucky charm" could you use to keep your cool and focus your mind on your fortunes (your health, loved ones?) rather than your fear? What is something meaningful you could keep with you to avert those evil images and give yourself peace of mind ... even if it's for five minutes?

One woman going through a nasty divorce kept a picture of her two children in her Day-Timer, on her desk, and on her car dashboard. Whenever she was despondent and wondering if she had the will to put up the good fight against her powerful ex-husband, she would look at their faces and remind herself of her responsibility and determination to build a better future for them and her.

Another carried a piece of paper with the words "Stay calm. Stay strong. You can't help anyone else unless you save yourself" in her pocket. Whenever she felt herself wavering she'd hold the paper in her hand and silently repeat the message on it until her resolve revived. "In my weakest moments," she said, "when I would question whether I had the courage to do this, I would just touch the note and be comforted. It was more of a touch-paper than a touchstone," she said with a smile, "but all the same, it was a lifesaver."

Inspirational quotes can also help us keep a positive perspective. In the middle of a crisis, we can take a minute to read the words of someone who has triumphed over tragedy to remind us that we can do the same. That person's example can keep us from sliding back down the slippery mental slope of despair. Select one of the following inspirational messages (or find one that resonates with you at www.BrainyQuote.com or at http://nobullying.com/cyber-bullying-quotes/

Post this quote where you can see it throughout the day, whenever you need it, so it will be in sight, in mind. Next time you're between a rock and a hard person, pull it out and center yourself in a mindset that helps vs. hurts.

- "The very least you can do in your life is to figure out what you hope for. And the most you can do is live inside that hope. Not admire it from a distance, but live right in it, under its roof." —Barbara Kingsolver
- "There are always two voices sounding in our ears—the voice of fear and the voice of confidence. One is the clamor

of the senses, the other is the whispering of the higher self."
—C. B. Newcomb

- "No one can make you feel inferior without your consent."
  – Eleanor Roosevelt
- "You've got to own your days, each one of them, every one of them, or else the years go right by and none of them belong to you." —Herb Gardner
- "An individual dies. . . when, instead of taking risks, he cowers within, and takes refuge there." —E. M. Cioran

Give Yourself an Instant Attitude Adjustment

"I need to take an emotional breath, step back, and remind myself who's actually in charge of my life." —-Judith M. Knowlton

When you're dealing with someone determined to take you out, it's easy to forget he or she is just one person. It's hard not to be consumed by the awfulness of what's happening. However that means the bully has accomplished what s/he set out to do— ruin your life.

Vow NOT to give them that power. Turn your thoughts to the people you love instead of this person who's being hateful. Keep your touch-stone, touch-shell or lucky charm nearby as a reminder, even in the midst of misery, that somewhere the sun is shining, children are playing, flowers are blooming. Your talisman can give you instant perspective and shrink this problem and person down to their deserved minuscule size. In that way, you take back control of your life and goodness prevails.

Action Plan and Discussion Questions

Do you already have something that serves as a talisman or touchstone? What is it? How does it help you keep your cool?

If not, when and where are you going to acquire something tangible to give yourself evidence you can be nice and strong at the same time?

Do you find it difficult to stop thinking about how this person has wronged you? Is there a quote or inspirational message you could keep in sight, in mind or carry with you to focus your thoughts on what's right with your world instead of what's wrong? Explain.

Chapter 14
STOP BLAMERS IN THEIR VERBAL TRACKS

"Our task is not to fix the blame for the past; it's to fix the course for the future."
– John F. Kennedy

Bullies are masters at blaming other people. They don't want to find solutions; they want to find fault. Instead of claiming "The Devil made me do it," they argue "*You* made me do it." They know that by focusing the fault on you, they keep it off themselves.

I's important to keep this in mind so you're not vulnerable to a bully's attempts to fix blame on you.

How to Hold Your Own When Being Blamed

1. USE AS FEW WORDS AS POSSIBLE. The wordier you are, the weaker you appear. Conciseness connotes confidence.

2. DON'T LISTEN TO REASON(S). Listening to reason is normally a good thing. But not when it comes to a habitual blamer.

Blamers always have rationalizations for why they did what they did. It's not that they were late. No, traffic held them up. It wasn't that they were rude. No, it was that "uppity salesclerk" who made them lose their temper. It wasn't that they didn't deserve the promotion. No, it was that lousy supervisor who played favorites. Bullies always have a reason for everything, and none of their excuses have anything to do with them.

3. APPEAL TO A BLAMER'S NEED TO SAVE FACE, NOT TO ANY SENSE OF FAIRNESS.
Trying to point out to a blamer that what s/he is doing is morally wrong can be a waste of time. The only thing that motivates bullies to change their behavior is seeing that they will suffer in some way if they don't stop. Bullies respond to negative consequences. Only when we reverse the risk-benefit ratio and they realize they're about to be penalized for their inappropriate actions will they choose to act differently.

A friend of mine who runs a large nonprofit told me of the time their newly appointed board president set up his own interview with the local newspaper and made numerous commitments on behalf of their organization. "The other board members were aghast that he didn't clear his comments ahead of time. Their initial attempts to convince him he was out of line and getting ahead of his team were dismissed.

"It was clear this loose cannon wanted to make his mark by taking advantage of the attention that came with his position. It was only after our previous president pointed out he was going to get censured by his own organization that he chose to tone down his lone wolf act. Diplomatic pleas for politically correct leadership had gone ignored. The only thing that convinced this ambitious individual to put a sock in it was pointing out he was about to be publicly embarrassed."

4. GIVE THEM AN OUT.
Since appearances are so important to bullies, it's smart to give them a way to justify in their own minds that this was their decision to do things differently. Remember the young lady who told her father, "I'm proud of graduating from Georgetown. If you're here to help me celebrate, you're welcome to stay. If you're not, leave." By giving bullies two options, both of which are acceptable to you, and letting them choose their course of action, they can comfort themselves with the perception they're still in charge.

5. ACT OUTSIDE OF THEIR EXPECTATIONS.
Sometimes we've got to be wild and crazy to get a bully's attention. They may be so accustomed to ruling the roost, they don't even listen to anything we say. A social worker who was supervising a shift at a juvenile detention home said two teenaged girls really got into it. They were wrestling on

the floor, pulling each other's hair, and punching each other. Nancy said she tried to pull them apart, to no avail. Several other employees joined the fray in an effort to stop the fight, with no success. Finally, at the end of her rope, Nancy started screaming at the top of her lungs. The two teens stopped and stared at her in amazement. Nancy said, "I don't even know why I did it, but it worked."

Plan to Be Unpredictable

Why did this work so well? Nancy had done the unexpected. When dealing with bullies, we need to act outside our customary range of behavior or we'll get the customary results. We can tell the truth until we're blue in the face and it won't get through a habitual blamer's mental armor. Surprising them with unanticipated behavior forces them to pay attention. We're not doing same old, same old, so they can't either.

Since blamers count on us being reasonable, we may need to be unreasonable. Since blamers count on us to be rational, we may need to be irrational. Since blamers count on us to shoulder the responsibility, we need to make them shoulder the responsibility.

A woman named Lisa said, "My roommate complained constantly about her job. She would itemize every little thing that had gone wrong, rehashing incidents and obsessing about what each person had said or done. A recurring theme was that everyone was a foul-up except her.

"When she had finished bashing everybody, she'd waltz off and I'd be left sitting there, down in the dumps. If I ever dared to suggest that she might be playing some role in all this and her censure was a little one-sided, she'd turn on me with 'Oh, great! So now my own roommate is criticizing me? Who else am I supposed to talk to if I can't talk to you?'

"I wish I'd known about the Rights/Needs Seesaw because it would have helped me see how one-sided her behavior was. Five minutes into it, I would have told her 'Enough!' and gotten up and walked away. She would have called me a few choice names, but that would have been better than letting her turn me into her own private dumping ground."

One of the best ways to persuade blamers to stop is to stand up, make a T with your hands (like referees do) and say "Time out!" or "Enough!" Those commands fit the situation because they're brief and unequivocal.

Unequivocal is such a great word. It means definite, explicit, incontestable, unambiguous. These are all the things we want to be when dealing with outspoken people who find fault with everyone but themselves. Remember, bullies and blamers are INTENSE. In a confrontation between intensity and uncertainty, intensity almost always wins. That's why we need to speak UP with self-assurance. No soft, meek, seeking approval voice with upward inflection. As the saying goes, be LOUD AND PROUD. When a blamer/bully senses you're unequivocal instead of ambiguous, they won't be so quick to dump on us because they know you have a mind of our own. (What a concept!)

From now on, understand you do not have to patiently listen to faultfinders who are bending your ear (and will).

One way bullies control you is by taking up your time. Think about it: the blamer plays the dominant role, the listener the passive role. Bullies control the situation (and you) by commanding your time and attention—whether you want to give it to them or not.

Off-loading problems on others is not appropriate—unless it's complicit. For bullies to expect other people to stop everything and listen to them ad infinitum is insensitive at best, selfish at worst. Only a bully would do this repeatedly, and only a bully would accuse you of being insensitive, unsympathetic or a lousy listener if you're unwilling to be a mute audience to his or her monologue.

As comedienne Paula Poundstone said, "I think we need a Twelve Step group for nonstop talkers. We're going to call it On and On Anon."

The next time someone starts talking on and on and on, INTERRUPT. This may come across as impolite, but continuing to give them a sympathetic ear will perpetuate their whines and reasons. if a trash-talker in your life doesn't like that you'll no longer willing to listen to them rant and rave, remember this word, "Tough."

Control the Conversation

"At the moment of truth, there are either reasons or results." – aviation pioneer Chuck Yeager

If someone has consistently been tactless, it's appropriate for you to take control of the situation, because if you don't, the other person will.

A security manager said, "You're right about not letting blamers get a word in edgewise. I handle a lot of the discipline problems for our organization. Believe me, these people always have a hundred and one reasons why whatever went wrong wasn't their fault. When I sit down with repeat offenders, I don't even let them get started on the whys and wherefores. If I listened to their excuses, we'd be there all day."

He continued: "As you say, If I don't control the conversation, they will. They do this by counterattacking. I had a woman in here who insisted it was unfair to blame her for pilfering hundreds of dollars of office supplies because 'everyone else did it' and there wasn't a rule forbidding it in the employee handbook. She was trying to make me out to be the bad guy in the situation."

He's right. Blamers purposely put you in a position where you are so busy denying their criticisms, you forget they're the one who's "done the crime." Their goal is to put YOU on the spot so they don't have to be.

One of the most important ways to cancel the blame-shame game is to detach instead of defend. As discussed earlier, manipulators know that if they blame you for an error, you'll be tempted to deny it. As soon as you do, they have succeeded in changing the subject and moving the spotlight off them and onto you.

Don't Open Mouth, Don't Insert Foot

Remember, if someone accuses you, "You love your ex-boyfriend more than you do me," don't protest with "That's not true!" If you do, he succeeded in dragging you into a "Yes, you do; no, I don't" debate. Instead say, "We agreed that discussing ex's serves no one. That topic is off-limits."

If the bully persists with "You're laughing in all your pictures with him and you never laugh when you're with me," say, "Drop it. We're not going there." Notice these responses are short and they don't challenge the *content* of what's being said. Don't wait until the other person stops talking (that could be a long time) to respond. If you're dealing with someone who goes "on and on and on," you need to interrupt and cut them off before they build up a head of blame-shame steam. They can't sell you a ticket for a guilt trip if you don't buy it.

Action Plan and Discussion Questions

Is there someone in your life who is a habitual faultfinder? How are you going to detach instead of debate his/her unfounded accusations?

Do you continue to listen to blamers? What are you going to do next time s/he starts talking on and on and on?

Do you sometimes buy tickets for guilt trips? How so? What will you do next time someone tries to make you feel bad for not giving in and going along with his/her demands or accusations?

Chapter 15
WHAT WE ACCEPT, WE TEACH

"Regret is the only wound from which the soul never recovers." --author *Sarah Ban Breathnach*

This is an important chapter because it asks you to step back from what's happening and look at it from a helicopter perspective.

Taking the long-view can help us avoid being reactionary which leads to regrets. A helicopter perspective can help us transcend the muck we're in, and get clear about how what actions will serve us and our loved ones, in the long run.

For months I asked just about everyone I encountered, "Can you think of someone who bullied you? What did he/she do? How did you respond? What worked? What didn't? Were you finally able to resolve the situation? How?"

A friend who writes a nationally syndicated column for teachers reported this unsettling story. This educator was asked by a couple what they could do about their daughter, who was terrified of an extremely aggressive classmate who had targeted her. The parents said the twelve-year-old (!) bully-ette's behavior went beyond adolescent name-calling and teasing. Her systematic scheming was downright diabolical.

The parents had already complained to their daughter's homeroom teacher. The teacher confronted the taunter, who not only denied any wrongdoing but had the audacity to accuse their daughter of making it all up in an effort to cause trouble because she was "so unpopular." The parents took their case to the principal, who essentially shrugged it off with "Your daughter needs to learn how to handle this kind of stuff because it happens all the time. We can't watch them every minute."

The parents were at their wit's end. They said, "Our daughter comes home every day crying and begs us not to make her go back. She has stomach aches every day and is losing weight." At this point, my educator friend interrupted and said simply, "Take her out."

You'll never guess what the parents' response was. "We can't take her out. This school has the best reputation in the area and we've already paid tuition for the whole year." After further discussion, my friend sadly concluded that this couple seemed more concerned about their pocketbook and their daughter's continuing to attend this prestigious school than they were with her psychological well-being.

This former school principal suggests that parents look at themselves and ask, "What are my actions or non-actions teaching my children?" The disconcerting message being sent to this poor girl was "Status and money are more important than standing up for yourself."

She added, "It's true that kids need to learn how to deal with challenges. It's also true that parents need to act on their children's behalf if they're suffering at the hands of someone else. Can you imagine how this twelve-year-old must have felt? She must have felt no one was listening, no one really cared, and she was all alone with no options."

Chapter Eighteen, "Is Your Child Being Bullied?" will provide specific suggestions on how children can protect themselves from trolls. For now, the question is, is what you're preaching what you're teaching?

What Example Are You Setting?

"In influencing others, example is not the main thing; it's the only thing." – *Albert Schweitzer*

A friend told me about an encounter she had as a child that negatively influenced her for years. She was ten years old and lounging in her favorite summer hangout, the town's air-conditioned library. She had walked there from her home, a few blocks away. She was looking something up on a library computer when a man walked over and stood next to her. She looked up, puzzled, wondering what he wanted.

He pushed a piece of paper into her hand and motioned her to look at it.

As soon as she saw what it was, it was as if he had hit her. He had drawn a crude picture of her in the nude, with an obscenity coming out of her mouth. She was so shocked, at first she didn't know what to do. Then she ran out of the library and all the way home. Sobbing, she stumbled into the house, found her mother, showed her the picture, and told what had happened. Who knows whether her mother had had a bad day or just didn't know what to say? Whatever the reason, she folded the picture up, put it in a drawer, and told her daughter to stop crying. That was the end of that. Except it wasn't. My friend said the silent message her mother sent was "When somebody does something bad to you, put it away in a drawer, stop crying, and don't say anything about it."

My friend told me, "It's taken me years to undo that lesson. I wish my mother had done something. I wish she had taken me into her arms. I wish she had called the library to report what had happened so the staff would watch for that man and keep him from traumatizing any other unsuspecting children. I wish she had sat me down and said if anything like that ever happened again, I should immediately go to the nearest adult and tell him or her what had happened. I wish she had done something—even if she didn't know if it was the right thing. Because the message I internalized was that this was my fault. I felt dirty, like I'd done something wrong to deserve this."

That mother may have just been overwhelmed at the moment and didn't understand that her example - and lack of action - would have long-term consequences. The point is to understand that if we do nothing when someone mistreats us or a loved one, we teach the perpetrator that it's acceptable, and we teach ourselves and the people around us that passively enduring mistreatment is the proper response.

Is that the message we want to send to bullies, ourselves, and loved ones? I think the message we want to send is "No! You cannot do this and get away with it. I will not look the other way. I will speak up. You will be held accountable." In the long run, this is the only way to convince bullies it's not worthwhile.

"I agree with this," said one woman. "My daughter plays travel team softball in California. We go to tournaments almost every weekend, and last year the team made nationals. Even though these girls are only sixteen years old, many are already being scouted by colleges.

"Last year, the girls' coach really had a mouth on him. He had played in the minors and took the game very seriously. He was constantly screaming at the players, even at his own daughter, who was the star pitcher. When team members would go up to bat, you could see how nervous they were by how they hunched their shoulders and kept glancing over at him. Players who made errors dreaded going back to the dugout because they knew they were going to get bawled out.

"His rampages made several of us bleacher-warmers uncomfortable, but none of us dared say anything because we were afraid he would retaliate against our daughter and not play her.

"One weekend the father of one of our players came to a game for the first time and sat next to me in the stands. I could tell he was steaming after the coach ridiculed his daughter for flubbing a throw. He waited until the game was over and then went up to the coach and asked to speak to him in private. He told the coach in no uncertain terms that an adult man calling a teenaged girl an idiot and telling her 'Your stupid mistake just cost us the game' was verbal abuse even if it was happening in an athletic arena."

Kudos to this father for having the moral courage to speak up. He was absolutely right to call foul, and absolutely right in his assessment that verbal abuse is unacceptable regardless of where it's taking place.

Be an Upstander, Not a Bystander

"One man practicing sportsmanship is far better than a hundred teaching it."
Football legend Knute Rockne

Contrary to what Knute Rockne said, I think the more we adults teach and practice sportsmanship, the more our kids will practice it.

I hope coaches everywhere understand how wrong it is to vent rage on their players. Doing so teaches young people that it is "normal" for adults to rant and rave and they (and their parents) are supposed to endure this abuse and not say a word in defense of themselves. Is this what we want to teach our sons and daughters? Do we want them passing this message on to future generations? Because they will. What is done to our youngsters will be done by our youngsters.

You may be thinking, "Every coach, male or female, yells at his or her players. That's what coaches do." It may be true that this is the norm. Does that mean it's a good thing? Does it make sense to condone ridicule just because it's common? When are we going to understand that verbal abuse is every bit as damaging as physical abuse? When are we going to take a stand and no longer look the other way when adults direct their rage at defenseless children?

If you've watched youth sports, you know it's not just the coaches who get carried away. You've probably witnessed over-ambitious parents who persecute their kids for blowing a big play. You've probably seen overzealous fans get wrapped up in the game, and the next thing you know, they're screaming at five-year-olds, "Lazy! Stupid! What a dumb mistake!"

I remember an article in the *Los Angeles Times* that reported more than 60 percent of kids give up organized sports by the time they're twelve years old. Why? The number one reason given was that they were tired of adults yelling at them. Isn't that a sorry state of affairs?

It's time to practice common courtesy instead of making young athletes miserable. We can stem the tide of temper tantrums if we personally commit to lobbying for change in our local school sports programs and hometown recreation leagues. Some communities have already taken the lead. They've instituted "quiet games" where parents vow not to say a single word from the stands or sidelines. The kids love it! Perhaps you can follow the example of that brave father who collared the softball coach. Perhaps you can speak up at your next league or team meeting and ask everyone to shape players instead of shame them by contributing cheers, not jeers.

Can you imagine the powerful message we would send by caring enough to hold ourselves and other adult authority figures accountable for treating children with the respect they deserve? We would be saying, "How we treat each other matters. Communication counts. We will speak to each other with R-E-S-P-E-C-T."

A June 12, 2015 column by the always-wise Carolyn Hax featured a submission from "FanNana" who had witnessed an "appalling" example of poor sportsmanship with both coaches yelling at the umpires at her granddaughter's softball game. "Everyone was stunned by this inexcusable behavior. Hope to hear your thoughts."

Carolyn answered with her typical wit and wisdom. "But ... how will their girls go D-1 if the umps blow the call!?!'"

She then went on to suggest that FanNana tell her granddaughter that she wished she didn't have to deal with her coach's loss of perspective. "Ask HER how she feels to give her a voice, and then write a letter to the proper authorities, whether that's the club, league, tournament organizers or the local governing body of the sport."

Carolyn ended with, "You're free to lament the decline of sportsmanship, but it's not enough. To rein in or remove bad actors, witnesses have to speak up."

Hear, hear. That's what it takes to be an upstander instead of a bystander. Don't stand idly by when witnessing acts of verbal abuse. Speak up to the people in charge and rally the people around you to do the same.

There is strength in numbers. The more you voice your unacceptance of verbal abuse, the more likely it is the people in charge will institute policies outlawing it.

An organization that does an excellent job of holding everyone accountable for respectful behavior is the Sportsmanship Brigade. Check out their pledge that holds everyone (including coaches, players, parents and fans) accountable for behaving honorably. http://sportsmanship.org/tools/pledge/ You might want to recommend this to the organizations you're involved in. It's a way of being an upstander for fair play.

Action Plan and Discussion Questions

Do you know someone who is verbally abusing others? Are you bearing silent witness? What message does that send?

Does your lack of action sanction this bully's behavior? Is it time to intervene so this person knows his/her verbal abuse will not be tolerated? Why or why not?

Does this unacceptable situation demand some moral courage for you to speak up? How can you summon up the strength to be an upstander instead of a bystander?

Who are you going to contact (coach, teacher, school principal, your boss) to propose that treating others with RESPECT becomes a mandated behavior? How are you going to lobby for this issue? What organization are you going to contact? What pledge will you take?

Chapter 16
DENY BULLIES ACCESS

"I told my doctor I broke my leg in two places. He told me to quit going to those places." —Henny Youngman

Do you need to follow that doctor's advice and STOP going back to the people and places that break your ... spirit?

Fellow speaker Scott Friedman has a different way of expressing this. If a perennial bully is giving us a hard time, he suggests we ask ourselves, "Is this deja moo? Have I heard this bull before?" If this person has a history of abusing us, why are continuing to give them access? As the saying goes, "Insanity is continuing to do the same thing and expecting a different result."

What's Your Return Policy?

"A lot of people are afraid to tell the truth, to say no. That's where toughness comes into play. Toughness is not being a bully. It's having backbone."– Robert Kiyosaki, author of Rich Dad, Poor Dad

A young woman shared this story: "My mother-in-law is manic-depressive. When she is in her 'down' phase, she is rather introverted. When she's in her manic phase, especially if she's not taking her meds (she hates them because they make her 'numb'), she turns into Attila the Hen.

"I'm a Realtor, so I'm gone a lot on weeknights and weekends showing houses. I'm good at what I do professionally, but I don't have that same level of confidence about parenting. Half the time I don't know if I'm doing a good job, and the other half of the time I feel bad for not being there for my kids as much as I'd like. She knows I'm sensitive about this and seems to purposely target my anxiety about it.

"My husband, Carl, has told me over and over that I can't let her get to me. The saving grace for him is that after one particularly vicious episode in which his mother told him she regretted the day he was born, his saint of a father took his son's face in his hands and said, 'Look me in the eyes and remember what I'm telling you. Your mother's behavior is not your fault, and there's nothing you can do to make her better.'

"My father-in-law had nailed it. Carl had always believed that if he just tried hard enough, researched long enough, or experimented with enough different approaches, he'd finally be able to reach his mom and she would turn into June Cleaver. His dad finally convinced him that his mom was not going to change and he had to stop giving her the power to devastate him. Carl still cares for his mom, but he's developed a thick skin and no longer lets her criticism get through.

"She's in her manic phase right now and is 'hell on heels.' She gets obsessed with projects, and yesterday her project was me. She sent this blistering e-mail that carried on about how our kids were spoiled little brats who were going to grow up to be monsters, and how I should stick to real estate and leave the parenting to someone else. It shattered me.

"My husband came home and found me weeping. I told him what had happened. He listened for a while and then said something that stopped me in my tracks. He asked simply, 'Why did you read the e-mail? You know what she's like.'

"I looked at him, dumbfounded. He wasn't being mean, he was just gently prodding me to realize that I had in a way played a role in this. Why had I read the e-mail? I knew she was in a manic phase. I knew these missives of hers were often vicious. Why had I reopened myself to her mean-spiritedness? My husband was right. I was culpable."

Why do we do this to ourselves? Why do we let people back in who have hurt us before? Many of us want to believe they will come to their senses, feel remorse, and opt to be kinder. Some of us still care and want to give them one more chance to change their evil ways. And some of us simply can't comprehend that human beings can consciously choose to be cruel even when it's to everyone's detriment, including their own.

Delete Haters, Trolls and Bullies From Your Life

"I am thankful the most important key in history was invented. It's not the key to your house, car, boat, safety deposit box, or private community. It's the key to order, sanity and peace of mind. The key is "Delete." — comedian Elayne Booseler

There's a well-known parable about the danger of continuing to give people access and the benefit of the doubt.

An alligator was about to cross a river when a scorpion showed up and asked for a ride. The alligator said, "You've got to be kidding. I'm not going to give you a ride. You'll sting me." The scorpion protested, "Why would I do that? I want to get across the river as much as you do." "No way," the alligator resisted. "I can't trust you." The scorpion reassured him, "Look, if I sting you, we'll both drown. Now why would I do a stupid thing like that?" The alligator grudgingly admitted the truth of this and agreed: "Okay, get on." The scorpion got on and the alligator crawled into the river. Halfway across, the scorpion stung the alligator. Shocked and dying, the alligator asked disbelievingly, "Why did you sting me? Now we're both going to die." His passenger, going down for the last time, gargled out, "I'm a scorpion. That's what I do."

You've heard the adage, "A tiger doesn't change his stripes"? Well, scorpions don't change their stings. The way to stop them from zinging us is to stop giving them rides on our back! Delete them from our life.

If someone in your life is sending you hostile e-mails or leaving you obnoxious voice mail messages, remind yourself that you are not obligated to read or listen to them. If someone has hurt you time and time again, stop inviting this person back into your head.

Follow the advice of a woman who finally took action to stop her ex-husband's persecution. "My former husband and I share custody of our children. They spend two weeks at his house and two weeks at mine. What complicates matters is that we both travel, so we often need to make changes in our schedule. On top of that, he's always late with his child support and alimony checks and I've got to keep after him to make those payments. That requires a lot of messages being sent back and forth, and he used to fill them with these venomous attacks. He'd bury some important detail in the middle of the call or at the end of an e-mail so I'd be forced to read or listen to the whole thing to find out what I needed to know.

"My divorce attorney recommended I copy his e-mails and record his phone messages so the court would have documentation of his harassment. My lawyer then drafted a letter informing my husband that from that day forward, his written and spoken communication to me needed to address only the logistical information concerning our children or financial arrangements. At the first derogatory word or opinion, the phone call would be terminated or the e-mail would be printed for our files and then deleted but not read.

"He tested this, of course, and claimed it was my fault our kids didn't get registered for summer camp because I had failed to sign and submit the application form he had attached to one of his hateful e-mails. My attorney copied him with his original message showing it had been deleted after the first name-calling paragraph. Every once in a while, he'll try zapping me again. However, the second he starts in, I cut the communication off."

Sometimes we give scorpions the ability to sting us even when they're not in the same room. I remember reading a fascinating article about a world-famous model who had spent a good deal of her adult life under the thrall of a Lothario who controlled her (almost) every move. In this interview, she related how she was on a shoot in Europe and was still letting this individual rule her life even though she was thousands of miles away. Out on the town one night with the crew, a photographer asked her something and she responded, without thinking, that so-and-so wouldn't let her do it. The photographer asked in wonderment, "What kind of power does he have over you?!"

Indeed. Do you have someone in your life who tries to control your every waking moment? Do you find yourself saying things like "She wouldn't let me do this"? "He made me turn that job offer down"? "She told me I couldn't go"?

Are you an adult? Why are you letting someone tell you what you can or can't do? Why are you allowing someone to make you do things you'd rather not do? Why are you permitting someone to pull your strings as if you were a puppet? Don't you have a mind of your own?

If you are in a relationship, by all means, coordinate your actions with those of your partner. However, don't let other people make your decisions for you and don't let other people run your life. The question is, "What do you think?" "What do you want?" "What do you believe?"

Instead of giving away your power and living a life not your own, have clarity that you are a grown-up and you're going to act like one. That means you treat people as equals, not superiors. It means you have the final say-so concerning what you do and don't do in your personal and professional life. It's time to take back the remote control.

One woman sighed upon hearing this idea and said it had given her much-needed perspective on her relationship. "I never realized how insidious his control of me has become. The words "let" and "make" have indeed crept into my vocabulary. He makes me drive his old pickup truck to work when I hate it because he says he needs the family car. He makes me accompany him on weekends and sit around while he flies model airplanes all day with his friends. He doesn't let me take night classes even though I really want to.

"I'm a middle-aged woman. Why do I let him control me? Because I'm afraid of him. He's never hit me— well, physically he's never hit me—but (her eyes open in amazement as she realizes this) he hits me with words all the time. I shrink in his presence. It just seems easier to go along with him because he gets so ugly if I don't."

Not only will the meek not inherit the earth, they won't inherit much of anything. Stop putting this person on a pedestal. Stop seeing this person as "larger than life." Say to yourself, "This person is my equal, not my superior. My needs count just as much as his, not less or more."

This woman doesn't have to put her husband down; she's just no longer going to let him put her down. She could say, "If you want to own a pickup, that's fine, but then *you* drive it from now on." "You're welcome to go to the field this weekend. I have other plans." "I'll be taking night classes, so I'll be gone on Tuesday and Thursday evenings."

The Little Princess Circle

If you're dealing with a bully, do yourself a favor this weekend and watch the film *The Little Princess*, available on *Netflix*. A young girl is taken to a school run by a cruel headmistress. The jealous woman locks the bewildered young girl in a dark, spooky attic, and announces her life, as she knows it, is over. The girl curls up on the hardwood floor and weeps. Through her tears, she notices a piece of chalk and determination glints in her eyes. She picks the chalk up, draws a circle around herself, and then settles back down on the floor inside her protective cocoon.

This is all done in silence, but it's clear the girl is establishing a boundary (a hula hoop of space) to block out the woman's hateful energy. Later in the movie, the resourceful princess summons up the courage to confront the headmistress who is terrorizing her. The movie makes a powerful statement about how we can maintain a sense of self when dealing with someone who's determined to break our spirit.

If you're dealing with someone who's trying to destroy your spirit, could you draw an imaginary safety circle around yourself? Could you picture their sadistic remarks bouncing harmlessly off your protective cocoon? Imagine this hula hoop in your mind. Imagine their criticism being deflected. Get clear; no one can hurt you if you don't care what they're saying.

Don't Play Their Game

"The way to work with a bully is to take the ball and go home. First time, every time. When there's no ball, there's no game. Bullies hate that. They'll either behave so they can play with you, or they'll go bully someone else." – Seth Godin

You may agree with Seth Godin's advice, but you're wondering, 'HOW do I take my ball and go home?"

One of the best examples I ever witnessed of this happened following a Tongue Fu!-Bully presentation I gave at the Professional Women's Conference at Moscone Center in San Francisco. I had been given a booth in the exhibit area in trade for speaking. A little gathering had assembled, and I turned it into a communal brain trust, asking people to share their challenges and success stories.

Many of these women worked in Silicon Valley in male-dominated high-tech industries. They had all experienced more than their fair-share of harassment.

One woman smiled as others shared their bully stories. Sensing she had a "secret," I asked, "What do you do if someone gives you a hard time?"

She smiled serenely and said, "I just look them in the eye and say, 'Five brothers.'"

We all burst all laughing. Got it. This smart woman let guys know right up front she had "been there, heard that" and nothing they could say or do was going to rattle her. *That* is a way of "taking the ball." *People can't play you if you don't play along.*

Action Plan and Discussion Questions

Is someone being hateful to you? Have you continued to take their calls, read their texts, posts and emails, spend time with them? Why?

Is this person a scorpion? Will she continue to sting you because that's what they *do*? Does this give you an epiphany about giving them access?

Do you find yourself saying "She won't *let* me do this" or "He *made* me do this"? Who is this person? Are you an adult? Why have you given this person control of your life?

How are you going to take back control of your own life? How are you going to take the ball and not play along so they can't play you?

Chapter 17
DON'T LET A BULLY ISOLATE YOU

"You should be nicer to him,' a schoolmate had once said to me of some awfully ill-favored boy. 'He has no friends.' This, I realized with a pang of pity that I can still remember, was only true as long as everybody agreed to it." -- author Christopher Hitchens

Bullies will often try to isolate you as part of their plan to own you and have you all to themselves. They don't want you to receive support (or warnings) from friends and family so they bad-mouth them in an effort to cause you to doubt them. Their goal is to diminish your loved ones so you don't have anyone else to trust, to turn to, to escape to.

They do this with constant little digs and with complaints about how boring, stupid or exhausting they are. They will discourage your visits to them and try to limit your time spent with them. They know this weakens you because you're not receiving any "outside" input. Destroying your support network is a form of propaganda. It's a deliberate attempt to weaken you by causing you to question everything you think you know.

That's why it's crucial to continue to reach out to trusted friends and family members. They can offer objective, balanced input that helps you see what this person is doing to you. They can assure you you're not "crazy" as the bully may be telling you. They can reassure you that it is this person who is being destructive ...and that you're the sane one.

"I don't know if I could have survived these last few months if it hadn't been for my friends," one woman told me. "You know the phrase 'They were there for me'? Well, my friends were everywhere for me.

"I've worked as a secretary at our local university for the last four years. I've always enjoyed my work and I get along well— well, I used to get along well—with the students and faculty. That all fell apart earlier this year when a new dean was hired for our department. I don't know how this man got the job, but he probably schmoozed the hiring committee with his smooth-operator act. He started coming on to me the first week he was in our office—not overtly in a way he could be caught, but in subtle, double entendre ways that left me feeling slimy.

"I was working late one night. He walked up behind me, leaned over the back of my chair, and pretended to look at what I was writing while trying to sneak a peek down my blouse. I turned and said, 'What are you doing?' He gave one of his sick grins and said, 'Just enjoying the view.'

"That did it. I pushed my chair back, gathered my things, and left. Or at least I tried to leave. He blocked the door and said, 'Come on, don't be so uptight.' I pushed him aside, ran out of the building, and filed a grievance against him the next morning.

"The next day I was called into the main office. I entered the room ready to report what had been happening over the past few months. I never had a chance. The dean had filed a grievance against me! I sat there in shock as the administrative officer read his complaint against me. In essence, the dean said I had come on to him and he felt he had no choice but to report my 'infatuation' out of self-protection.

"I tried to explain that the dean was the one who ought to be called on the carpet, but I could see that as far as the admin officer was concerned, it was a 'he said, she said' situation. I was put on probation and told I would be terminated if there were any other reports of this kind of harassment.

"I can't put into words how I felt. It was incomprehensible to me that someone would out and out lie the way he did and get away with it. It was even more incomprehensible that *I* would end up in trouble when *he* was responsible for the whole thing. I approached several secretaries and asked if they would testify on my behalf. They all said they felt bad about what I was going through, but weren't willing to jeopardize their jobs because they were afraid he would turn on them, too.

"Thank heaven for my friends. I spent hours on the phone pouring out my frustration. They were so patient. I'm sure there were times they had better things to do than hear the latest chapter in my battle with the school—but I guess they realized they were the only ones I could turn to."

Repeat After Me, "I Am NOT Crazy"

Do you have friends to turn to if someone's turned on you? Friends can be your saving grace if you're unlucky enough to find yourself in a nightmarish situation. Friends can reassure you that you're not crazy and you're not alone.

This is especially important because bullies tell us repeatedly that we're crazy. Their intent is to make us doubt our sanity so we're more susceptible to their propaganda. Many interviewees told me they felt like they were losing their mind—because the bully in their life kept telling them they were.

One woman gave up her business and flew to another country to live with a man she'd worked with in the foreign service. This woman had been a successful entrepreneur who had started and sold a million-dollar company. Within a few months of arriving, she was a complete wreck.

This man would tell her to schedule dinner plans and then deny ever saying that. He belittled her constantly with "Can't you do anything right?" On the way to social occasions, he would deliberately pick a fight and then sweep through the door, the charming hail-fellow-well-met, while apologizing for his partner, who was a "basket case." He kept saying, "You are some crazy broad." After months of his relentless attacks, this formerly confident woman started wondering if she was.

Don't Buy into the Propaganda

"The five most dangerous words in the English language: maybe it will go away." – sign in dentist's office

Propaganda is defined as "ideas or allegations spread deliberately to further one's cause or to damage an opposing cause." Propaganda is a bully's stock-in-trade.

Terrorists and cultists know that repeatedly bombarding someone with one-sided information in a vacuum of opposition eventually results in that individual adopting the partisan beliefs. Cult leaders deliberately subject recruits to around-the-clock indoctrination and cut off all contact with loved ones so recruits are out of touch with reality. They take advantage of the recruits' vulnerable, isolated, sleepless status to imprint the desired beliefs.

Bullies do much the same thing. They subject us to round-the-clock indoctrination and brain-washing. They try to isolate us by keeping us apart from loved ones. They knock us off balance by behaving in contradictory ways that make us think we've lost touch with reality. They tell us over and over, in our vulnerable state and in a vacuum of input to the contrary, that we're nuts. After a while, we feel like we've lost our mind, and we have. The bully has stolen it. It's in his possession.

So what to do? Don't go it alone. If you lose touch with your friends, you'll lose touch with reality. Your friends will keep you sane because they'll assure you that you are sane. They will give you balanced input so you can put thoughts in perspective. They'll help you see that it's not you who's unstable, it's the bully, who is deliberately undermining you in an effort to make you lose yourself.

Are You Being Brainwashed?

"If the emotions of fear, rage, or anxiety are kept at a high pitch of intensity for a long enough time, the brain goes 'on strike.' When this happens, new behavior patterns may be installed with the greatest of ease." – Aldous Huxley

For all the reasons we've previously covered, it can be a daunting task to take on a bully. They will NOT go away of their accord.

Most of us have no desire to destroy a fellow human being and we're devastated that someone's trying to do it to us. It's hard to match the obsessive zeal of a bully who's doing his best to brainwash us.

Leaning on friends is a way of tapping into their strength so we don't have to supply all our own. My favorite teacher used to say, "Encouragement is oxygen to the soul." When our energy tank is drained, we can fill 'er up with the encouragement of people who care. Perhaps most important, frequent contact with friends can render propaganda meaningless because we'll know it's not true.

It is now you and your friends against the bully—which makes you more formidable. If you're intimidated at the prospect of calling a support group, please know you'll be in safe hands and hearts. You don't need to take my word for this. Take the word of an extremely successful broker who discovered this for herself.

I had the privilege of speaking at a conference for some of the country's most successful female financial advisers. At a dinner one evening, we went around the table and shared how we'd gotten into the business. Every woman had a fascinating, against-all-odds story of how she'd made her mark in this mostly male enclave. We were all particularly impressed with one woman's story.

This now successful executive had sought a divorce from a vindictive husband years ago. Much to her dismay, he succeeded in getting custody of their three young sons when, as she said, "the only women in the South who didn't get custody of their children were drug addicts or prostitutes. Or," as she added ruefully, "uppity women who dared to divorce their powerful attorney husband."

Voice trembling at the memory of that horrible time, she said she went to Displaced Homemakers—the last place she, a formerly affluent woman, ever thought she'd end up. She took a placement test and was told she either needed to own her own company or be president. Her counselor suggested she call a broker in town, express interest in his profession, and ask if she could interview him over lunch. The broker agreed. During their meal, he said he loved his job because he was in control of his outcome and his income and he felt his work mattered and made a positive difference for others. She was sold. This now prosperous financial adviser (who's since reconnected with her sons) said she never would have had the insight or courage to make that call if it hadn't been for the support she received from Displaced Homemakers.

If for whatever reason you feel you have no one to turn to, rest assured. There are organizations designed for people just like you that are a google click away.

For example, I typed "How can I tell if I'm being abused?" into a search engine and this website came up in seconds. http://womenshealth.gov/violence-against-women/am-i-being-abused/ Check their homepage for a list of behaviors that constitute abuse. Know that the abuser in your life will be trying to convince you that YOU'RE in the wrong. Reading that list can be a relief of sorts because it confirms what you know deep down inside but's been "beaten" out of you ... that this situation is what's wrong.

You are going to feel such relief when you contact these organizations because they will believe you. They will understand your story because they have heard it before. They may not have heard your specific tale, but there are patterns to abusive behavior and they have heard every variation. They will support you through this mess. The people working for these organizations have often been bullied themselves, and are dedicated to helping others as they themselves were once helped.

Action Plan and Discussion Questions

Has the bully in your life tried to cut you off from friends and family? If so, explain.

Have you been going it alone? Could you benefit from leaning on we? Name a couple of friends you've lost touch with. How are you going to reconnect with them?

Has a bully in your life been emotionally blackmailing you and showering you with propaganda? What has he or she been saying to you? Have you started believing this indoctrination? How so?

How are you going to remind yourself that this person's agenda is to erode your belief in yourself? That what this person say has no basis in truth but is designed to cause you to question yourself and feel weak so s/he can keep you in their power?

Chapter 18
IS YOUR CHILD BEING BULLIED?

"School is about two-parts 'A,B,C's' and fifty parts 'Where Do I Stand In the Great Pecking Order of Humankind?" – *author Barbara Kingsolver*

Did you know the National Center for Educational Statistics said (in 2015) that:

- One out of every four students reports being bullied during the school year, and 37% say they have been cyber-bulled
- 64% of children who were bullied *did not report it*
- More than *half* of bullying situations STOP when a peer intervenes on behalf of the person being bullied
- School-based bullying prevention programs typically decrease bullying by up to 25%
- The most common reasons for being bullied were looks (55%) body shape (37%) and race (16%)
- 15% of students say they have skipped classes because they were afraid of being bullied?

Clearly, bullying is a problem. What makes the problem worse is that many parents are giving well-meaning but ineffective advice to their kids on how to deal with it.

In fact, on a weekend outing, a vanload of my sons' teen-aged friends told me, "Mrs. Horn, the advice adults give us about bullies is a joke. They tell us, 'If someone picks on you, just walk away.' Right!" they snorted. "If we walk away, the bully will come after us. Parents tell us, 'Report bullies to your teacher.'" They all rolled their eyes. "If we tell teachers what happened, they say they can't do anything because they didn't see it. If bullies do get in trouble, they get suspended— which is what they want anyway."

Were the boys giving me this report from an inner city school with gangs? No, they attended a public school in what is often lauded as one of the finest academic school districts in the country. This school boasts state champs in many sports and many National Honor Society members. It also has a Monday-to-Friday threat of bullying, just like the majority of students in our country.

Convince Bullies to Leave You Alone

One of the first things we can do about this is to stop handing our kids meaningless platitudes that minimize their trauma and give them the impression we don't understand what they're going through.

Many in-school programs have well-meaning literature, programs and short films suggesting that kids befriend bullies. That naive advice often backfires because most bullies aren't interested in being your friend, they're interested in being your worst nightmare.

Mary Loverde author of *I Used to Have a Handle on Life, but it Broke*, pegged it. "We'd love to believe that love will prevail and as long as you don't bother bullies, they won't bother you. In the real world, kids jockey for position. We may wish this weren't so, but kids constantly size each other up to figure out who's the alpha dog. Trying to ignore a bully invites, even encourages, aggression because it is perceived as avoidance."

I've come to the conclusion that we do children a disservice when we give them the impression that their only and best option is to stay away from bullies. That's just not realistic. Telling children to stay away from someone who's mistreating them gives bullies continued power and relegates your son or daughter to living in fear. I think it is far better to teach children how to take care of themselves so they can handle aggressors instead of hide from them.

You may agree with this in theory. The question is, how can children deal with bullies without putting themselves at risk? One way is to follow the example of your cat. What?! Read on to understand why I say this.

Adopt Your Cat's Courage

"You either learn to play hard ball or you become the ball." -- *author Crystal Woods*

Do you have a cat and a dog at home? Have you ever noticed how cats often rule the roost, even if the dog is larger and stronger? Watch what happens when a dog approaches. The cat arches her back and glares menacingly at the dog. If the cat holds her ground, the dog will often back off and not bother her because she has a "paws off" presence.

I saw this played out every day I walked my dog Murph in our neighborhood. We had several cats on our street. One, Mr. Gray Cat, had an imperial presence. When he saw Murph coming, he—there's no other word for it—expanded. He puffed himself up, stood his ground, and glared at Murph. Murph, who was twice his size, always gave him a wide berth because he exuded such a "Not here you don't" attitude.

On the other hand, there was a calico cat who panicked as soon as she saw us and took off running. Murph would always be at the end of her leash straining to get at her. Hmmm. Two different cats, two different attitudes, two different outcomes.

I think kids need to adopt the attitude of Mr. Gray Cat when dealing with a kid who's trying to be the top dog. Tell them to picture how cats can back down a dog three times its size simply by standing its ground and sending out a "Don't even think about it" attitude.

Standing your ground is such an important concept. A child who heads the other way when s/he sees a bully will often have the same effect as a cat trying to slink away from a dog. Cats know not to show fear or the dog will be after them in a second. Most dogs would win a battle with a cat if they tried, but they don't try when they can tell the cat will defend itself.

Most children are not interested in bullying others. Unfortunately, there are probably children who are interested in bullying them. At the dinner table tonight, talk about this cat-dog scenario. Ask your kids to picture the difference between a scaredy cat and a cool cat. Suggest that from now on they might want to act like a cool cat if someone starts picking on them. Stand in front of a mirror and ask them to adopt the pose of a scaredy cat. They'll probably duck their head, hunch their shoulders, and look like they're ready to flee. Now, ask them to pull themselves up to their full height and project a "Don't even think about it" look. Here a few of the ways kids can look like a cool cat.

SCAREDY CAT	COOL CAT
Run and hide	Stand your ground
Shrink back	Puff up
Slouch, hunch shoulders	Pull self up to full height
Eyes looking down or away	Eyes open and direct
"Don't hurt me" attitude	"Don't mess with me" attitude
Show fear	Show confidence

Martial Arts Can Teach Your Kids Physical Confidence

"You might as well fall flat on your face as lean over too far backwards." – James Thurber

You may be wondering, "Aren't there more tangible ways for my kids to protect themselves if they're being picked on?"

Matter of fact, yes. One of the most pivotal things you can do is to get your kids involved in activities that give them an athletic confidence, an assured physical presence that clearly projects, "I can handle myself."

Years ago, while I was being prepped for an appearance on the TV program *To Tell the Truth* (what fun), I noticed a photo on the makeup artist's mirror of him and his son receiving their black belts in karate. I asked about it and he told me how this had come about. His son had been the smallest kid in his class. As a result, he got pushed around a lot.

The father said, "In the beginning, I told him to mind his own business, but realized what useless advice that was when he told me, 'Dad, I tried to ignore them, but it doesn't work. Who likes to be ignored?' That's when I realized bullies who are ignored escalate their behavior so we're forced to pay attention to them. I signed us both up for martial arts classes. Within weeks, I noticed a change. My son held himself differently and projected a physical confidence that just hadn't been there before.

One day in gym, the school bully bounced a basketball off his head. Instead of backing away or backing down, he stepped up closer to the bully and said, 'Feel better? Is this what you have to do to feel good about yourself, pick on kids half your size?'

After that, it didn't matter that my son was one of the smallest kids in school. Tough guys left him alone because they knew he could take care of himself."

Do your children know how to take care of themselves? Registering your children and yourself in a self-defense or martial arts course is a good investment in bully prevention. Hopefully, you'll never have to use the skills you learn in class (unless you choose to compete in contests). However, the physical assurance you gain from knowing how to neutralize attacks will persuade most bullies to walk on by. Your "cool cat" confidence changes the risk-benefit ratio because you no longer look like easy prey. As this father said, "My son may not be able to stop bullies from hassling everybody. He can stop them from hassling him."

Another way we can help children achieve a cat-like confidence is to role-play real-life scenarios so they know what to say instead of being tongue-tied and tongue-twisted.

Turn Learned Helplessness into Acquired Courage

"When I was in high school I had a best friend who became a bully. I took a stand and took it upon myself to separate from her. I couldn't be associated with her because it wasn't the type of person I wanted to be." —Glee actress Amber Riley

Courage can take a lot of different forms. It can consist of speaking up to a bully or separating yourself from a friend who has become a bully. The bottom-line is, courage always consists of doing SOMETHING instead of doing NOTHING.

Learned helplessness is a psychological term that describes the dispirited mental state that results from being repeatedly put in situations in which we feel powerless. Anxiety is defined as "not knowing." Most of us have never been taught how to deal with someone who is threatening us. Since we don't know what to do or say to make bullies leave us alone, we feel helpless around them. This makes matters worse because bullies sense our fear and are emboldened by it.

Furthermore, confidence is defined in two words: "I can." Think about it. If you have a high level of competence in something, you feel confident in that situation. Most of us don't feel we're good at handling bullies. This lack of know how makes us even more afraid, which encourages more aggression.

What to do? Children can counteract feelings of hopelessness and helplessness by practicing situations in which they respond competently to verbal attacks. By rehearsing scenarios in which they think on their feet, they know what to do the next time someone tries to bully them.

One of our certified Tongue Fu!-Bully trainers is Christina Grimm, PsyD., a world-class softball player who played softball at UVA and UC-Davis. Christy once won the fastest pitch award at an international tournament in Florida and now coaches a college team in California.

I had been asked to present "Never Be Bullied Again" for the Youth Program of the annual National Speakers Association convention. I asked Christy to team-teach the session with me. Our goal was to make our session "eye-opening" instead of the normal INFObesity that's often presented on this topic, so we used the metaphor of baseball to demonstrate the dynamics behind bullying, and what to do about it.

We took the attendees outside, and recruited two talented athletes, one to catch and one to bat. Christy and the catcher took their positions, and she started firing the balls over the plate. You could see the kids' eyes widen as Christy popped that mitt with one fastball after another.

After a few warm-up pitches, she asked the batter to approach the plate. She fired one high and inside. (Please know, Christy is in control of her pitches, so even though this pitch was close to his head, he was not in danger.) He quickly backed away, a little shaken. Suffice it to say, on the next pitch, he was reluctant to get too close to one of her 65 mph rise balls. You could tell he wanted to be anywhere but there.

Christina turned to the group and said, "*What I just did to the batter – is what a bully is doing to you.* I want the batter to be afraid of me. I intentionally fire one in there and have her think I'm a little crazy so she's too busy being scared of me to get a good hit.

When a bully taunts you or teases you, she is firing a high-fast-ball at your head. And if you flinch and back away, she knows she's IN your head. She knows she owns you."

"Now, let me show you how to counteract the bully if you're the batter." This time, Christina took the bat and took the plate. And by that, I mean she *crowded* the plate. She got so close to the plate, she got in the pitcher's head. She exuded confidence and stared at the pitcher as if challenging him, "Go ahead, bring it on. I'm either going to hit it out of the park or you're going to hit me, but either way I win."

Christina said, "As a batter, I want to get in the pitcher's head. I want her worried about me so she can't get in her groove. I want her to see I am ready for anything she throws me; that I have complete confidence I can hit it out of the park. That's what you want to do if you're being bullied. Don't back away and don't back down. Project complete confidence that you're ready for anything they throw at you."

We then returned to the meeting room and asked kids to be honest. What mean things were said to them? I asked them to not hold back the ugly stuff. As the statistics showed, at some point, they were probably going to get called names about their looks, shape and race, maybe even their religion, physical disabilities and sexual orientation. Our goal was to come up with comebacks so they never again had to be embarrassed by what someone called them. Because if they were embarrassed by it, that meant the bully had gotten in their head and they'd keep doing it.

Is The Bully Changing The Way You See Yourself?
"Whatever look you were going for, you missed." – popular t-shirt

Christina said, "One of the most important things I learned while getting my Doctorate in Psychology is that the goal of a bully is to change how you see yourself, to cause you to question yourself. What you believe about yourself is the most important thing to protect. So, a primary goal of my programs is to help you figure out what your "tender points" are, and learn how to protect them, strengthen them, and turn them into opportunities to learn something about yourself while taking away the manipulative tools bully use to target that and hurt you."

Christina continued, "As a psychologist, coach and human being, I have been both witness to and a target of bullying. What is consistent about every case is that *the bully knows exactly what to say to make the biggest 'boom' in your life.* As the unsuspecting target, you are left reeling, cleaning up the mess, and sometimes fending off a new attack all at the same time. It can be so hard to get your thoughts in order, your feet on the ground and a strategy in place. But, you can. This is where Tongue Fu! –Never Be Bullied Again training can help. By identifying your tender points and learning how to be invulnerable to attacks on them, you can regain control of your experience and bullies can no longer get to you."

This weekend, sit down at the dinner table with your kids and tell them you're going to provide them opportunities to practice standing up to a bully. They wouldn't expect to be good at soccer or piano or any other skills without practicing. How can they expect to get good at handling verbal attacks if they don't have a chance to practice?

Ask your kids what mean things they hear at school. Ask which remarks bother them most so they can prepare for the real thing. Brainstorm responses so they have a repertoire of remarks that will convince bullies to take it somewhere else. Role-playing desensitizes them so they're no longer taken aback (look at the significance of those words) by taunts. The next time a bully challenges them, they will have "been there, practiced this," so they'll be able to think on their feet instead of being tongue-tied and tongue-twisted.

When I did this with my sons, I learned they were getting teased about their last name. Horn had become "horny" and when you're 11 and 12, this is embarrassing. Well, it's only embarrassing if you're embarrassed about it. We came up with a comeback. It wasn't brilliant, but it did the trick. From then on, when someone would call Tom or Andrew "horny," they would say, "That's my name. Please wear it out." After a while the kids dropped it because Tom and Andrew were no longer sensitive about it. Whatever the bully was going for, missed. Issue over.

Believe You Are Brave, Inside and Out

"Argue for your limitations, and sure enough, they're yours." — author Richard Bach

There's another way to help children bully-proof themselves. Author Victoria Moran told me a wonderful story about a famous actress. Victoria was interviewing her for her book *Lit from Within*, which discusses how we can be beautiful inside and out. Victoria was intrigued with this woman's style and wanted to know how she had acquired the reputation of being a room-stopper, the type of person everyone looks at admiringly because she has such a commanding presence. The woman confessed, "I'm not really beautiful. I realized a long time ago that life would be better if I was, so I decided to be beautiful, and people have believed it ever since."

Life will be better if children decide to be brave. Once they believe they are brave, other children will believe it, too. Children who have been targeted by a bully spend a lot of time reliving what the bully has done to them and worrying about what the bully will do to them. Focusing on these frightening images causes them to be filled with dread—the opposite of determination. The good news is, they can counteract this by filling their minds with images of them being brave.

As a parent, start catching your kids being "brave." Notice when they do something bold,. "That was brave going first down that big water slide." "Good for you for having the courage to run for office."

Remember, avoid the ghost words (e.g., "not" and "never") linked with unwanted behaviors such as "There's nothing to be *afraid* of," or "Don't let him *scare* you," or "Never let a bully *back you down*." Those well-meaning statements have the exact opposite effect of their intent.

Build up children's beliefs by using the words "courage" and "confidence " and "brave" when you see them exhibiting that, so they give themselves credit for it and start seeing themselves that way.

You Can Beat the Giants

"You're the weak one. You'll never know friendship. I feel sorry for you." - Harry Potter

If kids want to look and feel brave, they need to start telling themselves they're brave so they believe it. Suggest that every time they're in front of a mirror at home, they look themselves in the eye and say, "I am brave. I am brave. I am brave." Post signs with "I AM BRAVE!" in places (inside a notebook, on their personal computer, by their desk or bed) where they'll see this affirmation throughout the day.

This may sound like pop psychology, but it works. A fact of human behavior is that we act in accordance with our beliefs. We believe what we repeatedly hear, think, and are told. When we replace cowardly "I'm scared, I'm afraid" messages with confident "I'm brave" messages, the brain accepts what we tell it and our body behaves accordingly.

This was demonstrated by a successful executive who told me how he got his confidence. He said, "I owe it all to my mom. She read the book *The Magic of Believing*, and it changed her life and it changed mine.

"Our small-town Little League team won our local championship, so we advanced to the regional tournament, where our first-round opponent was the top-seeded Giants. The Giants were just that. They were all five to six inches taller than us and at least fifty pounds heavier. No one thought we stood a chance except my mom. She plastered posters all over our house that said 'Beat the Giants!' 'You Can Win.' My friends saw them and teased me unmercifully. I was so embarrassed.

"But guess what? We beat the Giants! Thanks to her, I learned early in life you can do what you want if you just believe in it hard enough."

Instead of seeing a bully as a "giant," shrink them in your mind. Instead of seeing them as "larger than life," see them, as Harry Potter did, as someone to feel sorry for. This diminishes their disproportionate power to dominate you. It "cuts them down to size" so they no longer have the ability to dictate how you feel.

Are Your Kids Getting Emotionally Mugged?

You may not agree with these suggestions to teach your kids to be a cool cat, stand their ground, learn martial arts or practice comebacks. I understand your reticence to recommend anything that might put your children at risk. The problem is, they're at risk whether you want them to be or not. It's up to you to prepare them to handle bullies so they don't live their life in fear of them.

Whatever you do, be sure to sit down with your kids and discuss this important issue. Start off by asking questions instead of giving advice. Find out what they've been dealing with and how they've been responding. Ask if their school has zero tolerance. What happens if they defend themselves from someone who is pushing them around? Brainstorm options about how they can protect themselves from troublemakers. Clarify whether they have permission to stick up for themselves if they're being picked on, and what such behavior looks like.

Whatever you do, please understand that doing nothing about this problem does not make it go away, it makes it worse. Give your children a fighting chance by preparing them to deal with intimidators so they feel powerful instead of powerless. They can't force others to treat them with respect, they can refuse to be disrespected.

Action Plan and Discussion Questions

Were you bullied as a child? What happened? How did it impact you then? What lingering effects has it had?

Do you have a child, niece, nephew or grandchild who is being bullied? Or, are you a teacher, coach, or youth leader who is in charge of a group where bullying is taking place? What's happening?

When are you going to sit down and have a conversation with these kids and discuss pro-active steps they can take to deal with it? What are you going to say? How are you going to listen so they feel comfortable being honest about what's being said or done to them?

How are you going to be an upstander on childrens' behalf and recommend their school or youth activity initiate a bully-awareness-prevention program? (Check the directory for organizational options.)

Chapter 19
What Can Be Done About Cyber-Bullying?

"Cyber-bullying is verbal and/or social aggression carried out via technology." – StopBullying.gov

Cyber-bullying has become such a complex, rapidly growing problem, it deserves its own book. The more I researched the topic, the more I realized the enormity of this issue – the swatting, trolling, ghost profiles and anonymous apps like Secret, Whisper, Shots, Ask.fm, Yik-Yak, Kik, Formspring – and its insidious impact.

Hardly a day goes by where there's not a headline about yet another over-the-top attack or stunt online. You may have heard about the Egyptian TV host who "punk'd" Paris Hilton. He invited her to go flying with him, supposedly for an aerial tour over Dubai. All of a sudden, alarms started going off. The plane "stalled" and then went into a deep dive. People were parachuting out of the back of the plane. Everyone aboard thought they were going to crash. A video shows Paris screaming, sobbing, begging for her life."

It was discovered the whole thing was an intentional prank that was *filmed* in order to be released online. Why? To get the perpetrator (and Paris) in the news, to drive millions of views, and so people around the world could LAUGH at Paris's reaction as she thinks she's about to die.

As I write this, *L.A. Times* has just published an article saying that TMZ uncovered documents that seemed to indicate Paris Hilton was in on the scam. The TV host, Ramez Galah, had actually pitched this idea to several celebrities in previous months, outlining what would happen and proposing what they would get paid to be involved.

Whether Paris Hilton was "in" on this prank or not, is almost beside the point. The video has generated 8+ million views, and was covered by almost every major media outlet worldwide. Which sends the message to other pranksters, "Go ahead, think up some outrageous stunt and you too can become famous and get on the news. You too will be rewarded with millions of page views and media interviews."

Is that really the message we want to send – that it's funny to watch someone think she's in mortal danger? In other countries, there are TV shows that, for laughs and ratings, make contestants think they're been marked for death by a sniper, where people are almost driven to a heart attack as they're stuck in a "haunted" elevator with a little dead girl. These shows turn us into virtual voyeurs. They desensitize us to cruelty.

This is the slippery slope of cyber-bullying. The insidious impact of people who have way too much time on their hands and spend it online on what Monica Lewinsky calls a "blood-sport" in her highly-acclaimed TED talk entitled "The Price of Shame."

http://www.ted.com/talks/monica_lewinsky_the_price_of_shame

You remember Monica? Whatever you think of her inappropriate relationship with the President of the United States, (when she was a 22 year old intern in the White House), she does not deserve the global mockery and hatred she endured in the following decade.

Monica realized she couldn't undo what had happened; she could be accountable for it. She's chosen to be an advocate on this issue that affects millions of people. She has turn her cyber-bullying experience into a teaching lesson that will hopefully serve as a cautionary tale.

So, what can you do in the face of this escalating social problem that is traumatizing many innocent victims? Here are two of the most helpful resources I've found on this issue:

www.CyberAngels.com. Curtis Silwa founded The Guardian Angels in 1979, to combat the safety risks caused by street gangs. In 1995, in respond to citizens' calls for assistance with online threats, (which can be even more insidious as it is often done anonymously and to unsuspecting children), he launched CyberAngels. It is one of the oldest, most respected online safety education programs, and has won numerous awards, including the Presidential Service Award. www.NoBullying.com reatures the 100 Best Articles on Cyber-Bullying. It updates the list frequently to feature the most recent. helpful advice. http://nobullying.com/100-must-read-cyber-bullying-articles/

How Informed Are You About Cyber-Bullying?

"Parent's just don't understand." – child featured on Dateline show titled, "My Kid Would Never Do That"

While proofing this chapter, I had the TV on in the background. I heard the phrase "cyber-bullying," and turned up the sound to discover CBS was airing a special entitled, *My Kid Would Never Do That.*

If you're a parent or youth leader, I suggest you and the kids in your group sit down together, watch this program, and have a conversation about it. Ask, "Does this happen to your friends, to you? What do you do about it? Do you intervene if it's happening to someone else? What can we do as a group to prevent this?"

The show features troubling insights from kids confessing how awful it feels to be cyber-bullied, to be told by peers, "You're worthless, a freak. I hope something sick happens to you. Why don't you kill yourself?"

In one of the most impactful scenes, Caitlin, a girl who runs a bully-prevention program at her school, watches a child at her table openly ridicule another girl. The bully (an actor) starts off by calling the targeted girl a "nerd" and then escalates into trashing her online. The targeted girl (also an actor) finally speaks up, rather meekly, "You know, I'm sitting right here. I can read everything you're saying online."

The bully shrugs, "It's just a joke" and keeps on texting nasty things.

A disbelieving Caitlin gives the mean girl a long, hard stare. The other girls at the table glance nervously at the bully and laugh along. Caitlin realizes that glaring isn't going to stop the mean girl, so she intervenes. Watch this clip to see what happens next.

http://www.nbcnews.com/dateline/video/my-kid-would-never-do-that-bullying-470712899860

What's abundantly clear from this clip is that unless someone has "practice" challenging a bully, they won't speak up, especially if people in the area are "siding" with the bully. Perhaps they're afraid the bully will turn on them or they don't want to risk being "uncool." Often, they don't know what to say – so they don't say anything.

It is Not "Funny" to Make People Suffer or to Watch People Suffer

Harris Interactive published a study that reported 81% of teens believe their peers cyberbully because they think "it is *funny.*"[B]

Cyberbullying is not funny. This cavalier attitude toward cruelty is removed from the very real consequences of what it's like to bullied virtually.

I had the pleasure of talking with Sherry Turkle, (author of the bestselling book "Alone Together"), following her keynote at the 2015 ASAE convention. Sherry reported research that shows there is a 40% drop in empathy in college students. Empathy is the ability to put ourselves in the other person's shoes and imagine what they're feeling. Sherry's premise is that communicating on digital devices literally and figuratively "removes" bullies from the object of their ridicule. They don't "see" the damage they're causing. It doesn't even register with them, much less phase them or motivate them to stop.

Remember the story of Tyler Clementi that I shared at the beginning of this book? Tyler committed suicide after having a private moment filmed and posted online. His roommate supposedly said, in his defense, that he shot the video as "a prank" and didn't anticipate it would have such drastic consequences.

Look at that word "anticipate." That's what empathy is. *Anticipating* how our actions will affect others, and adapting them accordingly if we predict they are not right or fair. Unfortunately, that room-mate got caught up in his "prank" and didn't empathize or anticipate the results.

This is why it's so important to become an advocate and educator about the drastic consequences of bullying. One of every 20 teens has seen a student with a GUN at school. 61% feel that school shootings are done in retaliation for being ostracized and bullied. Clearly, it is time to take a more pro-active role in teaching kids that cyber-bulling is not "funny," and to anticipate and empathize with the results of their online comments so they think first before hitting "send." http://www.bullyingstatistics.org/content/bullying-statistics-2010.html

Here are a few things you can do to pro-actively deal with this troubling issue. Once again, this issue "runs deep." If you are parenting, teaching or coaching young people, please take the initiative to lead a conversation that brings this topic "out into the open" so kids are not struggling with it on their own, where it can do "untold" damage.

1. Learn What Your Kids Are Doing And Inform Yourself about Online Platforms

"Sometimes the Internet can feel like a middle-school playground populated by brats in ski masks who name-call and taunt with the fake bravery of the anonymous." – author Susan Orlean

According to the Cyberbullying Research Center, the signs that your child may be being cyberbullied can include:[7]

- • unexpectedly stopping the use of their device(s)
- • appearing nervous or jumpy when using device(s)
- • appears uneasy about being at school or outside
- • appears to be angry, depressed, or frustrated after texting, chatting, using social media, or gaming
- • becomes abnormally withdrawn after use of device(s)
- • avoids discussions about their activities online

Educating yourself is the first line of defense. A fellow parent told me, "I'm not a techie. I barely know how to text. I don't even know where to start." She's not alone. Boomers who are not digital natives depend on schools to curb the cyber-bullying problem. Unfortunately, many school administrators are just as clueless as to how to counteract this. Furthermore, they can't legally intervene in online behavior that occurs away from school, even when it involves their students. As you can see, it's complicated. That why it's up to adults to take the initiative in this battle.

John Tullius, founder of Maui Writers Conference, helped me with this book. When we were discussing this issue of cyber-bullying he said parents should ask themselves, "'Do I know what Instagram, Snapchat, and Kik are? Do I know how to access them? Do I know exactly what my child does with them?' I didn't either, but I made a commitment to find out. It's a hassle and takes up hours of precious time; but think of all the effort you've put in, all the financial burden you've undertaken, all the love you've poured into protecting and nurturing your family. You may have picked out a safe community in which to live, maybe even behind gates, installed and paid for a 24/7 security system. You lock up every night, making sure your home is secure. But you may have put no effort into protecting your child from the most ubiquitous predator out there. Home invasion affects less than one percent of children, while it's a good bet your child is being psychologically invaded in his/her own bedroom, right now, to devastating effect."

The best way to learn about social media platforms is to visit the most popular platforms – and read the Getting Started and/or Frequently Asked Questions (FAQs) page. There are many individuals who are new to social media. The companies understand it's in their best interest to make it easy for you to understand how to use them … *safely*. Here are the links for the most-used social media platforms below.

- Twitter
- Facebook
- Instagram
- Snapchat
- Kik
- Pinterest

2. Remove the Mask of Cyber-Bullies So They're No Longer Anonymous

Anonymity is the curtain cyber-bullies hide behind. Bullies can launch systematic campaigns with impunity because victims don't even know who or where it's coming from. False or disguised email addresses and screen names can confuse as well as humiliate a victim.

Many cyberbullies feel there are few, if any, consequences for their actions because they can't be detected or identified. To them, it's no risk, all reward.

Fortunately, the shield of anonymity is dissolving, at least to a degree. Twitter, for example, allows you to report any tweets you feel are harassing by tapping the More icon (… and then selecting Report.)

Anytime you receive an offensive remark, take a screenshot. That is your documentation. It is crucial to take a photo or screenshot so you have hard proof of what was said. This makes your report objective vs. emotional and gives the authorities evidence they can use in court (if necessary) to hold the cyber-bully responsible. If the cyberbully denies sending the post, text, video or email, or deletes it, you have irrefutable evidence.

Nearly all computers are equipped with an internal screenshot mechanism, usually found on the top right of the keyboard. For example:

- **Windows:** The key is labeled "prt sc" or Print Screen on Windows computers. Press this key and then open Paint by clicking the Start button, going to All Programs, then Accessories and finally Paint. In Paint, on the Home tab, in the Clipboard group, press Paste. Now save your image. Alternatively, you can press Ctrl + V after opening Paint to paste the image.

- **Apple:** Mac users have a few options – Command+Shift+3 will take a screenshot of the full screen and save it to the desktop, Command+Shift+4 will allow you to choose what portion of the screen you wish to copy, and then will save that image to the desktop.

These screenshots can then be uploaded to the media platform, such as Facebook, as proof of the offending parties' trespasses. This is important to teach to your children, especially for use in online video games where chat logs are often fleeting and disappear in seconds. Most companies take bullying complaints seriously because they can damage the reputation of their product and cause a loss in users.

Mo Sahoo, a project manager for my business found an example of how taking a screen-shot can take down a troll. A teen was playing a popular game on Facebook. Because she was winning, her in-game name was on top of an online leader-board featured on a fan-based website. A troll, intent on discouraging her from playing, used Google to research her username. He found her username on a writing forum she was involved in. She had made the mistake of putting her address on her profile on this writing forum. The toll sent her a picture of her home, from Google Maps, and threatened her.

Thankfully, she had the presence of mind to take a screenshot of his threat and sent it to the game's support team. They reported the threat to the local police, who accessed the troll through his online account. The company who owned the gaming site cancelled the troll's access, banned him from further use, and deleted "strings" of other offenders associated with his attack. The young lady wasn't bothered again.

There are several lessons to be learned here. First, never put identifying information in a public place. Second, do not use the same username or password for multiple platforms as committed cyber-bullies can track that down through Google.

Bullying is Bullying – Whether It's Done Online or In Person
"Cyber bullies can hide behind a mask of anonymity online and do not need direct physical access to their victims to do unimaginable harm." – Anna Maria Chavez, CEO of Girls Scouts of America

The over-arcing message of this chapter? We adults have a responsibility to protect children from the insidious impact of bullies. We need to sit down and have conversations with kids so they feel safe revealing what's really going on at school, in their youth activities and online. Perhaps most importantly, we need to let them know there is strength in numbers; they are not alone, the adults in their life will listen to them and act on their behalf to protect them.

Although I've focused up to now primarily how cyber-bullying affects children, it is a problem for adults too.

I had the privilege of speaking at BlogHer15 in New York City. One of the keynoters was Brianna Wu, a video game developer and podcaster who has received 108 death threats in the past 9 months. She is often cited as one of the primary targets in an ongoing online campaign of emotional terrorism designed to threaten, harass and endanger prominent women in the gaming community. She said, "I'm doing everything I can to protect my life, except remain silent."

Her sister keynoter, Shireen Mitchell, founder of Digital Sisters and current chair of the National Council of Women's Organizations, said, "People need to understand that death threats are not a form of free speech. They're not protected."

Shireen is currently running SOVAW (Stop Online Violence Against Women) and is collaborating with legislators to showcase women who have had scary, offensive online experiences so trolls can no longer remain anonymous. Check out this article to find out more about their pioneering work. http://www.blogher.com/brianna-wu-and-shireen-mitchell-life-online-target-gaming-community-blogher15

As with kids, the key to counter-acting hateful online behavior by adults is to take a screen-capture. A woman going through a difficult divorce brought stacks of printed-out emails, texts, and social media posts to her initial hearing as proof of her ex-husband's vicious campaign against her. After going through the overwhelming evidence of his slanderous attacks, the judge awarded her custody of their children.

What's this mean for you? If you, or a loved one, are being cyber-bullied, please don't go it alone and don't stay silent. There are professionals who can help you deal with this. Please reach out, capture proof of the offensive online behavior, report what's happening, and get support instead of giving trolls the power to ruin your quality of life.

Action Plan and Discussion Questions

Do you know someone - yourself, a friend or family member - who is receiving offensive or hurtful messages online? What is happening?

Have you told someone about this? Were they helpful? Explain.

Do you know someone who has been targeted by an online troll who is spreading untrue rumors about them, who has published private information, or has solicited them for unlawful acts? Explain.

What pragmatic action are you going to take? Are you documenting or taking screen shots so you have tangible evidence of what's being said or done? What online networks, authority, or organizations will you to report this to - so the trolls will be held accountable?

Chapter 20
Stand Up For Yourself

"I learned that courage was not the absence of fear, but triumph over it. The brave man is not he who does not feel afraid, but he who conquers that fear."
- *Nelson Mandela*

Have you noticed that the difficult people in your life often launch their verbal assaults when you're seated and they're standing?

Why is that? It's easier for them to tower over someone who's lower than them. They are trying to take physical advantage of their dominant position to reinforce their superiority.

That's why one of the best things you can do to counteract the bully's attempt to dominate you is to literally and figuratively stand up for yourself. It's a way of saying, "I will not take this sitting down." It's a way of leveling the playing field so they are no longer looming over you.

An engineer named Matt chuckled upon hearing this and commented, "This reminds me of a co-worker at my previous job. He was rather short and compensated for it by swaggering around talking about the days when he had been in charge of this or that as a senior military officer. He was quick to point out your errors so he could correct them. One afternoon I was working on a set of blueprints and he came over and started pounding on my desk with his fist. He was upset because he'd just found out our project had some cost overruns. I wasn't going to sit there and take that because I knew the unapproved spending had been done by a different department.

"I stood up (I'm six-four) and started walking around my desk. I was going to tell him to get his facts straight, but I didn't have to. As I rounded the desk, he took off, muttering something under his breath."

What Matt must have known at some intuitive level is that getting up from a chair is a nonverbal way of letting the bully know you are capable of "standing on your own two feet." Staying seated during a tirade gives tyrants the upper hand and keeps you under their thumb. When you stand up, you are no longer beneath them. In fact, the taller you can make yourself, the less a bully can lord over you and the more likely s/he will decide they have better things to do elsewhere.

I had the privilege of playing in a golf tournament with Mariah Burton-Nelson, a former professional basketball player and now the VP of Innovation and Planning for ASAE. While waiting to tee off, I asked if she had any bully stories. She thought about it for a moment and then looked at me, mildly perplexed. "I can't think of any," she said. Of course not. Mariah is over six feet tall and is a confident, athletic woman who knows who she is. She simply is not bully material. One look at her sense of assurance and any bully would wisely leave her alone.

A friend pointed out, "I'm feeling some short-ism coming on. Mariah has an unfair advantage. She's over six feet. I'm barely over five." Good point. There are still things you can do to appear tall even if you're not. Petite people can be perceived as powerful and can prevent would-be intimidators from invading their space as long as they stand strong.

Criminals have revealed that they seek out marks who have what they call a victim's stance. Victims walk or sit slightly hunched over. Victims often keep their chin down and their eyes averted or unfocused. They often hold their arms close to their body in a protective pose. They walk with small, hesitant steps or wander mindlessly. Unfortunately, this cowardly-appearing posture attracts bullies.

Confident people don't cower, they tower. They stand straight with their shoulders back. Their chest is out instead of concave. They keep their chin up and look at the world straight on with a calm, steady gaze. They walk purposefully and energetically. Even when in a chair, they sit up and project authority instead of slouching. Their whole demeanor says, "I know and like who I am."

A popular teen magazine interviewed me for an article on confidence. My first suggestion to young female readers was to stop hugging their schoolbooks to their chest. That posture rolls their shoulders forward and makes them appear vulnerable. It's better to lug heavy textbooks in a backpack so they can walk tall with shoulders back, chin lifted, and strong, purposeful strides.,

If you have a bully in your life right now, ask yourself what signals your body has been sending. Have you been feeling defeated? Has your posture reflected and reinforced that image? Do you slump when you're with this person? Do you give away your nervousness by flinching or leaning away? Do you keep your head down in the hopes he or she won't notice you? (Note: It didn't work with your third grade teacher and it won't work with a bully either.)

A former security guard named Harold told me, "We need to keep in mind that bullies operate from a primal point of view. They measure their worth by where they are on the 'authority ladder' compared to the people around them. You're either higher on the ladder or lower. Bullies check out our body language in the first few seconds. If they perceive you're the 'bigger dog,' they'll usually leave you alone. If you indicate any hesitancy or weakness, they'll pounce. That's why it's so important to send the right signals. I train my security personnel to have a commanding presence. They can prevent a lot of fights just by the way they hold themselves."

Read again what Harold said: "They can prevent a lot of fights just by the way they hold themselves." Think about it. "You've got me in your hold" means you've got me in your clutches, in your control. Ergo, holding a powerful posture means you're in control of yourself, which means the bully won't be able to.

Stand Strong

"People can hate you, rate you, shake you or try to break you; but how strong you stand is what makes you." - Pinterest

How do you hold a powerful posture? By standing strong. One woman protested, "But I don't feel strong. How can I act strong?"

Good question and good news. As discussed in my book *What's Holding You Back?*, you can act confident even if you don't feel confident.

Many of us let our body *reflect* how we feel. We feel depressed or exhausted, and our body reflects that by drooping. From now on, get clear that you're going to use your body to *direct* how you feel. Renowned psychologist William James said one of the most important discoveries he made in fifty years of studying human behavior was, "It is easier to act ourselves into feeling than it is to feel ourselves into acting."

In other words, if we wait until we feel strong to act strong, we may be waiting a long time. Our goal is to stand strong - even though we may not initially feel strong.

How do we do that? By intentionally adopting a posture that exudes authority. Remember earlier in the book when we talked about how your children could act like a cool cat instead of a scaredy cat? Starting today, you're going to do the adult version of that.

Exude an Aura of Authority

"Please take responsibility for the energy you bring into this space." – Dr. Jill Bolty Taylor, top-ten downloaded TED Talk

Dr. Jill Bolte Taylor made the above request in her highly-regarded TED talk. As she pointed out, we bring a certain energy – either positive or negative – every time we walk into a room. And it's up to us to make sure the energy we're projecting serves us and the situation.

I loved developing this chapter because of the metaphorical significance of the phrases associated with authoritative body language.

Standing on our own two feet means just that. It shows we're standing our ground instead of giving in to the flight urge and being poised to flee. Having our eyes wide open means we're looking straight at what's happening in front of us instead of turning a blind eye toward it. Meeting a situation head-on means we're prepared to face it instead of looking for a way out. Stepping up to the plate (or the person) indicates a confident willingness to engage and is the opposite of backing down.

"I've heard about the importance of body language before," one skeptic commented. "I never thought of it this way, though—that I can regulate how I feel and how other people feel about me by regulating my posture. It makes sense. I may not be able to control my emotions, but I can control the way I stand, sit, and walk. And by choosing to adopt a more confident stance, I'll feel and be perceived as confident."

If you're near a mirror right now, take a minute to walk over and see for yourself the difference between a "cower" and "tower" position.

Cower	Tower
Feet close together	Feet Should-width apart
Head tucked down	Head up
Hands in fig-leaf position	Hands in basketball position
Shoulders rounded/slumped	Shoulders up and back
Stand small	Stand tall

See how weak and meek you look and feel in the "cower" posture? Notice how insecure you look when you duck your chin, droop your shoulders and let your chest cave in? Notice how the fig leaf position (clasping your hands in front of your pelvic region) makes you look and feel like you have something to hide? This "stand small" stance (where you're shrinking from the world) comes across as fearful, "Please don't hurt me." It actually attracts bullies who conclude you'll be an easy target.

I saw the devastating consequences of a "cower" posture when I spoke for a INC 500 conference, which honors the fastest-growing entrepreneurial businesses in the U.S. Seth Godin, Tom Peters and Jim Collins were the morning keynoters. They commanded the stage *and* our attention from start to finish.

The next keynoter was introduced. A woman walked out rather tentatively, leaned against the lectern with her feet crossed at the ankles (which made her look tipsy and off-balance), tucked her head (which made her look coquettish) and said with an upward lilt, "I was telling my grand-daughters yesterday how much I was looking forward to this ...?"

Almost immediately, the laptops and cell phones came out and people started walking out. Her tentative posture and opening had not captured our respect. Which was too bad because she's a brilliant executive, however her "cower" posture that morning undermined her perceived authority and lowered people's regard for her leadership.

That's the unfortunate impact of a "cower" posture.

Now, back to you. Look in the mirror and adopt a "tower" posture. Feel the difference? Don't you immediately feel and look more confident when you stand straight, square your shoulders and hold your head up? Now, hold your hands out in front of your waist, about a foot apart. This "basketball hands" posture is what I recommend to speakers to counteract nerves. It keeps your shoulders back and your hands open to what's happening. Adopt the athletic "ready stance," feet shoulder-width apart, knees slightly bent. Don't you feel more grounded, but physically alert, ready to pivot in any direction and be quick on your feet?

Adopting this "stand strong" stance helps you exude authority which reverses the perceived risk-reward ratio for bullies. Your physical confidence causes them to take one look and decide, "I don't think so. This one can handle herself. I don't want to risk getting shown up."

Action Plan and Discussion Questions

Picture your customary body language. What signals do you send? Do you stand strong or come across as weak and meek? Explain.

Do you have a bully in your life? If so, how does your body language change around this person? Do you sit or stand small? Give an example.

From now on, how are you going to tower instead of cower? How are you going to project an aura of authority that says "I know who I am, don't mess with me" so bullies can tell you're not an "easy mark?"

Chapter 21
ANGER CAN BE HEALTHY

"Anger is meant to be acted on, not acted out." -- author Julia Cameron

"I'm not angry," I insisted. "I just don't want to have anything to do with this person." The therapist I'd sought out to get perspective on what I was dealing with nodded knowingly, and jotted notes on his pad.

Therapists know that people who insist they're not angry may have stuffed their anger so deep they don't know it exists. They may have compartmentalized the anger because they need all their energy to function and get through the day. They may admit to feeling depressed or exhausted, not knowing that depression and exhaustion are often signs of suppressed outrage.

It's time to understand that anger is a natural response to our rights being trampled. It's actually the way our emotional system is supposed to work. If someone does something hurtful to us (or to people we love), our mind gets mad as a way of signaling "That's wrong." Anger is the original warning system for letting us know our line's been crossed.

Unfortunately, many of us have been intellectualized out of our anger. Anger isn't pretty. It can lead to yelling and screaming, which isn't "nice," so we mentally ratchet it in rather than run the risk of letting it out.

My book *Tongue Fu!* featured many quotes about anger, almost all of them associating anger with negative outcomes. For example:

- *"The greatest remedy for anger is delay."* —*Seneca*
- *"If you are patient in one moment of anger, you will escape a hundred days of sorrow."* —*Chinese proverb*
- *"For every moment of anger, you sacrifice sixty seconds of happiness."* — *Dale Carnegie*
- *"Anger is never without a reason, but seldom a good one."* —*Benjamin Franklin*
- *"You will not be punished for your anger; you will be punished by your anger."* – *Buddha*
- *"Every day we have plenty of opportunities to be angry or offended. But what you're doing when you indulge those negative emotions is giving something outside yourself power over your happiness. You can choose not to let little things upset you."* – *Joel Osteen*

These quotes are insightful, but they are one-sided. They only speak about the harmful aspects of anger (or, as a colleague once told me, "Anger is one letter away from danger.")

What I've come to understand is that there are times it is appropriate, even advantageous, to get angry. There are times we'll actually produce more sorrow if we don't speak up. An angry response can be more appropriate than an empathetic response when dealing with cruelty.

The problem is, many of us have internalized these cautionary quotes to such a degree that we perceive all anger as bad. We bury it, deny it, and think we've failed if we can't rise above it. After years of doing our best not to feel this dark emotion, we stop feeling it. We become numb because we have dulled our anger to a point we've suppressed all feelings.

It's time to understand what a terrible price we pay for believing we don't have the right to be angry. Believing this is tantamount to believing we don't have the right to feel aggrieved. It means if people hurt us, we're somehow supposed to take the high road and continue to respond compassionately - no matter what. In other words, be a saint.

Many of us believe deep down that anger is a base emotion that only "un-evolved" people show. Enlightened folks are supposed to be loving, right? An enlightened, loving spirit is indeed a worthy goal. An equally worthy goal is recognizing we have the right to not be loving when someone is harming our physical and mental health. It's time to stop apologizing for honest anger and start expressing it responsibly so we no longer suffer in silence when we are wronged.

I'm not suggesting we go around losing our temper at the slightest provocation. I am suggesting that outrage is sometimes justified. Shakespeare said, "To be furious is to be frightened out of fear." Our goal - when the situation warrants - is to no longer be afraid of becoming furious.

As stated before, quiet endurance of bad behavior condones it. The famous dramatic scene from the movie *Network*, for example, shows a frustrated broadcaster urging his viewers to stick their heads out the window and scream "I'm as mad as hell, and I'm not going to take it anymore!" It's an unforgettable scene, but does the dramatic gesture solve anything?

That pent-up outburst may have made him feel better, but it didn't help his cause, because it was reactive anger.

Reactive anger means letting loose pent-up fury without considering the consequences and without improving the situation.

Responsible anger is unleashing pent-up fury after considering the consequences and concluding it *will* improve the situation.

Acting *out* anger means getting mad at someone who did something we didn't want. It's usually focused on the *past*.

Acting *on* anger means expressing our emotion and then asking for what we *do* want ... in the *future*. It is pro-active rather than reactive.

FIVE STEPS TO EXPRESS ANGER RESPONSIBLY

These five steps can help you express A.N.G.E.R. constructively rather than destructively so you can be angry in a way that helps instead of hurts.

A = ASSESS WHAT HAPPENED. Ask yourself, "Why exactly am I upset?" Pinpoint the precise cause so you know what's making you mad. Did this individual break an important promise? Did he or she say something derogatory that crushed the spirt of a loved one? Identify the reason behind your anger so you can target the wrong you want righted.

N = NO EXTREME WORDS. Extreme words produce extreme reactions. *Always, nothing, never, no one, and everyone are sweeping generalizations that incite emotion.* If you say, "You always let us down," the other person will huffily point out the one exception that disproves your claim. "You had promised to take the kids to Disneyland over the weekend" will get better results than saying "You never keep your promises." Saying "How will you make this up to them?" is more constructive than "There's nothing you can do to make it up to them."

G = GIVE SPECIFIC EXAMPLES. The more precise you are, the more productive you'll be. Describe exactly what was done or not done. Sweeping accusations such as "You are so irresponsible" are open to interpretation and don't isolate the particular act/inaction that caused the problem. Say instead, "When they came home, they told me they don't want to spend weekends with you anymore, because you took them to your friend's house (who they don't know) and then ignored them while you watched the football game."

E = EXPRESS THE BEHAVIOR WANTED IN THE FUTURE. Once you give evidence of what was wrong, move on. Complaining about what happened won't undo it. Instead of punishing people for past mistakes, pinpoint how they can do better in the future. Say, "The kids want and need to trust you. From now on, if you change your plans, tell them before the weekend so they don't get their hopes up. As my dad used to say, "We can't motivate people to do better by making them feel bad." Focus on how they can do it right next time instead of how they did it wrong this time.

R = REVIEW TO MAKE SURE YOU GOT THROUGH. Trying to have the last word, "This better not happen again" leaves a sour taste and little incentive for the other person to cooperate. Asking "What are your plans for your next weekend with them?" gives the other person a chance to verbally commit to changed behavior.

Don't Deny Your Anger It, Direct It
"Anger is an acid that does more harm to the vessel in which it is stored than to anything on which it is poured." – Mark Twain

From now on, understand that holding onto anger, *not* acknowledging and articulating your anger, is what's dangerous.

"I was one of those people who was afraid to get angry," Tricia said. "I don't explode, I implode. My parents fought like cats and dogs. I would be in bed with my pillow over my ears and mentally beg them to stop. I vowed never to be like them. I went a little overboard, though, and was so nice to everybody all the time that I got walked on a lot. I finally snapped last year when one of our PTA officers went too far one too many times.

"I was president of our local elementary school PTA. Our program chair was notoriously lax about her responsibilities. I don't know why she volunteered for the position because half the time she didn't show up for the meetings. What's worse is that half the time the speaker she scheduled also didn't show up for our meetings. Patti called me two hours before our December program, traditionally our biggest event of the year, to say the parenting expert she had booked wasn't going to be able to come after all. Before, when things like this happened, I would just take charge and let her off the hook. Not this time. I was absolutely clear this was her responsibility.

"I told her, 'I am really angry that you waited until the last minute to tell me about this. Patti, you need to find a substitute, quick.' She whimpered, 'But how am I supposed to find someone? It's four o'clock and the meeting starts at six.' I said, 'Figure it out, and you better find someone good because we've got three hundred people showing up at the school cafeteria in an hour and a half, and if you haven't found someone, you're going to be the one to explain it to them.' Then I hung up. That felt so good. Patti must have done some scrambling because a former school counselor gave a wonderful program on how we could (guess what?) hold our kids responsible. Needless to say, Patti never tried to pull that again."

Kudos. Next time you feel that unsettling emotion in your gut that signals you've been wronged, don't disregard it. These A.N.G.E.R. steps can help you constructively express what you're feeling so the situation is addressed instead of ignored.

Who are You Really Angry At?

"Usually, when people are sad they don't do anything. They just cry over their condition. But when they get angry, they bring about a change. There's nothing wrong with anger as long as you use it constructively." Author Wayne Dyer

An interesting thing happened while I was on the book tour for *Take the Bully by the Horns.* I was interviewed on a lot of radio shows by male disc jockeys who were still haunted by "Georgie" (or the equivalent) who had made their life miserable back in third grade. These DJ's vividly retold stories of having their lunch money stolen every day; being "pantsed" and humiliated in front of classmates; and dreading riding their bike home because they knew the bully would be waiting for them.

Even those these incidents happened twenty or thirty years ago, these DJ's still simmered with resentment at these mini-tyrants who had terrorized them. One DJ confessed he had seen a therapist about this and she had suggested he "forgive and forget." He told her vehemently, "I will *never* forgive and I will *never* forget what that jerk did to me."

I asked gently, "You know what my psychologist friend would say about that? Maybe he's not the one who needs to be forgiven ..."

"What do you mean by that?" he asked, almost belligerently.

"Maybe you need to forgive yourself. Maybe that's who you're really angry at."

He said "That makes no sense. HE was the one who beat me up every day and made school a living hell."

"I know. However many men have told me they've come to realize they're angry at the bully because he 'got the best of them,' but they're also angry at themselves for not standing up for themselves."

The DJ retorted, "That sounds like pop psychology mumbo jumbo to me."

I laughed, "I understand. It's just that a number of people have told me they were only able to put what happened behind them, when they forgave themselves."

"I still don't get it. Why should they forgive themselves? They didn't do anything wrong."

"True, but in their mind, they wished they had handled it differently. They were angry for 'allowing' the bully to embarrass them. Once they gave themselves a little grace and admitted their anger and regrets, they were able to let them go.

Maybe you could remind yourself, "I was only 8 years old. What did I know about dealing with someone twice my size who was out to get me? I didn't know then what I know now. It's over. Move on."

That DJ got back in touch to say he wished we'd had an hour instead of ten minutes. He said the console lit up like a Christmas tree with all the incoming calls of people wanting to share their bully story. Hopefully, the tips helped them put their bully experience in the past.

Are you angry at someone who bullied you? Be honest. Are you also angry at yourself for not doing more about it?

Could you give yourself a break? Could you realize you didn't know then what you know now? That you did the best you could at the time? Could you forgive yourself, extract the lesson-learn so it serves you in the future, and move on? Could you adopt the lyrics in the hit song from the movie *Frozen,* "The past is in the past. Let it go. Let it go."

Action Plan and Discussion Questions

When was the last time you got angry at someone? How did you handle it? Did you yell and scream? Suffer in silence? Explain.

Did you grow up thinking anger was a normal part of relationships or something to be afraid of? Elaborate.

Is there a situation in your life right now that's making you mad, but you've been afraid to admit it? What is that? What steps are you going to take to act on (vs. act out) your anger so you deal with this emotion in healthy ways?

Did you also realize that, for whatever reason, you're also angry at yourself? Do you wish you had handled things differently? Could you remind yourself you did the best you could at the time … and choose to give yourself some grace and forgive yourself so can truly forget?

Chapter 22
PROTECT YOURSELF IN DANGEROUS SITUATIONS

"Panic causes tunnel vision. Calm acceptance of danger allows us to more easily to assess the situation and see the options." – author Simon Sinek

This suggestion to be calm in the face of danger is one of those ideas that is great in theory and hard to do in practice. Which is the purpose of this chapter: to mentally prepare you for dangerous situations so you can think on your feet and respond proactively, instead of panicking and reacting in a way that puts you and others at risk.

For example, a friend was driving home the back way with her ten year-old daughter when she saw a man viciously slapping a woman and throwing her against a wall. The man was screaming obscenities and the woman was trying to ward off his blows.

Without a second thought, Victoria stopped the car (this was on a dark street with no one else around), ordered her daughter to lock the doors, and ran over and yelled as loud as she could, "What are you doing? Stop this right now!" The man stopped and turned to her, startled. Much to Victoria's shock, the woman, with tears and blood streaming down her face, said, "He's my boyfriend. Leave us alone."

Victoria walked back to the car, dumbfounded. She started driving home, but had to stop a few blocks later and pull over to the curb because she was shaking (and shaken) so badly. She was mortified, not just because of the unexpected reaction of the woman with all its ramifications, but because she realized her well-intended intervention had put herself and her daughter at risk.

The moral of this story? Consider the consequences *before* confronting someone who's violent. The following tips can help you handle dangerous situations pro-actively. As Simon points out, the goal is to assess the situation and determine the options that do not put yourself and others in harm's way.

Honor Your Instincts

"You have the gift of a brilliant internal guardian that stands ready to warn you of hazards and guide you through risky situations." – Gavin de Becker, author of The Gift of Fear

I was channel-surfing one day and flipped to a TV station on which high-security consultant Gavin de Becker was being interviewed. I don't remember which show it was (he's been on *Oprah, 60 Minutes* and *20/20* many times) ... but I certainly remember what he said.

As CEO of a firm that provides security for politicians, executives and celebrities, he debriefs anyone who's had the misfortune of being assaulted or kidnapped. His first question? "Did you have any warning?"

Guess what? Almost everyone says, *"I knew something was wrong."* But they over-rode their instincts. They looked around and concluded, "It's broad daylight. What could happen?" Or, they reassured themselves with, "I'm in an armored car with a security detail. No one can get to me." In other words, their sixth sense alerted them to danger *but they ignored it.*

The point? Honor your instincts if they're waving red flags or shouting "Red alert." If your gut is telling you you're at risk, you are. Have you ever known your instincts to be wrong? If you feel something "in the pit of your stomach," get the heck out of there or prepare to protect yourself. Do not let your intellect talk you out of the warning signals your instincts are sending you.

As De Becker says, "Intuition is always right in at least two important ways; it is always in response to something, and it always has your best interest at heart." Hear, hear.

Rally Your Resources and Rely on Your Foresight

"Light is metaphorical. There is green light and red light. Then there is black light, which is mostly danger." – German artist Sigmar Polk

A woman named Laura said, "A co-worker in my building was raped in the parking lot after she left work late one night. Our company sponsored a self-defense class for all women employees in an effort to prevent that type of thing from happening again. They brought in a police officer, a karate instructor, and consultant who specializes in executive protection. Those classes were such an eye-opener for me. One of the most important things I learned is that you can't take for granted that you'll stay safe as long as you stay out of 'dangerous' areas.

"I had always thought, in a kind of unarticulated way, that as long as I didn't wander around some parking garage or deserted street at midnight, nothing bad would happen to me. Wrong. The policeman told us many assaults happen in innocent circumstances, like when you're taking your groceries out to your car in broad daylight."

The following tips can help you keep your antenna up for "black light" - danger - so you can act quickly on your own behalf.

1. STAY ALERT.

Would-be assailants look for people who appear distracted because a preoccupied person can be easily overpowered. You're a prime target when you are sitting in your car talking on your cell phone, searching through your purse, or texting because you're unaware of your surroundings. Pay attention when you're in public places so you won't be caught off guard.

2. CARRY AND DISPLAY A DETERRENT.

Contrary to popular thought, keys are not a deterrent because you have to get up close to use them. Leave at least one hand free so you can defend yourself if necessary. If you're carrying packages in both arms, it's hard to fight back. It's better to make several trips than to be burdened down with several full shopping bags. If you're in an unsafe area, carry an umbrella or a can of pepper spray so you have something to fend off an assault. Blowing a whistle or sounding the emergency alarm button on your keys can at least alert anyone in the vicinity that something's wrong.

3. GO WITH THE CROWD.

There really is safety in numbers. If leaving a theater or shopping center, walk to the parking lot or garage with other people. If you're by yourself, do not open your car doors from a distance with your remote because it signals which vehicle is yours and lowlifes can slip in the back door and hide. Don't be embarrassed to ask security personnel to walk you to your car if you're in an isolated area. Don't take the stairs in empty buildings. Yes, it's nice to get exercise, but some stairwells are notorious hangouts for predators.

4. FIGURE OUT WHAT THEY'RE AFTER.

Most criminals want either to snatch your wallet or hijack you to a secluded location where they can take their time with you and don't have to worry about getting caught. If you think they're after your money or property, drop both on the ground, say "Take it," and run in the other direction. You can always replace your credit cards, checkbook, etc. If they're after you, get tough. This is not the time to be sweet. The more difficult you are, the more discouraged they'll become. DO NOT GET IN THEIR CAR. Cause a commotion. Assailants looking for an easy target will hopefully decide this is too time-consuming and you're not worth the trouble.

5. GET MAD AND BAD.

Do not say something timid like, "Please don't hurt me." Meek words incite criminals because they show you're scared. If someone starts coming toward you, hold your hands out in front of you and yell, "Stop!" or "Stay back!" or "I have pepper spray!" Instead of pleading, "Leave me alone," go on the attack with words like "Go away!" If they try to grab you, yell "Fire!" or "Fight!" because people pay more attention to that than they do to "Help!" Some security personnel believe bystanders run away when they hear "Fire!" but run toward you when they hear "Fight!" because they want to watch. Whatever you do, don't plead helplessly. Roar in RAGE.

6. DON'T PLAY BY THE RULES AND DON'T TRY TO REASON WITH THEM.

If you are grabbed, do not play fair. Go for the groin. Stick your fingers in his eyes hard. If he grasps your hands, twist your wrist toward you because that can break his hold. Bend his fingers back. Stomp his feet with your heels. Bite exposed body parts. Scratch his face with your nails. Kick vulnerable areas like the knees or groin. Toss manners out the window and become a raving maniac. Trying to talk sense into him -"You don't want to do this" - won't get through. He is in a predator-like state and not in his right mind. It won't help to beg for mercy or appeal to his humanity. At the moment, he doesn't have any.

7. RUN FOR YOUR LIFE.

Whatever you do, don't let them drag you into a car or van. You'll be in even more danger if they succeed in taking you out of sight and away from witnesses who could intervene or at least report what's happening. Some security specialists suggest that even if the person has a gun, it is better to take your chances and run. Police officers miss their mark a large percentage of the time when shooting at a moving target from more than twenty feet away. Security consultants say your odds of surviving are better trying to escape than going to a secluded area with someone who has a weapon.

8. GO WITH YOUR GUT.

If you're about to get on an elevator by yourself and a suspicious-looking stranger steps on, step out and wait for another elevator. If someone knocks on your door, says his or her car is broken down, and asks to come into your house to use your phone, and it feels wrong, it probably is wrong. If someone appears to be following you, move out of the shadows and walk out in the open where you can't be yanked into an alley. Some police officers suggest you boldly whistle or sing out loud—anything to break the silence, which may be interpreted as fear by a criminal. If your insides are churning, there's usually a legitimate reason. Honor your instincts if they're warning you someone is not on the up-and-up. If the hairs on the back of your neck are standing up, don't risk your neck. Get the heck out of there.

9. BE YOUR OWN BODYGUARD.

The time to think about what you'll do if you're ever attacked is now, not when it happens. Develop a game plan so if you are caught by surprise, you won't be caught by surprise. If you rehearse your response in advance, your mind will do what it's been trained to do instead of going blank.

When traveling solo, pretend you're a security detail for a VIP (because you are a Very Important Person). Scout the location. Plan escape routes. Identify hazards. Don't allow the hotel clerk to announce your room number out loud when handing you your key. Ask for a room close to the elevator. You don't have to be paranoid; just know what you're getting into. Look around first instead of casually walking up to an ATM to make a deposit. If it seems all clear, go ahead. If someone loitering nearby doesn't feel right, take precautions and plan what you would do if threatened. Maybe you can make that deposit later. Maybe you can leave your car lights on or take your dog with you.

I know from personal experience the importance of keeping your wits about you when attacked. One beautiful summer evening, I decided to go for a solo run around our neighborhood. At that time I lived in Hawaii near Pearl Harbor in senior military housing. I set off just after twilight.

About twenty minutes into my route, I heard someone running up behind me. I thought it was probably a friend coming to join me and didn't look back. The next thing I knew, this person had put a hammerlock around my throat. Thinking this was someone's sick idea of a joke, I choked out, "Hey, that's not funny." This assailant, who was taller than me, tightened his grip, and I realized this was no friend.

My lifeguard training saved me. I ducked my head and dropped to my knees. This unexpected move and my sudden deadweight surprised the attacker and broke his hold. He clubbed me on the back of the head. Luckily, I had not turned toward him or he would have broken my nose or jaw. Instead, his fist glanced off my skull. I scrambled up and started running and screaming at the same time. At that point, my attacker must have figured I wasn't worth it and hightailed it out of there.

Lifeguards learn not to rear back when someone has us in a choke hold because that exposes our throat even more and cuts off our air supply. Part of lifeguard training was to practice breaking free from someone who has us in a death grip until it became second nature. Even though it had been years since I'd taken those classes, those much-rehearsed release maneuvers kicked in, thank heaven.

I learned a lot from that incident. I learned to stay alert to my surroundings instead of assuming I was safe. I was attacked on a street a few hundred yards from an armed guard stationed at the Pacific Fleet Intelligence Center. I was running past houses with open doors no more than fifty feet away—and no one heard a thing. Obviously, this individual was acting impulsively because his behavior did not make any sense. Thankfully, my years of lifesaving training came back to me in that moment of danger and I did the one thing he didn't expect.

Preparation is the father of safety. Prepare a game plan so you can handle dangerous situations pro-actively instead of panicking. Hopefully, you'll never encounter a violent bully. However, if you do, use these tips to increase the likelihood you'll emerge with your health and life.

Action Plan and Discussion Questions

Have you been assaulted? What happened? What did you do?

What will you do if you witness a violent act? How will you act quickly and proactively to get yourself and other people out of harm's way?

What safety measures will you take to minimize risk in potentially dangerous situations? How will you mentally prepare and honor instincts that are warning you something's wrong?

Part III
CHOOSE A BETTER FUTURE

"You are your choices." — Jean Paul Sartre

Chapter 23
CHOOSE YOUR BATTLES

"People are always blaming their circumstances for what they are. I don't believe in circumstances. The people who get on in this world are the people who get up and look for the circumstance's they want, and, if they can't find them, make them."
— George Bernard Shaw

All of the chapters in this section start with the word "Choose." Here's why.

The Library of Congress selected Victor Frankl's book *Man's Search for Meaning* as one of the most influential books of our time. You may be familiar with Frankl's story and his profound insight, "Our greatest freedom is the freedom to choose our attitude. We can't always choose what happens to us, we do choose how to respond to it."

Frankl certainly didn't choose to be held prisoner in a concentration camp during the Holocaust, and he did not choose to be starved or tortured. When he survived, he did choose not to let those horrific experiences defeat and define him. He chose to retain his belief in humankind. He founded Logotherapy and shared his insights with others in the hopes that what he and others went through could help others deal more positively and proactively with their challenges.

I don't know you, but I know *you did not choose to be bullied*. You did not choose to be targeted by trolls, work for a tyrant, or be hounded by a hater. You did not choose to be in a situation with a toxic individual who is poisoning your quality of life or putting your loved ones at risk.

If there's any good news, it's that *you can choose what to do from now on.* You can start looking for healthier circumstances. You can shift the way you deal with the bully and reverse the risk-reward ratio so the bully is motivated to leave you alone. You can document what is happening and report the bully's behavior to the authorities (with evidence) so they can remove the bully and/or hold the bully accountable.

That is the purpose of this section – to switch your attention to the steps you're going to take to create a future that is more in alignment with your values, rights and needs.

This chapter offers a series of "Choose Your Battle" questions that can help you make informed choices about what to do next.

The importance of taking the time to answer these questions emerged during an all-day workshop for school administrators. The audience had been divided into small groups so we could brainstorm how to deal with specific challenges. One principal was facing a no-win dilemma: "I have a teacher who should be fired, but my hands are tied. We have documented reports from students and parents testifying to her incompetence. I've arranged counseling, hired a teacher's assistant, and monitored her classroom. Nothing's helped. She's got two years left to retirement and she's determined to stick it out and get full benefits. She is accusing me of persecuting her and has vowed to file a grievance with the union and contest this case in court if I try to remove her. What can I do?"

As you can imagine, his conundrum created a heated discussion. The group suggested a variety of approaches, but the beleaguered principal had already tried most of them with no success. In the long run, the group reached a reluctant consensus. A participant summed up the group's feelings. "I've been in a similar situation and I know how frustrating it is. I eventually decided that going through the very lengthy legal process to fire this one incompetent teacher was not in the school's best interests. As leaders, we have to make constant judgment calls about what constitutes the best use of our limited resources. My bottom-line decision was, I would rather take the several hundred hours I would have invested in that acrimonious court battle and spend it on the many dedicated teachers who are trying to make a positive difference for their students. My mentor used to tell me, 'No one ever said this was going to be easy. That's why we get paid the big bucks.' " At this, everyone in the room laughed rather ruefully, because as you probably already know, educators don't get paid nearly what they're worth.

You may be thinking, "That's an awful decision! What if my child was in that teacher's classroom? Are they just going to ignore this woman's incompetence?"

Believe me, the educators disliked this course of inaction as much as you. In an ideal world, the principal would have taken the necessary steps to replace the teacher, her students would have received the quality instruction they deserved, and everything would have turned out copacetic. In the real world, it doesn't always work out that way.

The principal's reluctant conclusion wasn't a perfect solution to the problem, but it was the best of the "pick your poison" options. He was triaging his attention, time and resources and choosing to focus on what he felt was the best use of them.

This is one of the hardest aspects of dealing with bullies. Sometimes they "win." Sometimes, even when they're clearly in the wrong, we're not prepared to do what we have to do to deal with them, or we're not in a position to pay the cost of holding them accountable.

This isn't fair. In fact, it's quite frustrating. But it happens. And the only way we can live with choosing not to pursue a course of action to hold a bully accountable is to project what would result from doing so. You may conclude it's wiser to walk away than spend thousands of dollars and months of fruitless effort that does more damage than good.

A friend told me a chilling story of a senior bank officer who was unfairly fired. This executive returned from a week-long professional meeting to discover the bank president had publicly accused him of being on a boondoggle. Even though his time away had been approved, the CEO continued to hang him out to dry . The executive decided this couldn't go unchallenged. He went into the CEO's office to complain and was fired on the spot.

This bank manager, who is in his fifties, has now been out of work for months. He has two kids in colleges he can no longer afford; he no longer has company-sponsored health insurance; and he has no prospects in sight. He has almost depleted his savings and had to put his house up for sale. The last I heard, he was planning to move back to his hometown so he could work in his brother's business.

This is a scary scenario. The rash words of one minute undid a thirty-year career. The thing is, he's not sure he'd do it differently. He certainly isn't glad he got fired, and he isn't glad he and his wife have experienced such bleak months of misery. However, he doesn't regret not playing ostrich. He's not sure he could have lived with himself if he had buried his head in the sand and pretended he didn't know his CEO had openly accused him of lying. Perhaps he could have approached his boss in a more diplomatic fashion, but he suspects the outcome would have been the same. The bank president had an agenda, and wouldn't have put up with any type of protest, no matter how mild or artfully phrased.

What's the moral of this story? Know the personality of who you're dealing with and anticipate consequences *before* confronting him or her.

To Speak or Not To Speak: That is the Question

"I made decisions I regret, and I took them as learning experiences. I'm human, not perfect." – Queen Latifah

What's a situation in your personal or professional life that isn't right, fair, or kind? Are you going to play ostrich and ignore it, or are you going to face the situation head-on and confront the person responsible?

The following questions can help you decide whether it is or isn't in your best interests to pursue this. These criteria aren't guaranteed to help you make perfect decisions, but they can help you think things through so you reduce the chance of a making a rash decision you'll regret later.

Choose Your Battle Questions

1. What is this person doing that I find offensive or unfair?
2. Is this person aware that what he or she is doing is unkind, unfair, or inappropriate? Is the behavior intentional?
3. Is this individual's objectionable behavior a one-time incident or an ongoing issue?
4. Have I already made reasonable attempts to inform this person of the inappropriateness of his/her actions? Has he or she made any effort to change, or has s/he rejected my verbal olive branch?
5. How is this person's behavior affecting me? Could I be overreacting or is my response justified?

6. Could there be extenuating circumstances explaining his or her behavior that I'm not taking into account? Could these circumstances temporarily excuse how this person is acting?

7. What will happen if I do nothing? Is that an acceptable option? Can I live with myself if I don't speak up?

8. What do I hope to achieve by confronting this person? Be specific. How best can I communicate my message to achieve that goal?

9. What are the risks and potential negative outcomes of confronting this person?

10. Am I willing to pay those consequences? Why or why not?

11. Is there any realistic chance this person will make an effort to improve how he or she treats me and others (voluntarily or involuntarily)?

12. Could pursuing this be a "Don Quixote" exercise in futility? Ultimately, do I believe that I won't be able to favorably impact this situation no matter how long, hard or smart I try?

13. What are the resources needed to win this "battle"? What will it cost in terms of money, time, emotional toll, legal fees, energy, and brainpower to achieve my desired outcome? This is a measurable question. Figure out in terms of dollars, hours, weeks, months (years?) what it would take to triumph.

14. Is it my job to educate this person? Does someone need to hold him or her accountable, and I'm that someone?

15. Will pursuing this put me at risk or endanger my loved ones? How so? Have I discussed this dilemma with the people who will be affected by my decision? If my efforts don't prove successful, will I and my loved ones regret doing this?

16. Are there other options I haven't explored? Is there a way to address this issue without endangering my job, marriage, family, health, or livelihood?

17. Have I discussed this with a peer or professional who could have innovative, workable insights about how to turn this situation around?

18. Will time heal this wound? Will this situation improve if this individual is left to his or her own "vices"?

19. Are there penalties or advantages for delaying? Do I need to act now? Could waiting help me approach more wisely?

20. Is there an objective third party who could bring impartial perspective to the conflict? Could someone who's not emotionally involved mediate a satisfactory resolution? Who is that person and how can I ask him or her to intervene?

Ellen DeGeneres said, "Some people prefer to live in drama because it's comfortable. They stay in a bad relationship because they know what to expect every day, versus leaving and not knowing what to expect."

Answering these questions can help you decide whether you're staying in a bad situation because it's "easier." What's the saying? "The devil you know is better than the devil you don't?"

Personally, I rather not be in a relationship with a devil. However, this is YOUR decision. Take the time to answer these questions (perhaps with a trusted friend so you talk out loud and hear yourself think) so you can make an informed choice about whether you want to stay in an unacceptable known, or opt for an unknown you hope will be better.

Make Informed, Not Impulsive, Decisions

"Never cut a tree down in the wintertime.
Never make a negative decision in the low time.
Never make your most important decisions when you are in your worst moods."
Robert H. Schuller

Schuller's right. Making an important decision when you're mad is rarely wise. A woman named Sandra said, "This is the thought process our family went through trying to decide whether to hold our mother's health care providers accountable for medical malpractice. Our mom had been told she had multiple sclerosis when she actually had a slow-growing brain tumor. It was finally correctly diagnosed and the doctor recommended immediate surgery. Unfortunately, they were unable to remove the whole tumor, so the doctor ordered follow-up radiation.

"Our mom did not want to undergo this often debilitating treatment, but we decided the doctors were the 'experts' and 'knew best,' right? They ended up irradiating the wrong spot and Mom endured weeks of gut-wrenching nausea for nothing. The doctor advised another operation. Once again, Mom pleaded not to be put through this ordeal, but finally succumbed to the pressure to have the second surgery. It turned out to be the nightmare she had sought to prevent.

"Over the next few months, there were countless foul-ups. Staff members were caught smoking marijuana. Mom was left lying in a hallway for hours following a painful angiogram. She almost drowned in her own fluids after an intern misdirected a shunt, draining brain fluid into her lungs. Mom died the fate she dreaded, hooked up to multiple tubes in the intensive care unit, on a ventilator, and unable to speak.

"Following the funeral, we discussed whether we were going to file a lawsuit. The doctors may not have been bullies in the normal sense, but her rights had certainly been violated by this clear case of medical malpractice. In the end, we realized that money wouldn't bring our mother back. We didn't want to profit from her suffering and we didn't want to spend months (years!) in court reliving her pain. We decided the best course of action was to send prayerful apologies to Mom for what she had endured, to express our regrets to her that we hadn't listened to HER wishes, and to vow that none of us would ever again abdicate our authority or ignore our instincts when making health decisions."

Action Plan and Discussion Questions

What's an unfair, unkind, or unacceptable situation in your life? Is the person responsible aware of what s/he is doing? Do they care?

Review the Choose your Battle questions to see if taking action is in your best interests. What are some reasons to follow up on this? What are some reasons to let it go? What did you decide and why?

Is there another relationship in your life you're not happy with? After answering these questions, did you conclude it's too big of a risk or not worth your resources to pursue a course of action? Can you live with that choice? Explain your decision.

Chapter 24
CHOOSE TO TRUST

"Whoever battles with monsters had better see that it does not turn him into a monster." -- Nietzsche

We don't want to distrust everyone, but we also don't want to risk being betrayed again. Where's the balance?

First, it helps to understand we are most vulnerable when we have "blind faith" in everyone. A friend learned this the hard way when she signed up for a free time-share offer. The deal was, she'd get meal vouchers and a two-night stay at an island resort if she'd attend an introductory ninety-minute sales presentation.

Dot signed up and showed up on the appointed weekend. She spent the first day swimming, reading, and kicking back by the pool, and then headed over to the briefing. (She would have been charged full price if she had skipped the sales talk.)

Dot told me, "I had heard these were hard-sell pitches, so I was prepared for their pressure tactics. Sure enough, after the slide presentation, the sales rep started in with every trick in the book to make us feel obligated to buy a unit. I knew this was part of the deal and I figured sitting through the sales pitch was fair trade for the free weekend.

"What I hadn't counted on was how ruthlessly the sales rep badgered us. He targeted two elderly widows in the audience and pounded them with really manipulative questions like, 'Don't you love your grandchildren? You don't know how much time you have left.

Why let your money sit in a bank when you could use it toward building happy memories?'

"One of the staffers noticed my growing distaste for the sales rep's deviousness. She walked over and said, 'You're not going to buy anything, are you?' I looked her straight in the eye and said, 'No way.' She put her hands up in mock surrender and said, 'Come with me, then. You can sign out and leave early.'

"We walked into the office, she closed the door, and we sat down to finish the paperwork. She started chatting me up, and the next thing I knew, she was peppering me with questions about how could I pass up such a good deal. I finally escaped, but not before realizing she had tricked me. I hadn't been vulnerable to their tactics initially because I'd anticipated them. Once I left the room, though, I let my guard down because I thought it was all over, and she tried to take advantage of my weakened defenses. As they say in *Star Trek*, my shield was down."

Many salespeople are ethical individuals who want to satisfy their needs and their clients' needs. As Dot learned, though, there are people out there who care only about *their* agenda. These people see us only as prospects to be sold, quotas to be met, obstacles to be overcome. If we don't accept this and stay vigilant, we'll be knocked off balance every time it happens.

Believe in Basic Goodness

"Trust is the glue of life. It's the most essential ingredient in effective communication. It's the foundational principle that holds all relationships." — author Stephen Covey

You may agree with Stephen Covey that trust is the glue of life, but you're wondering, "How can I trust again when I was blind-sided by someone who told me they cared about me?"

A woman told me, "This trust issue is a real problem for me. I don't want to go around suspecting everyone, but I was taken to the cleaners by my own uncle. He showed up in the hospital the day my husband died and said he'd take care of everything. He suggested we move my husband's clients over to his management account so I wouldn't have to 'worry' about them. He offered to take care of the bookkeeping for a while since he knew I had 'more important' things on my mind. In those next few months, he stole over a hundred thousand dollars. I couldn't believe a family member would take advantage of a widow with two children. He seemed so solicitous at the time. I never suspected he was out to get our money. I don't know who to believe anymore after I was so wrong about him. It's hard not to be a pessimist after going through something like that."

Have You Been Burned by a Bully?

"If we believe that tomorrow will be better, we can bear a hardship today." — *Thich Nhan Han*

What to do? How can we continue to trust when not everyone is trustworthy? How can we continue to believe in the best of mankind when we've been bested by a bully?

The answer to this was explained quite eloquently to me by a friend. As I told him about my surreal experience with a bully, he paraphrased William Blake's enduring insight, "We are all born innocent. At some point, we encounter evil. At that point, we have a choice. We become an embittered cynic or we choose to become an *informed innocent.*"

I love that phrase *informed innocent.* It helped me put my experience with that bully in its proper perspective.

Remember, the goal of a bully is to CHANGE YOU. I did not want my experience with that bully to change me into a cynic who saw the world as a dark place. I believe life is a blessing. I wanted to continue to see the world as a good place.

Blake's insight helped me understand that there are evil people in the world — and there are also ethical people in the world. I choose to focus on, and spend my time with, the ethical people. I choose to believe the best of people instead of letting one bully destroy my faith in the basic goodness of human*kind.*

You may be thinking, "Okay, I see the value of being an 'informed innocent.' The question remains, 'What can I do if I'm dealing with someone who turns out to be dishonest?'"

On way to hold people accountable for their dishonest tactics is to say, "What you're trying to do won't work." Naming a manipulator's game neutralizes it. As soon as Dot recognized the sales rep's unsavory tactics, she could have laughed out loud and said, "Oh, I see what you're doing. You brought me in here so I'd let my guard down, and you're starting up again now that I'm relaxed." The salesperson would have denied it, but Dot's recognition of the strategy would have defeated it.

Add this phrase to your repertoire and trot it out whenever someone tries to manipulate you. You've heard the phrase "Preparation is half the battle"? Preparing with this phrase can keep you out of battles. If, in the midst of a negotiation, someone tries to force a false deadline on you, simply say, "I know what you're trying to do and it won't work." Catching them in their act will neutralize their attack.

Be Vigilant
"Be vigilant. If you smell something, say something" – Jon Stewart

There is another way to reduce your vulnerability. Identify your emotional Achilles Heel. You see, bullies specifically target your perceived weakness. If you are embarrassed about a particular "fault," they will hammer away at it because they know you're sensitive about it.

One man said, "This really helped me understand why my mom would call me selfish whenever I didn't do what she wanted. I never wanted to be perceived as selfish, so whenever she flung that in my face, I'd end up going along with what she wanted."

I told him this was a double whammy. Not only do bullies ferret out and attack your weakness, they often project their weakness on you and accuse you of the very thing they're guilty of. It's the classic "pot calling the kettle black" scenario.

Instead of buying into her attempt to invalidate him, I suggested he remember how other people regard him. His wife, children, and friends all know him to be kind and caring. Instead of buying into her dishonorable tactic to tear him down, he should take her accusation on balance and realize it's truer of her than it is of him.

There's a saying, "Trust in God, but tie your camel." I think that's a pretty good policy. Choose to trust people until they give you a reason not to. But also pay attention to your instincts. If your gut is waving red flags, if this person is displaying the classic characteristics of a controller, then be wary. That personality type does not play by the same rules of integrity that you do. With then, cut the cards and stay vigilant.

And if someone you trust does blind-side you with a hurtful accusation, ask yourself, "Is she projecting her behavior on me? Is this designed to knock me down? Is she saying this because she knows I'm touchy about it? Is what she's saying in line with how other people feel about me?"

These questions can give you the clarity you need to determine whether their denunciation is more reflective of them than it is of you. And if this person has a pattern of making these types of "knock you down" accusations; it means they're not to be trusted because they do not have your best interests in mind; they have their interests in mind.

Action Plan and Discussion Questions

Are you a trusting person? Has that been a conscious choice? How so?

Have you have encountered evil or been blind-sided by a bully? How did it impact you? What do you think of the concept of being an "informed innocent"? Does it work for you? Why or why not?

How are you going to continue being a trusting individual who chooses to see the best in people, instead of becoming a cynic who sees the world as an dark place?

How are you going to stay vigilant so you're not vulnerable to people who break your trust or who don't deserve your trust?

Chapter 25
CHOOSE TO TAKE CARE OF YOUR HEALTH

"To keep the body in good health is a duty... otherwise we shall not be able to keep our mind strong and clear." -- Buddha ·

What are you doing with the hurt and humiliation caused by dealing with this difficult person? Are you writing in a journal and purging the pain onto pages? If so, good for you. "Writing out the storm" is a wonderfully tangible way to get the muck out of your mind.

How else are you exorcising the toxic waste that accumulates as a result of having haters in your life? Exorcise is defined as "to get rid of something troublesome, menacing, or oppressive; to free yourself from an evil spirit." Wow. This is exactly what we need to do with the bully in our life.

A friend discovered one of the best ways to exorcise her demons was to exercise. You've undoubtedly heard this before and may feel like skipping this part. Please take a few moments to read it because it will show how physically working out is a great way to psychologically work out our stress.

My friend moved from her beloved Hawaii to Atlanta to take care of her seventy-five-year-old mother who was suffering from Alzheimer's. She told me, "The day I arrived, I discovered the situation was even worse than I'd anticipated. My brothers had drained Mom's bank account and allowed her home to fall into a deplorable state of

191

disrepair. Worse yet, they obviously perceived me as a threat and tried to take me out of the picture by telling Mom the only reason I'd come home was to claim my inheritance. My mom, who was sliding in and out of reality, would sometimes look at me and ask, 'Did you really come home just to get my money?' I knew this appalling idea had been planted in her mind by my brothers, but it didn't make it any less painful."

My friend told me, "I didn't know what to do. I didn't have any relatives who could intervene, and I'm not sure how much my mom understood what was happening anyway. I was the one taking care of her day in and day out, but my brothers had convinced her that I was trying to put her in a rest home to 'get her out of the way.' The only thing that kept me sane was going for long runs."

My friend had actually completed the Ironman Triathlon, a grueling race on the Big Island of Hawaii that combines a 2.4- mile swim, 100+- mile bike ride, and a marathon-length run—all completed within twenty-four hours in the windy, start lava fields by Kona. She said, "The first couple of miles, I'd be 'in my head' replaying what was happening. Then I'd get back in my body, start noticing my surroundings, and my anger would rush out of me like water from a broken wading pool. I could actually feel my consciousness expanding back out into the world instead of banging around in my brain. By the end of a run, I would have realized that as horrible as this situation was, there were still things in my life to be grateful for."

Do Sweat It

You've probably heard the phrase "Don't sweat it." Forget that. Do sweat it. Sweat occurs when we exercise aerobically at a level that causes our heart to beat at 60 percent or more of its maximum, which: oxygenates the brain and body and deepens our breathing. Research shows that breathing deeply is one of the best ways to release stored tension. Furthermore, aerobic exercise gets us out of our head (which is either swirling with anger or swamped with despair) and into our gut (which is how we regain our center). Sweating helps us excrete toxic emotions and replenishes the energy that's been drained by our bouts with bullies.

The bully's MO (modus operandi) is to break our spirit (our life force) because he or she knows we won't offer any opposition if we're emotionally exhausted. Think about it. If you're dealing with a bully right now, what is your mental and physical state? Do you feel "down"? Do you feel like no matter what you do, you can't win? Do you understand this is how bullies keep you in their clutches? They wear you down so you won't be up to the task of taking them on. Bullies want you to feel beat before you even start, so you don't start.

That's why it's imperative to become physically active. As long as you remain lethargic and sedentary, it will be impossible to reverse the situation because challenging bullies requires energy you don't have.

A man approached me after a seminar and said, "I have to tell you the ten minutes we spent on 'Move It to Lose It' was worth the price of admission. When I married my wife, I was an athlete. That was my identity. I grew up in the mountains and was always outdoors doing something from the time I was seven years old. That all changed a couple of years into my marriage. At first I just thought my wife was jealous of the time I spent on sports because she wanted me to spend more time with her. She wasn't the outdoorsy type and always grumbled when I set off with my friends to rock climb or go for a trail run.

"Over time, she became more and more vocal about her disdain for athletes. We'd pass people running on the highway and she'd make some caustic remark about how 'vain and selfish' they were and how they must be single because married people with responsibilities didn't have time to indulge in such hedonistic activities.

"I started cutting back on my activities because I wanted my marriage to work and I thought that meant compromising. I bought into her accusations that I was being selfish and that I valued my friends more than I did her. It got to the point where I would go for weeks without doing anything outside. My friends kept telling me I was whipped, but I never saw it.

"I realize now that it wasn't just that she didn't share that part of my life. She was scared I'd meet someone else who loved sports, and I'd leave her. And she was jealous and threatened that I was happy and she wasn't. I don't know whether it was on a conscious or unconscious level, but she did everything in her power to destroy that side of me."

He shook his head ruefully, "After five years of this blah life, I didn't even recognize the guy looking back at me in the mirror. I got to the point where I didn't care if it was selfish; I just knew I couldn't live the rest of my life like this. In a kind of sick way, I realized my wife liked me fat and unhappy because it kept me home—kind of a male 'barefoot and pregnant' thing. If I ever get married again, it's going to be to someone who likes being active instead of to someone who tries to make me feel like a terrible person for doing something I love."

This man's story is important for several reasons. Bullies don't want us to move forward with our lives, they want to keep us where we are—with them. They do their best to prevent us from spending time in activities we love and with people we love for several reasons. Joy is defined as "the emotion evoked by well-being, success, good fortune" and the "prospect of possessing what one desires."

Bullies see activities and people that bring us joy as competition. They do their darndest to break our bonds to buddies and hobble our involvement in hobbies because they don't want us doing anything that:

- strengthens our sense of self and lessens their control over us
- gives us a sense of success, which makes them superfluous
- makes us happy and causes us to realize how unhappy we are with them
- threatens their grip on us because we have activities outside of them that bring us joy
- brings us into contact with people who notice our partner's jealousy and possessiveness and warn us how toxic it is

This is like a triple whammy. Bullies deprive us of our friends and family (our support network), of the hobbies we love (our identity and source of well-being), and of physical activity (the wellspring of vigor)—so we become inert and stay in the relationship. Their strategy is to de-spirit us so we simply don't have the strength necessary to break free.

Protect Your Energy – Direct Your Energy

"Build on failure. Use it as a stepping stone. Close the door on the past. Don't try to forget mistakes, just don't dwell on them. Don't let them have any of your energy, or time, or space." - singer Johnny Cash

Bullies try to drain or steal your energy, which is why it is imperative to start protecting and directing your energy to activities and individuals that support rather than sabotage you. It's time to:

- spend time with friends and loved ones
- re-involve yourself in hobbies that give you a sense of joy

- engage in aerobic activity a minimum of three times a week so you build the fitness that gives you the physical and psychological fortitude to resist a bully's efforts to bend you to his or her will.

You may be thinking, "I don't have the time or energy to exercise. I'm so busy or tired, it's all I can do to get through the day." That's understandable. Do you realize, though, that if you're waiting for the time and energy to exercise, they will never show up? Do you know of any people with spare time on their hands? Do you understand that lethargy is a result of no exercise, not a reason to avoid exercise?

Do you understand walking or working out is a form of *liberty*? It's a way to free yourself from the hold of a bully who is trying to rob you of your independence and lock you up spiritually, emotionally, and physically.

As long as you stay sedentary, you will stay trapped. You'll be trapped by your own unwillingness to do the one thing that will give you the wherewithal to change your situation. All the good intentions in the world mean nothing if you don't have the inner resources to carry out your determination. That's what energy is, the means to activate intentions. Energy is defined as "the capacity of acting or being alive."

The bully's goal is to enervate you. Enervate is defined as "lacking physical, mental, or moral vigor." Bullies win when they succeed in enervating you, lessening your strength, vitality and vigor, because it means they have broken your spirt so you don't challenge them.

One of the ways to win this battle (and please understand, that's what this is, a *battle*. You may not have wanted that but that's what's happening - a battle of wills) is to take responsibility for reversing the vigor mortis 5%ers cause with their belittling and bullying..

The question isn't whether you have the time or energy to exercise. The question is, Do you want a better life? Do you want to feel strong again? Do you want to take control of who you are? Do you want to have the will to prevail?

If you do, get a move on ... *today*. Movement cures morbidity. Moving your body supplies you with the energy and strength to counter a bully's attempts to sap your energy and strength.

Be sure to team up with a buddy for your daily walk, workout, or sport. It's the key to sustaining good intentions because it makes exercising more fun and helps you keep your commitment to show up. Finding an exercise partner is especially important when battling a bully because s/he is going to do everything in his or her power to sabotage your attempts to get fit.

Bullies see your efforts to become physically active as a direct threat to their supremacy. They often resort to scurrilous tactics to derail your determination to improve yourself. They may call you names, say it costs too much, or takes up too much time. They may accuse you of being frivolous, vain, narcissistic. They will say you "should" be taking care of the kids, the chores, the house or them. They may tempt you with alternatives (sleeping in, dates) to keep you at home.

Be clear that getting and staying healthy is your right and responsibility. Keep your touchstone with you to remind yourself that you're not going to allow anyone to undermine your resolve to be healthy. Picture the Rights/Needs Seesaw and see that you are simply taking care of yourself, and any attempt to keep you from being active is simple another attempt to keep you inert. Understand that confidence comes from being vital. You have the power to make that happen today if you start dedicating thirty minutes a day to being physically active.

Remember to steel yourself. What I mean by that is that bullies will try to put down your uprising. They don't want you to change the status quo, they like things just the way you are. That's why it crucial for you to be clear in your resolve **to** get fit, get active, get healthy.

As the saying from the movie *Ghostbusters* goes, "Who ya gonna call?" Are you going to call that neighbor who's told you before she wishes she had the discipline to get up early in the morning and walk? Are you going to call a friend who once expressed interest in a dance class? Are you going to call your local community center and sign up for that karate class? A healthier future is a phone call away. Make it happen now.

Action Plan and Discussion Questions

Are you physically active? If so, what do you do and how often? How does it make you feel about yourself?

Do you feel depressed or lethargic? Why do you think your energy is low?

Is there a person in your life who is sapping your strength? Who is this person and what is he or she doing?

What physical activity could you do to excrete toxins, replenish your energy, and rebuild strength? When, where, and how often are you going to do this?

What is a hobby or recreational activity you love to do that could bring joy back into your life? When, where, and how often are you going to do this?

Chapter 26
CHOOSE TO TURN HATE INTO HOPE

"Hate in your heart will consume you." – actor Will Smith

As mentioned before, hating helps nothing. It's like drinking poison and waiting for the other person to die. It's okay to be angry with a bully; it's not okay for that anger to metastasize into an all-consuming hatred.

Disparaging other people——no matter how much they deserve it— only reflects poorly on us. Even if listeners agree with what we're saying, at some level they're wondering, "I wonder what s/he says about me when I'm not around?!" Bad-mouthing bullies doesn't improve the situation or change their behavior, it only poisons our peace of mind and alters people's perception of us.

This chapter has suggestions on how to take what was done to you and turn it into something that serves a good purpose. Hating serves no good purpose. Sharing your lessons-learned with others so they can prevent this from happening to them does serve a good purpose. Advocating for people's right to live in peace and be treated with dignity and respect does serve a good purpose. Turning hate into the more productive emotion of hope does serve a good purpose.

Upon hearing this idea, a seminar attendee protested, "I thought you told us we're supposed to hold a bully accountable. Are we just supposed to ignore what a bully's done and pretend it didn't happen?"

I clarified: "I'm not suggesting we passively accept or ignore a bully's behavior, I'm suggesting it's counterproductive to dwell on what was done to us. It takes us down the rabbit hole of how unfair, undeserved or awful it was. It keeps their poison in our system. I'm talking about taking your resentment and turning it into resolve."

"This was one of the hardest aspects of this whole nightmare," confessed the financial adviser whose attorney husband had taken her children away from her and then added insult to injury by stashing them in boarding school in another country.

"When I visited them, everything in me wanted to set the record straight. I yearned to tell them I wasn't the one responsible for the whole mess—their father was. He was telling them terrible things about me, and I desperately wanted them to hear my side of the story. He told them I had driven us into bankruptcy, which was a total fabrication. I tried to explain to the kids that he was the one who ran up our credit card bills and drove us into debt. My ten-year-old son looked me in the eyes and said, 'Mom, Dad says one thing and you say another. I don't know who to believe anymore, so I don't believe either one of you.'

"Hearing that broke my heart. It was especially painful because I always tried to be honest and behave with integrity. To hear my own son tell me he didn't trust me anymore was devastating. I decided at that moment that what my kids needed more than the truth was one parent who was acting like a responsible adult. They didn't need to be put in the middle of what was going on between their father and me. They already had one parent who was saturating them with vindictiveness; they didn't need their other parent doing the same thing. A psychologist friend kept telling me, 'They'll figure it out on their own. You have to trust that refusing to stoop to your husband's level is the best thing you can do for them right now.'

"Her advice offered little consolation at the time. Hoping that my sons would eventually learn the truth and know who I was offered little comfort. What if it never happened? What if they had been so poisoned against me they never gave me a second chance? I can hardly express what it was like imagining this could happen. However, the alternative of trashing their dad and driving my sons deeper into this universal skepticism was not an option. Thankfully, my friend's prediction came true and my sons and I are closer than ever now."

One woman said, "I agree with this in theory, but it's hard to do—especially if someone has ruined my reputation, cost me my job, and made my life hell."

I'm not saying it's easy. I'm saying it's necessary if we're to move on and not let the bully "win." Get clear that the bully does win if you seethe with resentment and become hate-filled. Choosing not to become bitter is one of the few things you can control about what's happened to you. How do you pull this off? By surrounding yourself with friends, exorcising your demon(s) with exercise, and engaging in joyful activities that counterbalance the dark forces the bully brought into your life.

Bring Beauty Back Into Your Life
"You couldn't ignore me if you tried." — t-shirt

A workshop participant once told me he thought the above t-shirt slogan, "You couldn't ignore me if you tried" is a bully's motto.

Bullies deliberately stir up drama because they love being the center of attention. They don't want people to ignore them, they want people to not be able to stop thinking about them.

That's why it's crucial for you to mentally "ignore" the bully in your life by giving your mind better things to think about.

A way to not allow this person to drag you down to his or her level is to commit to being the quality of person you want to be—even though the other person isn't.

One way to do that is to bring beauty into your life.

"Everything is beautiful at the ballet" is line from the Tony Award-winning play *A Chorus Line*. It is sung by a character who escapes her hard life by going to the ballet. It's her way of sinking into the delight of dancing instead of sinking into despair.

She's right. We can counteract the impact of "the dark side" (think *Star Wars*) by deliberately focusing on what lifts us up instead of on what brings us down. Simply said, it's hard to be depressed when we're immersed in, and surrounded by, things that delight our mind and soul.

When I was in the midst of my own trial by fire, I was lucky enough to be renting a house that had a yard full of roses. Seeing my sons off to school and then watering and pruning those rosebushes became my morning ritual. How peaceful it was to spend those few minutes in the early morning air lovingly tending those healthy plants.

Every morning I'd clip a few just-right buds and display them around the house in colorful vases. I always placed a fresh rose by my computer where I could look at it during the day. If my mind started wandering to the latest injustice or outrageous incident, I would gaze at the rose and lose myself in its beauty. Those colorful gifts from nature nurtured my spirit and offered tangible reminders that while there may be beasts in the world, there is also beauty.

The Future Starts Today, Not Tomorrow

"Even though the future seems far away, it is actually beginning right now." – *youth activist Mattie Stepanek.*

One of the most important ways to counteract the debilitating aspects of being bullied is to start envisioning a better future, *today*. You may be thinking, "Easier said than done." True that, but you can start now by doing and envisioning little things that help you feel better.

Remember the bank officer who had been fired by his CEO for "boondoggling," even though he had been attending a business meeting? He told me, "I spent the first week, after being told to clear out my desk, pacing back and forth in our house thinking of all the ways I could retaliate against this guy. I was so wired I couldn't go to sleep at night. I'd lie there staring at the ceiling, hatching vengeful, get-even plots. The second week, my wife handed me a trowel and wisely told me to take my anger out on our garden.

"That's what I did. I went to Home Depot, bought just about everything in sight, and spent every morning that next week on my hands and knees weeding, terracing, planting, and watering. In retrospect, it was one of the most therapeutic things I could have done for myself. Working with my hands and working with living, growing things got me back down to earth, so to speak, and gave me perspective."

Smart man. It's true that getting back down to earth, whether it's working the land or walking the land, can immerse us in what's good about life on earth instead of what's bad. As the *Chorus Line* lyric implies, everything is marvelous in the mountains, everything is fantastic in the forest, everything is lovely at the lake.

Art Buchwald once quipped about a political leader, "I worship the quicksand he walks on." Forget that. Worship the ground *you* walk on.

Resolve to appreciate earth's pleasures instead of allowing a bully to take up residence in your heart and head.

Research shows that nurturing yourself in nature has psychological benefits. There's actually a word for this. It's called "shinrin-yoku" which is roughly translated into "forest bath." Check out its Wikipedia entry (you can't make this stuff up!) where it states that *"Every study reports a reduction in stress, anger, depression and sleeplessness"* when people walk in the woods. Are you thinking, "I live in the middle of a city. We don't have woods." Well, you have parks, right? New York City has Central Park. Washington DC has Rock Creek Park. San Francisco has Golden Gate Park. Los Angeles has Griffith Park.

If you can't stop thinking about what the bully has said or done to you, give your brain something better to think about. Head out to your local park, get moving, and turn that "black light" into "green light" energy.

You Can't Control Your Thoughts – You Can Direct Them

"The thing to do, it seems to me, is to prepare yourself so you can be a rainbow in somebody else's cloud." – Maya Angelou

Why not take Maya Angelou's advice one step further, and become a rainbow in your own cloud?

In my book *ConZentrate* -the result of fifteen years of research into how to focus when we want, on what we want - I shared my finding that it's impossible to *stop* focusing on something that's bothering us. The more we tell ourselves NOT to think about something, the more we think about the very think (!) we don't want to think about.

If you tell yourself, "I'm not going to get upset about how my boss humiliated me in front of my team," those words UPSET and HUMILIATE jump out. You'll end up getting upset because you're reliving how your boss humiliated you in front of your team.

The words "not," "stop" and "won't" are ghost words. Please understand, your mind can't focus on the *opposite* of an order. If you give yourself (or others) an order with a ghost word (e.g., "never," "not") in combination with a negative word, you will get a negative result.

If you tell yourself, "I am not going to cry," what does your mind hear? CRY. You might as well get out the tissues.

If you tell someone, "Stop yelling at me," what are they going to do? Keep yelling at you. If you say, "I won't let her make me feel guilty," you're well on your way to feeling guilty.

So, what to do instead? Direct your attention to what you *do* want instead of what you *don't* want.

In particular, if you're dealing with a bully, hater or troll, you need to switch your focus to what's *right* in your life instead of what's *wrong*.

I'm not saying it's easy. I am saying it's necessary.

Remember, the bully's goal is to dominate your thoughts. Bullies want you afraid of them. They want you worrying about them. Taking up your time and mind is their way to control you and continue to have power over you.

The way to lessen their control and power is to fill your mind with other things. From now on, you're going to focus on the loving people in your life instead of this loser.

Write Down What's Right in Your World

"It's rare to find a consistently creative person who is also an angry person. They can't occupy the same space. If your anger moves in, generosity and creativity often move out." – author Seth Godin

We talked in Chapter 22 about the importance of acting on anger instead of denying it. One of the best ways to act on anger is to write it out so you get it out of your system.

This weekend, go to a Barnes and Noble, Target, Walmart or Hallmark store and buy a notebook that makes you feel good when you look at it. Or, for all you Amazon Prime fans, buy one at your favorite online retailer. This is going to be your personal Blessings diary.

Draw a line down the center of the first 20 pages. Put "BULLY" on top of the left column and "BLESSINGS" on top of the right column.

Now, on page one, write on the left what the bully has done and/or said that's hurt or angered you. This make take a while and that's okay.

Put down all the terrible things this person has done or said. The goal is to get the hurts out of your head and heart where they're sapping your spirit, stealing your energy, monopolizing your thoughts. Be sure to number (e.g.., 1, 2, 3, 4) all the things this person has done to harm you.

Now, write down at least TWICE that many things in the BLESSINGS column on the right. Think about the kind people in your life who support you and want the best for you. Think about your health. Can you walk, see, hear, feel, smell? Think about what's right with your work, school, family, smarts, talents, abilities. Think about the flowers in your garden, the trees outside your window, the sun shining through the skylight. Put down everything you're grateful for.

Your goal, every day, is to reduce the number of items on the left and increase the number of things on the right. You are, literally and figuratively, *shrinking* the bully's impact on your life. You are visually reminding yourself there's more right with your world than wrong.

Yes, this takes time, but you're spending time thinking about this individual anyway, and it's not doing you any *good*. I promise you, keeping a bully-blessing ledger and consciously reducing the column on the left until there's nothing left to write, is time and energy well spent, because it's going to help you get the bully out of your head *for good*.

Another insight from my book *ConZentrate*, is, "*You may not be able to control what thoughts come into your head, you can control how long they stay there.* You *can* control whether you continue to think about individuals and incidents that bring you down - or whether you switch your thoughts to individuals and incidents that lift you up.

In a way, overcoming poisonous people and toxic encounters is about METRICS. It's hard to direct thoughts that are swirling around in your head. Getting them down on paper in juxtaposed columns makes it easier to *see* which are serving you and which are sabotaging you.

Another insight from *ConZentrate* is that "Our attention is where our eyes are." When we're thinking about the bully's latest offense, our eyes are often unfocused; we're "in our head."

When we get those thoughts into print (or onto the screen) – in easy-to-compare columns – we're better able to direct our thoughts to what contributes to our peace of mind (instead of to what compromises it).

As time goes by, your goal is to have fewer and fewer offenses on the left side of your ledger and more and more appreciations on the right.

That is how you diminish a bully. By enlarging and expanding what's right in your life so your blessings are bigger than the bully. By switching attention from your grievances to your "gratefuls."

Shift Your Focus From Bullies to Blessings

"The world is full of fear, negativity and judgment. I think people need to start shifting into joy and happiness. As corny as it sounds, we need to make a shift." – Ellen Degeneres

Choosing to focus on blessings may sound simplistic or "corny," as Ellen put it, but it works. For hundreds of years, our wisest philosophers have agreed that our thoughts determine our quality of life. For example:

"Life consists of what a man is thinking all day long." – Ralph Waldo Emerson

"To affect the quality of the day, that is the art of life." – Henry David Thoreau

"The mind is everything. What you think about, you become." - Buddha

"Drag your thoughts away from your troubles. It's the healthiest thing a body can do." – Mark Twain

In addition to keeping a ledger of blessings in a personal journal, you may also choose to post a calendar where you'll see it every day, maybe in your kitchen or by your computer?

Once again, pick a calendar that calls to you. It may have inspiring quotes or beautiful scenes of places you'd like to visit. Just select something that is meaningful to you. Each day, take 2 minutes to write down a few words of something that went well that day. It could be:

- a customer said a heartfelt thank you.
- your daughter brought home a painting she made in art class.
- you went for a swim and loved the way the water supported you.
- you finished a household project you'd been procrastinating on
- you had lunch with a long-time friend

I suggested this in my *Tongue Fu!* book, written almost 20 years ago. I have heard from many people who told me this simple action made a powerful, positive difference in their lives.

One man worked for a well-known university that was also a medical research center. He told me, "Everyone assumed I had the perfect job because of the prestigious place I worked. What they didn't know was my boss bullied me non-stop, forcing me to work long hours, ridiculing me every step of the way. He did it because he knew he could get away with it. If I left, there would be a hundred people waiting to take my job and there aren't many openings for someone with my work specialty.

Your book helped me choose my battles. I decided I was going to stick it out one more year while I saved money and explored other job options. But first, I had to figure out how to not get totally depressed by having to deal with this maniac every day. I got a calendar and promised myself that before I went to bed every night I had to write down something that went right that day. It gave me something TANGIBLE to look at and focus on instead of the nightmarish thoughts swirling in my head. It gave me daily reminders that I actually did have something to be grateful for and that someday I'd be a free man."

This may sound simplistic. It may be. It also works.

Become a Blessing to Someone Else

"I speak not for myself but for those without voice... those who have fought for their rights... their right to live in peace, their right to be treated with dignity, their right to equality of opportunity, their right to be educated." – Nobel Peace Prize winner Malala Yousafzai

Another way to counteract the toxicity a bully brings into your life, is to become an activist. That is what Nobel Peace Prize winner Malala Yousafzai chose to do...at seventeen years old.

You may be familiar with Malala's story. She wrote a blog saying Pakistani girls should be given the opportunity to attend school. In retaliation, a Taliban gunman boarded her school bus, asked for her by name, and shot her. Thankfully, she survived and has become a global advocate for girls having a right to an education. The UN initiated a petition in her name and *Time Magazine* featured her as one of their "Most 100 Most Influential people in the World."

TV host Jon Stewart interviewed her on *The Daily Show* and was enormously impressed with her eloquence and resolve. He said, "I know your father is backstage and he's very proud of you, but would he be mad if I adopted you?"

So, what's that have to do with you? Instead of spiraling into depression or retreating in fear after that horrific experience, Malala chose to mobilize others around this issue. Here's another story about someone who's chosen to turn a message into a mission and movement.

What Can You Do When You've Had Enough?

"I have had enough." – Golda Meir

Actress Amy Poehler has also resolved to be an advocate. She believes that when you've "had enough," you can continue to complain about what's wrong (thereby contributing to it and perpetuating it), or you can do something constructive about it.

In a June 14, 2015 *Parade* magazine interview, Amy told reporter Neil Pond that she and fellow TV producer Meredith Walker were concerned about the negative messages young girls were getting from the media. However, instead of bemoaning how wrong it is to have a culture of "total image bombardment about trying to be perfect," and how wrong it is for 13 year old models to be glamorized for their bodies, they decided to provide an antidote. They created an online TV series called "Smart Girls at the Party" and interviewed young girls about their aspirations and achievements ... instead of their appearance.

Their TV series has now become www.AmySmartGirls.com, a thriving website that interviews successful businesswomen, provides templates for DIY projects, and posts articles from teen contributors.

Amy says, "Life can feel so desperate and scary as an adolescent. Smart Girls is creating content I would have liked to have seen at that age. It's an attempt to be a joy-spreader, that's for sure."

You may be thinking, "I'd love to do something like this, but I'm no Amy Poehler. I don't have her resources."

You don't have to be a famous actress to become an activist at your school, workplace, community ... or in your own life. The goal is to counter-balance the negativity in your life by increasing the positivity. You can help turn the tide against bullies and counteract their negative impact by sponsoring or supporting individuals and organizations who are mobilizing campaigns for mutual respect.

One of the most pro-active things you can do to transcend the toxicity of a bully is to figure out how to prevent this from happening to others. Become a 'mama bear" on behalf of bully awareness and prevention.

Psychologists have long understood that one of the best ways to crawl out of a depression (no matter how well-deserved) is to help someone else. In fact, peace activist Pete Singer said, "I believe we have a responsibility to go beyond the 'thou shalt not's — that is, not harming others — and do what we can to help others."

Agreed. Want specific ways to be an advocate so that what was done to you isn't done to others? That's the subject of our next chapter.

Action Plan and Discussion Questions

Is there someone in your life you're tempted to hate? Who is that person? Why are you filled with resentment toward him or her?

Do you understand that hate serves no one? Can you resolve to become an "informed innocent" and choose to focus on what's right with the world instead of what's wrong? Please elaborate.

How will you immerse yourself in earthly pleasures to get perspective? Will you garden, walk in the woods, buy flowers and keep them nearby?

How will you become an "advocate for something" instead of a "hater against something"? Will you get a journal or calendar to write out your anger and switch your attention to your blessings vs. the bully?

Chapter 27
CHOOSE TO TAKE THE LEAD TO ADDRESS BULLYING IN YOUR ORGANIZATION

"Just one habitually offensive employee critically positioned in your organization can cost you dearly in lost employees, lost customers and lost productivity." Christine Porath and Christine Pearson, "The Price of Incivility" Harvard Business Review

Are you a business owner, manager, coach, teacher or team leader?

Would you like to know how to reduce bullying in your workplace, association, sports league, classroom, committee and community board?

If so, you're in the right place. Let me first share an example of someone who nipped a form of bullying in the bud, and then share specific steps you can take to set up proactive policies that make it crystal clear that incivility and bullying will not be tolerated in your company.

I've had the privilege of working with many outstanding leaders over the years. Long-time association executive Judy Gray, (now President of CEO on Call) is the best I've ever seen at earning respect from her employees, board *and* members. One of the reasons she's held in such high regard is she creates a culture where everyone is held accountable for high standards of personal and professional conduct. Here's an example of the "tough love" Judy demonstrated at the annual conference of an organization she had just been hired to lead. She told me:

"During the opening night dinner, the emcee brought the sponsors to the stage to thank them. No one paid any attention. In fact, most of the 400 attendees kept talking. The noise was so loud, it drowned out the proceedings on the stage.

I knew I couldn't 'let this go.' When it was my turn to take the podium the next day, I announced to the group, 'I'm new to your organization, so you may be surprised to hear I was embarrassed last night when no one could hear our sponsors being thanked. I was told this has been the norm for many years. Some members even said they felt this behavior would 'never change' even though sponsors had complained about it.

Many of you have sponsors for your own events. You know how you would want them treated, and how they deserve to be treated. May I respectfully request that tonight when our sponsors are introduced, you show them the respect they want and deserve? We'll ask the hotel to stop the music, bring the lights up, and bring the sponsors on stage for you to show your appreciation. Please stop your conversation for those few moments. Afterwards, you're welcome to go back to your meal and to having fun networking. Thank you.'

That night, the lights dimmed, the music stopped, everyone stopped talking, and the sponsors received full attention and appreciative applause."

"Was that a risk?" Judy asked me. "Was I worried members would feel 'scolded' and I would get off on the wrong foot my first week on the job? A little. But I was more concerned that no one had addressed this situation before and it was continue unless something was done about it. Many people came up later to thank me, and added that they were going to follow my example and make sure their sponsors were properly acknowledged in the future."

That's what often happens when someone has the courage to take the lead and hold people accountable for respectful behavior. Others choose to follow their example because it results in a "give and get respect culture of mutual respect" where everyone involved wins.

Incivility is a Slippery Slope to Bullying

"As citizens, we have to more thoughtful. I turn on the TV and see these grown people screaming at each other, and think, well, if we don't get our civility back, we're in trouble." — singer Emmylou Harris

Are you thinking, "Talking while sponsors are being introduced hardly qualifies as bullying."

You're right, incivility is NOT bullying; however it is a slippery slope to bullying.

How so? At the root of incivility is a lack of empathy. People are saying (or shouting) what they think, without first asking themselves how it would feel if this was directed at them. Incivility shows a disregard, a lack of concern, of the ramification of our actions.

As Emmylou Harris pointed out, all you have to do is turn on the TV to see people screaming and scheming, berating and belittling. It has become the norm.

The question is, do we really want this to be our norm? Do we really want a culture where screaming, scheming, berating and belittling is the norm?

We have to put a stop to it somehow, somewhere. If you are in charge of a group, it is up to you to "take the lead" and address this issue in a pro-active way so people in your group understand bullying, at any level, is NOT going to be their norm.

That's what Judy Gray did with those convention attendees. And they were all better for it.

Ralph Waldo Emerson said, "We are all looking for someone who will make us do what we can." I believe MOST people are looking for their managers, teachers, coaches and chairs to take the lead in creating courteous cultures and respectful teams.

Replacing rudeness with respect is not just a psychological issue, it is a bottom-line financial, productivity, performance, loyalty issue for your organization.

Christine Porath and Christine Pearson interviewed HR executives, CEOs, doctors, lawyers, judges, law enforcement officers, architects and engineers to track the causes and costs of incivility at work.

Their two most important findings? "Incivility is expensive, and few organizations recognize or take action to curtail it."

They reported that, "98% of the people we interviewed had experienced uncivil behavior at work. Nearly everyone who had, reacted in a negative way, in some cases *overtly retaliating* including:

- 47% intentionally decreased the time spent at work.
- 80% lost work time worrying about the incident.
- 63% lost work time avoiding the offender.
- 66% said that their performance declined.

- 78% said their commitment to the organization declined.
- 12% said they left their job because of the uncivil treatment.
- **25% admitted to taking their frustration out on customers.**

Ouch! It gets worse. Porath and Pearson reported that "Fortune 1000 firms spend 13% percent of their work time—the equivalent of seven weeks a year—mending employee relationships and otherwise dealing with the aftermath of incivility. Costs soar, of course, when consultants or attorneys must be brought in to help settle a situation."

Think about this. If companies are spending 13% of their time dealing with the aftermath of *incivility*, imagine the exponentially worse bottom-line costs and consequences caused by *bullying*.

6 Steps to Creating a Culture of Respect

"The greatness of a man is not in how much wealth he acquires, but in his integrity and his ability to affect those around him positively." – singer Bob Marley

One of the primary goals of this book is for you to choose to be pro-active rather than re-active when it comes to bullying. We don't want to wait until bullying becomes a problem in our organization. We want to prevent it from becoming a problem – or we want to mitigate the damage if it's already a problem.

That's why it's in everyone's best interests – including yours - to take the initiative to create a culture of respect where you work, live and play.

What is a culture of respect? You and your group members are welcome to create your own definition, however I like how Bob Marley defined it. It is a group of individuals "who all seek to affect those around them positively." Simple, yet effective.

One of the best ways to counter-act bullying is to create a culture where respect is the *norm* and bullying is the un-tolerated *exception*.

Here are six ways to create a culture where everyone commits to affecting those around them positively rather than negatively. Print these guidelines out. Discuss them in hiring interviews, in orientations and training workshops, in staff meetings and performance evaluations. Create an open, ongoing discussion where everyone chooses to adheres to these behavioral norms so everyone benefits.

1. Set an example other wants to follow.

"In influencing others, example is not the main thing, it's the only thing." – *Albert Schweitzer*

Ask yourself, "What precedent am I setting? Am I treating people with respect? Am I listening to other points of view or "running the show"? Am I finding solutions or finding fault? Am I keeping commitments or breaking them and giving excuses?"

Porath and Pearson found that 25% of managers who admitted to bad behavior said they were "just doing to others what had been done to them." Their logic was, "Why should I be kind or courteous to others when my boss is a jerk to me?"

The first step to creating a culture of respect is to be a walking-talking example of it. That includes finding out your co-workers', employees' or team members' names and greeting them when you see them. One of the most repeated findings in surveys that report a disproportionate percentage of disengagement in a company is, "No one even knows my name. I feel like I'm invisible."

2. Find out what's going on "behind the scenes."

"I believe it is better to tell the truth than a lie. I believe it is better to know than to be ignorant." – *H. L. Mencken*

Many people who are being bullied are too scared to speak up. They're afraid they'll lose their job, be viewed as a problem, or be punished for "tattling." Many fear that if the bully finds out, s/he'll exact revenge, especially if the bully is their supervisor.

The problem is, if you have bullying issues on your team, and don't know about them; you can't fix them. As Mencken points out, it's better to know than to be ignorant.

Judy Gray suggests you meet privately with team members who are in a position to tell you the truth about what's really going on. Ask them for the "W's." The more precise they are in reporting exactly what happened, the more likely it is authorities can take action because they have documented proof instead of sweeping generations like "She's mean to me." What are the W's? What? Where? When? Who?

What exactly was said and done?

When and **Where did this happen?**

Who said or did this? Who witnessed it?

What happened as a result of the inappropriate behavior? Did members drop off a committee because they didn't want to deal with this person's dictator-like leadership style? Did customers cancel their account because they were treated so rudely? Did two employees quit because they were fed up with being belittled and berated?

3. Develop and enforce a company-wide "rule-book" that defines bullying behavior and outlines consequences.

"You grow up with these people, so you want to give them a second chance. But a third chance? A fourth chance? A fifth chance? You think, come on; they'll get better. You coach them and they don't." – former IBM CEO – Samuel J. Palmisano

This "You coach them but they don't get better" quote was Palmisano's response when *Washington Post* reporter Lillian Cunningham asked, "What mistake guided a leadership lesson that's stuck with you?"

As he pointed out, the well-intended urge to give people second, third and fourth chances is why it's so important to create a rule-book that clearly defines expected behavior and exactly what will happen if those expectations are ignored or violated.

Without written expectations, it's too easy to let your good nature overlook egregious behavior Continuing to give people "benefit-of-the-doubt" chances sends the wrong message because it means rule-breakers keep getting away with unacceptable behavior.

While writing this book, I asked hundreds of people in different industries – tech, healthcare, retail, education, financial services - if their organization has policies regarding bullying. Most people laughed. Which is a bummer, because people can't be expected to follow rules if there are none.

Let's put this in perspective. Imagine getting in your car to drive somewhere, only to discover there are no lines on the highways. No lights or stop signs. No speed limits or pedestrian cross-walks.

It wouldn't be safe, would it? People would get hurt because no one would know what to do or not to do.

The reason cyclists, pedestrians and drivers can co-exist (for the most part) on the road is because there are rules and everyone follows them.

The irony is, many personal and professional relationships have no rules. At home, a spouse can get upset over something that happened years ago, that you've already apologized for. Your boss can hurl abuse, and you're supposed to sit and take it. A committee chair can not let anyone else talk , yet no one feels comfortable telling her to put a sock in it.

This is why it's so important to create a manual that outlines the rules of behavior. My son Andrew founded Dreams for Kids-DC, a non-profit that gets kids with disabilities off the sidelines and into the games of life. They've helped thousands of kids get out of wheelchairs and up on water skis, onto a soccer field, hockey rink and basketball court.

One of the first things Andrew did was to create a manual that included policies about everything from gossip to the importance of being on time, every time. New hires, interns and volunteers are required to read the manual before their first day on the job and are quizzed on it during their orientation. Here's what the manual said about gossip:

1. Gossip and Bad-Mouthing

- We don't talk negatively about other people in the office, period.
- The only time it is acceptable to talk negatively about other people in the organization is if you are voicing concerns to the appropriate senior staffer. If you have concerns, be prepared to back them up with evidence, not just subjective opinion.
- Talking behind peoples' back has a destructive impact on morale, and diminishes everyone's trust in one another. As the saying goes, "Anyone who gossips *to* you will gossip *about* you." If you "talk stink" to someone, how can that person ever trust you wouldn't do the same about them?
- Disparaging others is not in integrity and will not be tolerated.

Andrew has moved on from DFK-DC to found several other organizations including Ability List (think Craigslist for those with disabilities) and Tribute ("the world's most meaningful gift").

https://www.tribute.co/about-us/   A new staffer told him, "I was so impressed when you told me in my initial interview that this was a "gossip-free" workplace. It's one of the reasons I chose to work here instead of taking another job."

4.   Offer training in respectful communication skills.

"Communication is a skill you can learn.   It's like riding a bicycle.   If you're willing to work at it, you can rapidly change the quality of ever part of your life." – Brian Tracy

Porath and Pearson said they were amazed that one quarter of the "offenders" they surveyed said *they didn't recognize their behavior as uncivil.*

That's not surprising when you realize we learn math, science and history in school, but very few schools have courses in how to be civil.

The good news? It's not too late. Learning respectful communication is a *learnable skill* that can be acquired at any age.

It is worth investing in training. Everyone in your organization benefits when you do. Customers appreciate being treated courteously and reward you with their repeat business. Employees experience higher satisfaction and less stress because they know how to prevent conflict and create cooperation. Business owners are rewarded with reduced turnover and absenteeism, and increased customer/employee loyalty. Children can learn better and look forward to school when they're freed from the anxiety that accompanies being bullied.

The training can be done via internal workshops, online study courses, presentations by guest experts, video and podcasts, and/or with everyone discussing a book on this topic at your staff meetings.

An owner of a small law firm told me she had bought copies of *Tongue Fu!* for her staff. She told me, "Over the last few months, we worked our way through the book at our Monday morning staff meeting. Each week a different employee led a 15 minute discussion of 'her' chapter. I gave them autonomy to conduct the discussion any way they wanted. We all got a lot out of hearing how others had used the ideas with clients or family members. It was a real bonding experience."

5. Agree to group norms at the beginning of projects and programs.

"The quality of a leader is reflected in the standards they set for themselves." Ray Kroc, founder of McDonalds

Setting standards at the outset is one of the many reasons I respect the Day 1 Campaign. They understand the power of getting it right from the beginning. They understand we can't expect people to adhere to guidelines that don't exist.

Check out their website – www.Day1Campaign.com - to find out their recommendations for success including:

- A person in authority needs to be involved
- The person in charge clearly states what behavior is expected and what behavior is not tolerated
- The announcement needs to take place early in the tenure of new students, employees, athletes or project members
- Participants must verbally confirm they understand and agree to the policy

My dad used to tell me "Whether or not people support a decision depends on whether it's being done *to* them or *by* them."

To increase ownership of your behavior guidelines, involve participants in creating them so they're motivated to comply because the standards were set *by* them instead of being delivered *to* them.

Encourage concrete suggestions. The more tangible or measurable the rule, the better. It's hard to enforce vague rules such as "Don't be rude." What does that mean? Does it mean no email or texting during meetings? Does it mean passing a talking stick during meetings to prevent people from interrupting each other?

Porath and Pearson shared in their HRB article that they have resorted to using soccer's "yellow cards" and "red cards" to alert meeting participants they're out of line. They say, "In academia, professors can get overly impassioned in an effort to prove their intellect, point or superiority. A yellow card is a warning. It means, 'Rethink your phrasing, tone and intensity.' A red card is pulled out when someone is a repeat offender. It means 'Zip it. You're out of here.'"

6. Reward wanted (vs. unwanted) behavior

"Start with good people, lay out the rules, communicate with your employees, motivate them and reward them. If you do all those things effectively, you can't miss." – Lee Iacocca, former CEO of Ford

It sounds so simple, doesn't it? Anyone reading Iacocca's quote would think, "Of course that's the way to be an effective leader."

Well, just because something is common sense doesn't mean it's common practice.

A high school student who was a "good kid" once told me his "black sheep" brother got all the attention. "It's so unfair," he told me. "I get good grades. I play sports. I'm on the student council. He's into drugs, skipping school and stealing stuff. My parents spend all their time (and money) getting him into counseling, hiring lawyers and trying to keep him out of jail. I get ignored and taken for granted. They never come to my games or school events. What do I have to do to get noticed? Break the law?"

My heart went out to this young man. He had a point. "Offenders" can take up a disproportionate amount of a leader (or parent's) time. People in charge can become consumed with trying to turn "offenders" around and/or trying to mitigate the damage they cause. It's easy to overlook, and take for granted, the individuals who are not causing trouble. After a while, people who are "doing things right" feel they're getting penalized for their good behavior.

That's why it's equally important to have policies that reward "good behavior" in addition to policies that deal with "bad behavior."

I had the privilege of working with Jill Nelson, founder of "Ruby Receptionists" which has been one of *Fortune Magazine's* "Best Small Companies to Work For" three times. One of the many reasons Jill and her team have earned this award (and have had double-digit growth every year since they opened) is because they reward positivity and catch their employees doing something right.

As Jill says, "Our core values are not something you hear about on your first day and then get filed away in a drawer. We use them to make all of our decisions, big and small. Every team member knows them by heart, and is given a petty cash fund to use as they please to wow their clients. That trust is returned ten-fold by enthusiastic employees who love their work and show it to everyone they deal with."

How about your organization? Does it have a mission statement that outlines its core values and characteristics of expected behavior? Are those values posted where everyone keeps them "in sight, in mind" or are they filed away in some desk drawer where they're "out of sight, out of mind?" Are employees given autonomy and trusted to act in alignment with those values? Are they rewarded when they do?

7. Have the hard conversation. Penalize bad behavior.

"Michael, if you can't pass, you can't play." – Coach Dean Smith to Michael Jordan in his freshman year at UNC

I love that quote. It shows that Coach Smith was ready to bench his best player if he didn't agree to follow the rules of being a team player.

Ultimately, it is the leader's job to make sure that *one* person's refusal to obey the rules isn't undermining the entire group's performance.

If you're the leader, the ball is in your court. Team members look to YOU to hold a bully accountable. If you don't, there's a ripple effect where they start wondering why they should continue to care when someone is repeatedly breaking the rules and nothing's done about it.

Unfortunately, some leaders are conflict-averse. They may be secretly afraid of the bully. The bully may be their star player, rain-maker, renowned surgeon, top sales person. They're don't want to risk losing this individual who is in some way contributing to the success of the organization. The bully may be so intimidating, visible, aggressive or powerful, the leader dreads confronting them.

I had an opportunity to speak on this topic at the 2015 ASAE (American Society of Association Executives) annual meeting in Detroit. On the shuttle bus from the airport to the convention hotel, I got into a conversation with several people in nearby seats. They were intrigued when they discovered the topic of my workshop, so I gave them the "Are You Dealing with a Bully?" quiz right here on the bus.

Every single one of these association execs was dealing with a bully situation – whether it was a board member, committee chair or employee. One told me, "Our CTO is a tyrant, but he has the keys to the kingdom. He set up our computer system and he's the only one who knows how it works. If we fired him, he's so vindictive we're afraid he would probably purposely crash the system."

That's a typical "lose-lose" scenario that bullies cause where you're darned if you do (remove them) and darned if you don't (remove them). That's why Judy feels "managerial courage" is one of the most important qualities you can have. As she says, "managerial courage" means doing what is right for your team even when you know it will be crushingly hard to deal with the repercussions. It means honoring the greater good of the group and caring more about being respected than liked."

When I asked Judy Gray how you create the courage to hold "offenders" accountable, she said, "We all need to ask ourselves, 'What kind of leader am I known for being? Am I satisfied with that? What kind of legacy am I leaving? Who am I honoring here?" We're all on a journey of becoming the kind of leader we want to be known as. Unfortunately, we don't just ARRIVE and then get to relax. Leading effectively is an ongoing process. None of us becomes wise or effective by chance. It requires making tough decisions in tough times, decisions that feel right, that honor the greater good and that we can live with instead of regret."

An Example of a Termination Meeting

"It's not the people I fired that caused the problems. It's the people I should have fired and didn't." – author Harvey Mackay

I asked Judy to share a sample dialogue of how a termination might go when it's clear that repeated warnings have been ignored and an employee is continuing to behave badly. As you can imagine, there's a caveat with this. These are guidelines, not a formula guaranteed to work in every case. Please take this in context and use your executive judgment about how best to handle the specific situation you're dealing with.

1. Be sure to mentally prepare. Remind yourself, "This is a professional conversation. I am not this person's parent. *I will not be drawn into the drama.* I am acting on behalf of what is best for our organization and will handle this straightforwardly and objectively."

2. Consult with an attorney who has a specialty in HR or employment law to clarify what to say – and what not to say. Present the documentation you have collected to prove you have evidence that this is based on cumulative facts and actions, not opinion. Ask the

attorney whether the person should be given an option to resign vs. being fired (and how this affects unemployment benefits/payments).

3. Arrange for a witness – NOT a co-worker – to be present. This could be an attorney, union rep, board member or organization officer.

4. *Write out what you plan to say in advance.* Have it reviewed by an attorney. Give a printed copy of this to the witness and the person being removed. Announce, "I'm going to read from this" and then do so. That may seem draconian but it ensures you won't stray from your script and react to an inflammatory accusation that lands you in legal hot water.

5. Ask the person to meet you in your office toward the end of the day, e.g., 4:30 pm. If you work in a small office you might want to ask other employees to leave early to ensure privacy.

6. Say the person's name, (for example, "Jane,) and then say, "We've tried to work with you regarding the inappropriate behavior we discussed in this office twice in the past three months."

7. "We have not seen the improvement we requested and you agreed to. Your behavior is unacceptable and not a match for your job description and our standards. So, today will be your last day."

8. At this point, explain logistics concerning their access to COBRA or other benefits regarding retirement/insurance benefits or 401K's they may have been involved in.

9. Start wrapping things up with, "In closing, I do appreciate the things you have done for our office that helped us, and regret that your actions have made it impossible for this to work out in the long term. Do you have any questions for me?"

10. If they attack, "This is all your fault," "I'm going to sue you," or break down into tears, "How am I going to support my family?" simply say, "I understand you're upset and that will not change this decision. This whole process has been documented. This is final. The board is fully aware of and supportive of the actions we're taking today."

11. Bring the conversation to a close with, "We need your keys and passwords. Our security officer will be glad to help you pack up your things - or we can pack your personal belongings and have them delivered to your home. Which do you prefer?"

12. It is crucial that you – and/or a security guard – escort this person to his/her desk, cubicle or office. Do not allow this person access to their computer, to company files, or to any equipment that contains confidential records or data.

13. Call a staff meeting the next day and let employees know, "Jane is not employed here anymore, and you are not to discuss details of this with anyone. Is this understood?" Explain who will be handling Jane's job and the plan to replace her so there is a smooth transition.

Judy told me this step-by-step process helped her handle a potentially volatile situation. "One time I had to fire an abusive manager who handled one of our key accounts. Complicating matters was that he had insider knowledge of our association, and was in a position to really hurt us if he took it to a competitor. I consulted an attorney, and was so glad I did because we prevented what could have turned into a fiasco."

As you can see, the steps to removing someone who has a history of bullying behavior can be complex, so I've recommended several resources from *Forbes, Entrepreneur, HBR,* INC.com and Monster.com in the directory at the end of this book. Please reference these if you need to remove someone from your organization.

Judy added an important insight. "If a valuable employee suddenly leaves your organization, request an exit interview to ask 'Why?' Assure this person there will be no penalties for telling the truth. Many companies in male-dominated industries have experienced an expensive "brain drain" from women who up and quit because they've been bullied. They often don't report what's happened, they just take it and take it and take it, until they've had it. Then it's "Enough!" and they give notice. These individuals often say they didn't speak up because they felt no one would listen and nothing would change."

Judy's observation mirrors a U.S. Department of Labor Statistics study that found that "46% of employees who quit their job said it was because they didn't feel listened to."

That's why it's crucial to ask departing employees what contributed to their exit. If they were driven to take this drastic action because a co-worker was making their life miserable, that employee's behavior needs to be addressed before it causes more damage.

Buckminster Fuller said, "You can never change things by fighting the existing reality. To change something, build a new model that makes the old model obsolete."

That's the purpose of this chapter. If you want to prevent incivility (which slides into bullying) in your organization, follow Bucky's advice and build a new model that makes the old norms obsolete. How are you going to use these six steps to do that?

Action Plan and Discussion Questions

Are you in charge of a group? How so? Are you a manager, business owner, coach, committee chair? Describe the organization of team you're responsible for?

Do you already have polices, standards, rules, in place regarding the types of behavior that are allowed, encouraged? What are they?

If your group doesn't have a mission, policy or manual in place, how are you going to involve team members in developing one?

What are some of the specific, concrete guidelines you're going to feature that outline the group norms? How, when and where will you announce those?

Do you have an "offender" who is not honoring your rules? How are you going to have the hard conversation and hold this person accountable so you honor your group instead of this one individual?

Chapter 28
CHOOSING TO LEAVE CAN TAKE MORE COURAGE THAN STAYING... AND CAN BE THE BEST THING YOU EVER DID

*"I stayed, because I thought things would get better, or at least not worse." --
lead character in Anna Quindlen's book Black and Blue*

You may be saying, "Okay, I've read all this and I agree these techniques would work with most people; but what if this is a lost cause? I don't know if *anything* I do will make this situation better. "

Fair enough. This chapter will show how people in similarly daunting situations have taken action to improve their lives, and how you can, too.

As one woman suggested, she wished she had screwed up her courage and held the bully accountable instead of feeling she screwed up because she hadn't.

Don't Give In When Subjected to Public Pressure
'What is this word 'No' you speak of?' — toddler t-shirt

A woman had gone on a skiing vacation with her family. A blizzard had wiped out all but the last afternoon of skiing, so they hurried up to the slopes to try to get in a few runs while the weather allowed. While renting their equipment, their youngest daughter confided she was scared because it had been several years since she had skied and she didn't remember how to stop. The woman reassured her daughter that a couple of trips down the bunny hill would bring her confidence back and she seemed satisfied.

Unfortunately, by the time they waited in long lines to rent equipment, they had less than two hours on the slopes. She explained to her husband that their ten-year-old wanted to get her ski legs back on the bunny hill first. Her husband replied angrily, "We don't have time for that. She can go up to the top with me and I'll teach her how on the way down."

Her daughter looked at the mother with wide, frightened eyes. The wife tried to reason with her husband: "This is her first time on skis in quite a while, and she needs a chance to practice her stops and turns." Her husband turned on her and raised his voice in a threatening manner. "Don't you trust me? Don't you think I know what I'm doing?"

The woman tried to reason with him one more time, "It will take only fifteen minutes and she'll feel better about going up."

Her husband was livid at this point. He was not accustomed to being told, 'No." He leaned into her, his face red and angry, and said loudly, "I've been skiing for thirty years! Do you think I'd put my daughters in danger? You're overprotecting them again!"

At this point, both daughters were looking at her with a mixture of fear, embarrassment, and dread. People in the area were starting to stare. She didn't want to yell back so she backed down to avoid a scene. She patted her frightened daughter on her arm, told her it would be okay, and sent her off. . . with her daughter's look of hopeless betrayal carved in her heart.

Two hours later, the last skiers had come down and her husband and daughters had still not shown up. She searched the lodge and the ski racks. She walked back to the car and checked the lodge again, thinking she had somehow missed them. They were nowhere to be found. It started to get dark, and the ski patrol mounted up and headed up the hill. In desperation, she went to the first aid office and her worst fears were confirmed. There had been an "incident" on the mountain and her daughter was being brought down the hill on a ski sled.

Thankfully, her daughter was not seriously injured. In fact, she had had a mysterious "fall" shortly after getting off the lift, had developed hypothermia, and was unable to continue. The ski patrol brought her down mostly for safety reasons.

This woman never did confront her husband over the issue because it was "in the past, and getting upset with him after the fact wouldn't have changed what happened. Her daughter was already traumatized and she "didn't want to make things worse." She did get upset with herself, though. Her failure to stand up to her husband and for her daughter could have resulted in a tragedy. It was not her daughter's responsibility to stand up to a grown man— it was hers. She had been so afraid of making a scene that she had given in instead of protecting her daughter from his bullying.

She said, "In retrospect, I realize how afraid of his anger I was. I tried to 'keep the peace' at any cost. And what a cost. Anytime he was told 'No' and didn't get his way, he would get loud and ugly. No matter how miserably he behaved, I always tried to smooth things over to prevent things from escalating. And my daughter almost paid the price for my unwillingness to stand up to him. That was my wake-up call."

Remember the old adage "Children are to be seen and not heard?" That's what bullies want their partners to do. They want you to quietly go along with their agenda, and kowtow to their authority. If you ever question their judgment, they often intentionally ramp up their behavior in an effort to embarrass you so you'll back down in order to prevent a scene.

Forget that. *Make a scene!* Say, "You're darn right I don't trust you. Not when your ten-year-old daughter is telling you she's scared and you're not listening. She is going to practice on the bunny hill first so she can get her confidence back, and you are going to back off!"

If he gets louder in an attempt to cause you to cave and attacks with, "I know ten times more about skiing than you'll ever know," interrupt and get louder and in his face and say, "Then you know that no one should go down a slope they're not ready for." Then disengage and take charge of the situation by doing what you're going to do. Go with your daughter to the rope tow or the chair lift and don't look at the bully.

The key to causing a scene so you will be heard is to say what you're going to say and then exit. If you stay in a bully's vicinity, he will feel honor-bound to reassert his authority by continuing to bluster. Once you've said your piece, leave. He can mutter and harrumph all he wants —but you're not around to hear it.

I can't emphasize this strongly enough. *Be willing to cause a scene.* If you don't, the manipulator in your life will know how to get the best of you. He or she will wait until you're around people and then purposely bait you because he or she knows you don't have the stomach to verbally duke it out when others are watching.

Ask yourself, "Am I going to let this individual continue to manipulate me? Am I going to be more concerned about what people think or with making sure my rights and the rights of my loved ones are respected? Am I going to allow this person to put me and the people I care about at risk because I'm afraid what bystanders might think?"

Remember, you're not the one causing the scene. The bully is the one causing the scene—and you're just responding in a way to prevent him or her from doing it again.

A man said, "I can really relate to this. I was aware that my wife had grown increasingly resentful of the bond between my young daughters and me, but I had no idea how bad it was until we went on vacation to Disney World. Our first day, we were waiting in the hotel lobby for the shuttle bus and I had to use the rest room. When I came out, I heard my daughters and my wife singing a little ditty. I wasn't able to hear it so, curious, I asked my daughter to sing it for me. She sang, 'Daddy's going away and he's never coming back, Daddy's going away and he's never coming back.'

"Aghast, I looked at her and asked, 'Where did you learn that?' Looking warily at her mother, she said, 'Mom taught it to us. We sing it every time you go to the bathroom.'

"Stricken, I turned to my wife, who quickly tried to do some damage control. 'It's just a joke. Don't make such a big deal about it.'

'A joke?' I said. 'I don't think that's very funny.'

"My wife went on the offensive at this point and tried to make me the bad guy, 'Come on, you're upsetting the girls. It was nothing.'

I pressed, 'I can't believe you would teach them something like that.'

Pretending to be the voice of reason, she said, 'Come on, it's our vacation. Don't ruin it by overreacting. We're trying to have a good time.'

"My girls were visibly distraught, looking back and forth at us and obviously fearing their big day was going to turn into a disaster. At the time I decided they shouldn't have to pay for their mother's gamesmanship, so I swallowed my my indignation, and we set off for our 'fun' visit to Disney World.

"In retrospect, I wish I had said, 'Girls, we are going to go to Disney World today, but first we're going back to our room so your mom and I can have a talk.' I wish I had read my wife the riot act and told her in no uncertain terms that what she did was terrible, that she was endangering our daughters' sense of security by using them as pawns, and that she better never do something like that again.

"That's what I *wish* I had done. In reality, I did nothing because I was trying to shield my girls from their mother's machinations. I realize now that backing down in that situation led her to launch even more underhanded ploys to destroy my bond with my daughters."

Bullies specialize in this type of diabolical, double-bind maneuvering. They corner you by staging something like this and then making it seem you're the unreasonable one if you react.

The movie *What's Love Got to Do with It?* tells the story of Ike and Tina Turner, with the lead roles being played by Lawrence Fishburne and Angela Bassett. It is the best depiction of the abuse cycle I've seen.

Outsiders often offer simplistic, stereotypical solutions to anyone in an abusive situation. They say, "Why don't you just leave?" They conclude this person must have low self-esteem or it's not *that* bad.

Well, it's more complex than that. This movie (now on Netflix) reveals the insidiousness of this type of "holy acrimony." It shows:

- A controller's initial charming courtship of a woman he "must have"
- His growing resentment of the woman who is outshining him and no longer treating him as the alpha male
- His smoldering rage, which erupts with him hitting her in an effort to "beat the sass" out of this woman, who is, in his mind, emasculating him and "showing him up"
- how hard the female tries to please him in an effort to recapture the love they once had—or at least to salvage the marriage
- how hard the female tries to appease him to keep his volatile temper at bay
- knock-down-drag-out fights, after which life "goes back to normal" and everyone acts as if nothing has happened— because both of them wish it hadn't
- the female making public and private excuses for why this man who purports to love her is hitting her: "He's under a lot of pressure." "No one understands him." "It's those drugs."
- a failed escape by the woman, who is punished when she's caught, which makes her feel even more trapped and helpless

- friends and family growing increasingly concerned and frustrated with their futile attempts to convince their loved one to leave
- the reluctance of the woman to "walk out" and abandon the marriage/partner she wants to succeed and has years invested in
- the mitigating factors (e.g., booked commitments, record contracts) that make splitting a daunting, logistical nightmare
- how the woman finally reaches her breaking point and starts fighting back. She pays a price, but at this point, she doesn't care
- how the female starts regaining personal strength through her faith in herself and a better future
- the woman reconnecting with friends, which gives her perspective about how awful her life is, which gives her the courage to get away for good
- the man's efforts to win her back—and how quickly his sweet-talk cajoling turns into angry abuse when she rebuffs him
- a penultimate scene in which the man bluffs his way into her dressing room the night she is to star at the Ritz. He takes out a gun and threatens her. Meeting his eyes, she shows no fear and tells him to go ahead and do what he's going to do
- the man's befuddlement when he realizes he can no longer wield his influence with her. He's the one with the gun, but he's powerless because she's no longer afraid of him
- the woman going on to lead a successful life as her own person

Get Away for Good
"Nothing ever goes away until it has taught us what we need to know."
– author Pema Chodron

This particular film happened to be about a male abuser and a female victim; however, gender is not the issue. The issue was the insightful depiction of the roller-coaster cycle of abuse that only stopped when the woman summoned up the strength to get out of the situation.

SAM HORN

Please read Pema Chodron's incisive observation. The bullying situation will *not* go away until we learn what it's supposed to teach us.

In my personal and professional experience; what the situation is supposed to teach us is, **"WE are in control of our quality of life. If we repeatedly try to forge a healthy relationship with someone, and, for whatever reason, that is not happening; then it is our responsibility to remove ourselves from that toxic situation."**

This book has offered a variety of ways to revere the risk-reward ration so bullies either choose to leave us alone or choose to treat us with respect – because they know they'll be held accountable if they don't.

If that is not going to happen, then stop beating your head against this wall. Read the writing on the wall and get out – or get the bully out.

I'm not saying this is easy. I am saying it's necessary. Over the years, I have heard thousands (really) of stories of people who told me they wished they had done something sooner about the bully in their life.

They kept hoping things would get better. They kept tip-toeing around the bully. They kept waiting for someone else to rescue them or to hold the bully accountable. They kept hoping the bully would respond to their win-win attempts, "come to his/her senses" and change.

Months, years, *decades* went by with the bully continuing to have a disproportionately damaging effect on everyone around him/her.

No more!

If you are ready to reclaim your quality of life, consider the following suggestions. Hopefully, they'll help you get away *for good*.

PLAN YOUR ESCAPE. You wouldn't leave for a vacation without planning. Don't leave your relationship without planning. Can you save or set aside money so you'll be financially secure? Can you set up living arrangements in advance so you and your children (if you have any) will be safe? Is it feasible to kick him or her out instead of being forced to vacate your home? If you have to act on the spur of the moment, that may be better than nothing. However, it's in your best interests to think things through so your actions are wise, not rash.

DON'T BE LURED BACK. This individual will probably do everything in his/her power to woo you back. Don't be tricked by this temporary kindness. Abusers can be master manipulators who can act however they need to in order to retrap you. They may even be sincerely apologetic, but that doesn't necessarily mean things are going to change. Being sorry isn't enough. What tangible steps is he or she taking to address issues?

COUNT ON TOUGH TIMES. No one said this was going to be easy. Asking for favors is anathema for many of us. We hate to "put people out." Now is the time to lean on others and graciously accept offers of assistance. "Yes, I'll come live with you. Yes, I will take you up on your offer of a loan." As my sister learned during a bout with breast cancer, if we don't let our friends help us in our time of need, they feel helpless. Let loved ones do for you—they want to help.

REMIND YOURSELF OF THE BAD TIMES, SO YOU DON'T WAFFLE. The mind doesn't remember pain. A woman I know swears this forgetfulness is God's way of making sure pregnant women will be willing to go through labor again. Once we're out of an abusive situation, we tend to gloss over the really ugly parts. This preference for "looking on the bright side" is one of those Catch 22 characteristics that is a strength until it is taken to an extreme and causes you to minimize just how awful the bully situation was.

Our mind simply doesn't want to believe cruelty exists. Over time, we grow distant from the terror of that time—which can be dangerous because it sets up the "it wasn't so bad" scenario. Normally, we don't want to dwell on hurtful incidents, but in this case it's important to remember how bad it was so you're not tempted to return.

REMEMBER, THERE IS NO EXCUSE FOR ABUSE. Keep your Clarity Rules with you. Frequently remind yourself that you are pulling a Tina Turner and taking responsibility for your life. You believe life is a blessing and people treat each other with respect. This person has repeatedly shown s/he will harm. Since the other person won't change, you must.

CONSULT A MENTAL HEALTH PROFESSIONAL. If your car breaks down, you take it in to a repair shop. If your toilet doesn't work, you'd call a plumber. If your heart is broken and your head is spinning, schedule an appointment with a professional who has been trained to deal with matters of the heart and head. Samuel Goldwyn once quipped, "Anyone who goes to see a psychiatrist ought to have his head examined." Anyone who *doesn't* see a mental health professional after going ten rounds with a bully ought to have his or her head examined.

TAKE STEPS TO ENSURE YOUR PHYSICAL, FINANCIAL, AND LEGAL SAFETY. This is not a good time to be naive. An attorney friend said, "I wish I had a hundred bucks for every person seeking a divorce who told me, 'It's not about the money.' I tell them, 'That's a noble thought. I understand that, right now, all you're thinking about is your safety and getting out of this relationship. I understand that you're not greedy and vindictive and you don't want to retaliate; you just want to get away from this destructive individual.'

"And then I tell them, 'Those are admirable characteristics; but they're naïve. It better be about the money. A year from now, who is going to pay for health insurance? Who's going to pay rent, buy the food, purchase clothes? Who's going to provide for your children if something happens to you?' I tell them I know a divorced fifty-year-old woman who's had a painful abscessed tooth for months because she doesn't have the money to get it fixed. I tell them they better do their research and find a strong attorney who can hold his or her own going up against a snake who will manipulate the system and play dirty tricks. I suggest they sit down with a financial planner who will open their eyes as to what their financial future will be like as a single person or parent. The time to think about all this is before you try to get out of the relationship, not after. I'm not trying to scare them; I'm just giving them a reality check."

Take the Initiative

"Some people never take initiative because no one tells them to." — *coffee mug slogan*

A woman said, "It looks like you're suggesting this option of ending the relationship. What if we don't want to end the relationship? What if we still love this person or want to try to keep the family together?"

Actually, what I'm suggesting is that you take the initiative to reclaim your quality of life. The bully is not looking out for your best interests. I hope the techniques in this book motivate the bully to change the way s/he treats you. If, for whatever reason, they don't, then I do think it's in your best interests to remove yourself from this toxic situation.

There are better people, better jobs, better relationships, better health waiting for you that honor your rights and needs, instead of violate them.

If you stay to stay with this person and in this situation, then resolve to use the techniques in this book to even out the balance of power. Keep the Rights/Needs Seesaw in mind so you are more aware of bully behavior that can see what is being done to keep you down and out. Rein in your desire to please and keep the peace. Interrupt when they start ranting and raving. Do not give them a bully pulpit. Put your hand up and "Do the You" to enforce your boundaries and keep them from encroaching on your physical or emotional space. Keep your Clarity Rules and touchstone nearby to give yourself the confidence to be brave.

Action Plan and Discussion Questions

Are you trying to summon the courage to get out of an unhealthy relationship? What are some of your fears?

Do you have someone in your life who puts you in a double bind in public because they know you'll give in rather than make a scene? Who is that person? Describe a time they did this.

Are you prepared to hold this person accountable from now on, even if it does mean making a big deal about it in public?

Can you relate to what happened in the movie *What's Love Got to Do with It?* Have any of those things happened to you? Explain.

Are you ready to "pull a Tina Turner" and garner the courage to get out of an unhealthy relationship and take charge of your life? How so?

Summing Up
IT'S UP TO YOU NOW

I was bullied so badly my dad used to have to walk me into school so I didn't get attacked. I'd eat my lunch in the nurses' office so I didn't have to sit with the other girls. Apart from my being mixed race, my parents didn't have money so I never had the cute clothes or the cool backpack. You have to make it push you to become a stronger person, in whatever way that may be. – actress Jessica Alba

Jessica Alba used her childhood bullying experience as incentive to become a stronger person.

You may know her as an actress and model. Did you also know she is the founder of The Honest Company?

I had the privilege of seeing Jessica interviewed at SXSW. She told the story of how her baby had a painful diaper rash that would not go away. Her pediatrician told her that her baby was allergic to the chemicals in baby wipes, and mentioned he saw this problem a lot.

Jessica thought, "This is unacceptable. Why aren't there products for our babies that don't have toxins in them?" She searched and couldn't find them, so she decided to create a eco-friendly company that made them. This was an idea whose time had come, but no one took her seriously. In fact, she was targeted by a version of the bullying she received back in school. People mocked her efforts online and suggested she put a bikini back on and go make another movie. They ridiculed her lack of education and predicted she'd never getting funding.

Alba wouldn't give up and didn't give in to their unflattering characterizations. She persevered, found the right business partner, the former head of Legal Zoom, and has now grown the company to a valuation of three *billion* dollars.

The point? Jessica Alba is clear about who she is and how she wants to show up. The bullies only "win" if you buy into what they're saying, if it changes you and keeps you from being the quality of person you want to be.

The primary message of this book is that, as bad as things may be, there are still things you can do to take back control of your life. The message is also that YOU need to take these steps because the situation won't improve by itself. The proverbial white knight won't ride in and save the day. You are the only one who can save this day. What's happening may not be your fault, it is your responsibility to fix.

American short-story writer O. Henry said, "Life is made up of sobs, sniffles and smiles, with sniffles predominating."

I disagree. I believe the proportion of sobs and sniffles to smiles is up to us. On any given day, there might be cause for all three. The question is, which will we allow to dominate and direct our thoughts? What will we choose to give our attention to? Which will we focus on?

Have you learned what you stand for – and what you won't stand for – as a result of dealing with this individual? Are you clearer about who you are? Are you more appreciative of what's right in your life? Has this nightmare revealed your true friends to you? Will the lessons you've learned serve you the rest of your days? Are you sharing those lessons-learned so others won't be poisoned by the toxic people in their life?

Then this experience has served a purpose, hasn't it? It wasn't for naught. You have emerged, or can emerge, from this ordeal, with strength, wisdom and a renewed appreciation for life's blessings, and for individuals who choose to act with integrity and treat each other with respect.

Make Music with What's Left

Those who follow the part of themselves that is great will become great. Those that follow the part that is small will become small. — fourth century Chinese philosopher, Mencius

There is a wonderful story about the gifted violinist Itzhak Perlman who gave a memorable concert at Avery Fisher Hall at Lincoln Center in New York City. Perlman was stricken with polio as a child; as a result, he has braces on both legs and walks with the aid of two crutches. Perlman is a shining example of an individual who has followed and developed the parts of him that are great. He is universally respected for his talent and poise under pressure, which were magnificently demonstrated on this particular evening.

After laboriously making his way onto the stage, Perlman settled into his chair and was warming up when one of his violin strings broke. People in the audience thought he would probably have to go through the complicated process of leaving the stage to find another violin or replace the string, but he did neither. Instead, he collected himself for a moment, and then motioned for the conductor and orchestra to begin playing.

Jack Reimer of the *Houston Chronicle*, who reported what happened, said, "Of course, anyone knows that it is impossible to play a symphonic work with just three strings. I know that, and you know that, but that night Itzhak Perlman refused to know that. You could see him modulating, changing, recomposing the piece in his head, getting new sounds from the strings they had never made before."

When Perlman finished, there was initial silence and then everyone in the room rose in a spontaneous standing ovation, wildly cheering his extraordinary performance. In response to the applause, Perlman said simply, "You know, sometimes it is the artist's task to find out how much music you can still make with what you have left."

Please know you still have music left to play, and it is time to get on your way.

Travel the Highway of Hope

"How do you find your way back in the dark? Just head for that big star straight on. The highway's under it, takes us right home." —Arthur Miller

While I was wrapping up this manuscript, a 21 year old wearing a gray sweatshirt and jeans walked into Emanuel African Methodist Episcopal Church in Charleston. South Carolina. After sitting through a Bible study group, he took out a handgun and shot and killed 9 people, setting one woman free so she could "tell others what had happened."

The next morning, police arrested a suspect, Dylan Roof. They later discovered a manifesto on a website he had built that detailed his white supremist views. The U.S. Department of Justice is investigating the shooting as a hate crime. According to Wikipedia, Roof confessed to the attack and said his purpose was to "start a race war."

The church's community, including family members of the victims, refused to return the hatred or wage a war against him. In fact, at Roof's bond hearing, 5 family members spoke to him directly and said they were praying for him and forgave him.

In an incredibly moving ceremony at the College of Charleston, President Obama delivered the eulogy for Minister Pinckney. He spoke eloquently, passionately and pleadingly about our need to embrace grace to buoy us in our dark times. He then started singing the healing words of John Newton's "Amazing Grace."

"Amazing grace!
How sweet the sound,
That saved a wretch like me.
I once was lost, but now am found;
Was blind, but now I see."

This transcends politics. For now, please set aside your feelings about President Obama (whatever they are) and just focus on what he chose to do in that moment. He could have ranted and railed against this individual who had taken the lives of innocent people who had never harmed him. People who, to the contrary, had welcomed him into their midst and were kind to him.

Instead, he shared his confidence that "the outpouring of unity and strength and fellowship and love ... from all races, from all faiths, from all places of worship, indicates the degree to which those old vestiges of hatred can be overcome."

Your Future is in Your Hands

"The future starts today, not tomorrow." – Pope Paul II

Hopefully, the situation you're dealing with isn't as violent as that. However, you face a similar choice. You can rant and rail about this individual who has harmed you ... or you can opt for the buoyancy of hope that can, as Obama said, "transform dark, desolate valleys into sunlit paths of inner peace."

I hope this book has helped you develop the courage, clarity, and communication skills to hold bullies accountable for their behavior. I hope it has helped you take responsibility for creating and re-claiming a better quality of life. I hope it helps you take steps TODAY to free yourself from bullies who are trying to run and ruin your life.

The sun is shining as I write this, and it will shine for you too if you'll just take your bully by the horns -- and take back your life.

Best wishes! And as Arthur Miller so eloquently suggested, I hope you'll travel the highway of hope. I hope you become an "informed innocent" who chooses to focus on blessings, not bullies, and who chooses to be ... *a force for good.*

Action Plan and Discussion Questions

Are you ready to extract value from this experience, and learn whatever lesson there is to learn, so it serves you? Explain.

Are you clear that you will not wait to be rescued – and that you will take responsibility to take back control of your life?

Think back over this book. What is one specific suggestion that was particularly insightful or helpful for you?

What will you do differently from now on to articulate and enforce your boundaries so people cannot manipulate or intimidate you?

What is one piece of advice you would give someone else if they are dealing with a bully who is putting them down?

How will you remind yourself to stay strong? Are you going to post the Clarity Rules where they're in sight, in mind? Are you going to remind yourself you have the right and responsibility to create the quality of life you want and deserve – and no one has the right to abuse you?

Please create a plan of action so you know exactly what you're going to do to protect and perpetuate the health of you and your loved ones.

BULLYING RESOURCES

This section is a compilation of the best resources on bullying we found during our research. You will find statistics, best practices, practical tips and virtual communities of support.

1. #Day1 – www.day1campaign.com
The #Day1 Campaign requires four main elements 1) A person in authority, 2) clearly saying what behavior is expected and what is not tolerated, 3) done early on (on Day 1), 4) and getting a verbal confirmation back that the instruction is understood.

2. The Trevor Project – www.thetrevorproject.org
The Trevor Project saves lives through its accredited, free and confidential instant messaging/text messaging crisis intervention services. The largest safe social networking community for LGBTQ youth and one of the most comprehensive anti-bullying resources, the Trevor Project was founded by the creators of the Academy Award-winning short film, TREVOR.

3. PACER Center – www.pacer.org

The PACER Center was created by parents of youth with disabilities to help other parents facing the same challenges. The staff at the Center, which was founded in 1977, primarily have children that have disabilities so they have a complete understanding of who they serve.

4. STOMP Out Bullying! – www.stompoutbullying.org

Stomp Out Bullying is the leading anti-bullying and cyberbullying organization in the U.S. focusing on reducing bullying in schools and teaching effective solutions to responding to bullies. Focusing on empowerment, Stomp Out Bullying works aggressively to prevent creating environments that support bullying.

5. Matthew's Place – www.matthewsplace.com

Matthew's Place is an online community that focuses on LBGQT youth from the ages of 13-24. It's unique 50-state resource and service directory, inspirational messages from LFBT and allied professionals and chat sessions with celebrities are all inspired by the intense need for information, support and services for LBGQT youth.

6. GLSEN – www.glsen.org

GLSEN is the leading national education organization focusing on ensuring safe schools for all students. Created by a small group of teachers in Massachusetts in 1990, GLSEN conducts extensive and original research to create evidence-based solutions for K-12 education.

7. Welcoming Schools – www.welcomingschools.org

Welcoming Schools provides information and resources for schools to create a more inclusive, safe community. Initiated by a group of parents and educators to meet the needs of students with limited family structure, Welcoming Schools focuses on providing tools to address bias-based name calling and bullying.

8. PFLAG – community.pflag.org

PFLAG is the nation's largest family and ally organization with a three-fold mission of support, education and advocacy. PFLAG has over 350 chapter with 200,000+ members in all 50 states. PFLAG started with Jeanne Manford marching with her son, Morty, in a pride parade. After many gay and lesbian people ran up to her asking that she talk to their parents, she decided to begin PFLAG as a support group.

9. GLBTQ Online High School
– www.glbtqonlinehighschool.com

GLBTQ Online High School is the world's first online high school specifically for discriminated-against youth. Currently focusing on fundraising, the school provides a comprehensive college-preparatory experience for all students who feel discriminated against.

10. Peace First – www.peacefirst.org

Peace First is a national non-profit organization that exists to create the next generation of peacemakers. By operating under the mindset that children are natural problem solvers and creative thinkers, Peace First teaches young people the skills of peacemaking by empowering educators and parents to teach these values and creating social messages that raise expectations for young people to demonstrate compassion and empathy.

11. StopBullying.gov – www.stopbullying.gov

One of the most comprehensive websites with information about bullying, statistics and general know-how on stopping bullying.

12. Pacer – www.pacer.org/bullying

PACER provides innovative resources for students and teachers in combating bullying by recognizing it to be a serious factor in development, both academically and socially. Pacer is one of the largest digital resources on bullying and is also the sponsor of National Bullying Prevention Month in October.

13. Band Back Together – www.bandbacktogether.com

BBT is a group blog that allows anyone to share their stories. By sharing these experiences the hope is that people can find common ground and realize that they are not alone.

14. Project Cornerstone – www.projectcornerstone.com

Project Cornerstone works with 200 schools and community partners to influence the personal behavior of adults towards children and teens, strengthens youth-serving programs and impacts public policy.

15. Center for Safe Schools – www.safeschools.info

The Center for Safe Schools provides valuable resources that specifically address bullying prevention, cyberbullying, school safety, and creating a safe school climate.

16. Character Counts – https://charactercounts.org

The Character Counts! Approach to bullying is to create a school culture where bullying is simply not accepted or tolerated. Through Character Development seminars and day-in workshops, Character Counts! is changing the culture of our schools.

17. Cyberbullying.US – www.cyberbullying.us

The Cyberbullying Research Center is dedicated to providing up-to-date information about the nature, extent and causes of cyberbullying among adolescents. The centers website is a clearinghouse of information about bullying with the latest in scientific studies and research.

18. American Academy of Child and Adolescent Psychiatry – www.aacap.org

The AACAP is a non-profit organization, established in 1953. It is composed of 8,000+ psychiatrists who pride themselves on giving direction to and responding to new quickly to new developments in addressing the health care needs of children and their families.

16. SafeKids – www.safekids.org

SafeKids is a website devoted to safety advice and tools for the use of the Internet. Through guides for parents and kids, SafeKids teaches families how to safely use the Internet without exposing oneself.

17. It Gets Better Project – www.itgetsbetter.org

Inspiring advice for LGBQT youth from mentors and older individuals who have "been there." The message is that as bad as things may seem, it will get better and it's always worth pushing through your pain.

18. Committee for Children – www.cfchildren.org

Resources that promote building empathy and character building in order to facilitate a "comprehensive bully plan."

19. Human Rights Campaign – www.hrc.org

The Human Rights Campaign is a venerate non-profit typically associated with fighting for the rights of humans in third world countries. They are, however, also one of the best resources with comprehensive articles and research on combatting violence and bullying.

20. Teaching Tolerance – www.tolerance.org

Tolerance.com, a subsidiary of the famous Southern Poverty Law Center, features many articles on professional bullying as well as film kits and classroom resources to combat bullying.

21. Highmark Foundation – www.highmarkfoundation.org

The foundation, a charity, focuses on leading ideas in public health and human service initiatives, and uniting global, local and national organizations with similar missions. Many grants focus on bullying.

22. BullyBust – www.bullybust.org

BullyBust is an awareness campaign designed to reduce bullying in schools by teaching students and adults how to stand up to bullying and promote upstander behavior.

23. Bully Police USA – www.bullypolice.org

This watchdog organization advocates for bullied children and provides links to state anti-bullying laws, along with a rating of each law's effectiveness.

About the Author

Sam Horn created the trade-marked *Tongue Fu!®* communication system that has been taught around the world. Her book on that topic was endorsed by Tony Robbins, John Gray and Jack Canfield and has been featured in *Chicago Tribune, Washington Post, Publishers Weekly, Readers Digest, Chicago Tribune, Foreign Service Journal* and *Investors Business Daily*.

Executive Book Summaries said *Tongue Fu!®* was "a gold mine for anyone who deals with the public" and said it "added to the legacy of ideas on dealing with people left by Abraham Lincoln, Benjamin Franklin, Dale Carnegie, and many others."

Sam also authored the book *Take the Bully by the Horns: Stop Unethical, Uncooperative or Unpleasant People from Running and Ruining Your Life* in 2002. It received a cover endorsement from Dave Pelzer, author of *A Child Called It*, who called it "the prefect guide on how to avoid negative confrontations and face those who intimidate and manipulate you – without sacrificing your integrity."

Sam has presented conflict resolution and bully awareness-prevention programs for hundreds of organizations including Boeing, ASAE, the U.S. Embassy in London, Henrico County Schools, the IRS, Capital One, American Bankers Association, KPMG ad the U.S. Navy.

Want to receive updated articles and videos on how to deal with bullies? Visit www.SamHorn.com to view Sam's TEDx talk and to access her podcasts and frequently updated blog to receive more insights on how to deal with people who don't want a win-win … they want to win.

Want Sam To Present These Techniques For Your Organization?

Would your employees, co-workers, association members and program participants like to know how to give and get the respect they want, need and deserve? Would they like to know how to get along better with just about anyone, anytime, anywhere? Would they like to know how to prevent bullies, haters, and trolls from mistreating them?

If so, contact us at Cheri@IntrigueAgency.com or call 1 805 528-4351 to discuss your group's needs and arrange for Sam to bring her insights to your organization or meeting.

You can trust Sam to deliver no-nonsense techniques that teach your audience members exactly what to say and do so they know how to deal with difficult people – without becoming one themselves.

Discover for yourself why Sam was twice the top-rated speaker at the International Platform Association convention, and why she has been hired by international associations and Fortune 500 companies to keynote their annual meetings.

Want to Get Certified to Teach the *Tongue Fu!*® - *Never Be Bullied Again* **Techniques?**

Over the years, many people have asked us, "Can I be trained to teach these trade-marked techniques so I can present programs for my organization's employees or for convention audiences?"

The answer is YES.

We have certified *Tongue Fu!*® - *Never Be Bullied Again* trainers around the world – in England, Canada, Australia and throughout the United States. They include judges, professional speakers, Realtors, FAA executives, coaches, Six Sigma experts, small business owners, educators, management consultants and restaurant owners.

Contact Cheri Grimm at 8045 528-4351 – or at Cheri@IntrigueAgency.com – to request a schedule of our certification trainings. They are conducted in person and virtually.

Please note: If you plan to use these techniques internally within a school, youth league or non-profit organization, and will not be paid to teach these programs, please inquire about our discount.

Also note: If you are a coach, professional speaker, entrepreneur or management consultant, you can earn a wonderful living doing work you love by adding these proven topics to your repertoire of services.

We Want to Hear From You

Was there a particular idea in this book that resonated with you, that helped you resolve a situation with a challenging person?

Did you get clarity as a result of the ideas in this book that helped you reclaim and recreate your quality of life?

If so, I'd love to hear your success story. It makes my day to know these ideas have helped people know they're not alone, they do have options, and they can take back control of their life.

Please contact me at Sam@IntrigueAgency.com with your success story or feedback. With your permission, I'll share your lessons-learned in a future blog or program so others might benefit from your experience.

Or, feel free to ask me to keep your story private and I'll do so.

I hope this book has made a positive difference for you. If so, you are welcome to write a review on Amazon and recommend the book to others. Best wishes to you.

Made in the USA
San Bernardino, CA
28 September 2015